Hammer Films'
Psychological Thrillers,
1950–1972

ALSO BY DAVID HUCKVALE

*The Occult Arts of Music: An Esoteric Survey
from Pythagoras to Pop Culture* (2013)

*Ancient Egypt in the Popular Imagination: Building a Fantasy
in Film, Literature, Music and Art* (2012)

*Visconti and the German Dream: Romanticism, Wagner
and the Nazi Catastrophe in Film* (2012)

*Touchstones of Gothic Horror: A Film Genealogy
of Eleven Motifs and Images* (2010)

Hammer Film Scores and the Musical Avant-Garde (2008)

*James Bernard, Composer to Count Dracula:
A Critical Biography* (2006; paperback 2012)

Hammer Films' Psychological Thrillers, 1950–1972

David Huckvale

McFarland & Company, Inc., Publishers
Jefferson, North Carolina

LIBRARY OF CONGRESS CATALOGUING-IN-PUBLICATION DATA

Huckvale, David.
Hammer films' psychological thrillers, 1950–1972 / David Huckvale.
    p.   cm.
Includes bibliographical references and index.

ISBN 978-0-7864-7471-4 (softcover : acid free paper) ∞
ISBN 978-1-4766-0421-3 (ebook)

1. Thrillers (Motion pictures)—Great Britain—History—20th century.   2. Motion pictures—Psychological aspects.   3. Hammer Film Productions.   I. Title.

PN1995.9.S87H73 2014   791.430941—dc23   2013047471

BRITISH LIBRARY CATALOGUING DATA ARE AVAILABLE

© 2014 David Huckvale. All rights reserved

No part of this book may be reproduced or transmitted in any form or by any means, electronic or mechanical, including photocopying or recording, or by any information storage and retrieval system, without permission in writing from the publisher.

On the cover: Poster art for the 1961 Hammer film *Scream of Fear* (aka *Taste of Fear*) depicting actress Susan Strasberg (Columbia Pictures/Photofest)

Manufactured in the United States of America

*McFarland & Company, Inc., Publishers
Box 611, Jefferson, North Carolina 28640
www.mcfarlandpub.com*

To Lionel Cummings

Table of Contents

Introduction 1

1. The Uncanny in *Les Diaboliques*
   (dir. Henri-Georges Clouzot, 1955) 11
2. Echoes and Inspirations in Four Hitchcock Classics 22
3. Houses in *The Man in Black*
   (dir. Francis Searle, 1950) 41
4. Misogyny in *Stolen Face*
   (dir. Terence Fisher, 1952) 48
5. Narcissism in *The Snorkel*
   (dir. Guy Green, 1958) 55
6. Psychiatry in *The Full Treatment*
   (dir. Val Guest, 1961) 67
7. The Gothic in *Taste of Fear*
   (dir. Seth Holt, 1961) 73
8. Love and Landscape in *Maniac*
   (dir. Michael Carreras, 1963) 87
9. Sex and the Dead in *Paranoiac*
   (dir. Freddie Francis, 1963) 96
10. Loss and Deception in *The Kiss of the Vampire*
    (dir. Don Sharp, 1964) 106
11. Dreams and Visions in *Nightmare*
    (dir. Freddie Francis, 1964) 113
12. The Oedipus Complex in *Fanatic*
    (dir. Silvio Narizzano, 1965) 122
13. Architecture in *Hysteria*
    (dir. Freddie Francis, 1965) 128

14	Domesticity and *The Nanny* (dir. Seth Holt, 1965)	137
15	Homophobia in *The Witches* (dir. Cyril Frankel, 1966)	147
16	Doppelgängers in *Crescendo* (dir. Alan Gibson, 1970)	152
17	The Past in *Fear in the Night* (dir. Jimmy Sangster, 1972)	160
18	Insanity, Incest and Christianity in *Demons of the Mind* (dir. Peter Sykes, 1972)	167
19	Peter Pan in *Straight on Till Morning* (dir. Peter Collinson, 1972)	175

Notes 183
Bibliography 188
Index 191

Introduction

The Psychological Gothic

Hammer film productions are rightly famous for Gothic horror but, sandwiched between the company's various vampires, menacing monsters and striking studies in the occult, it also produced a series of psychological thrillers, which Hammer's managing director, Sir James Carreras, dubbed "mini–Hitchcocks." This was an unfortunate sobriquet, for though these films certainly reflect, if only in part, the example of Hollywood's quintessential but nonetheless very British Master of Suspense, such a categorization suggests that they are mere imitations when, in fact, there is much more individuality and invention to them than that. However, without Hitchcock's *Rope* (1948), *Vertigo* (1958) and *Psycho* (1960), Hammer's *Taste of Fear* (dir. Seth Holt, 1960), *Paranoiac* (dir. Freddie Francis, 1963) and *Maniac* (dir. Michael Carreras, 1963), to name but three of the titles in this category, might never have existed. This was not so much because they were indebted to Hitchcock's overall style and subject matter, as because Hitchcock's *Psycho* was such a phenomenal success when it was first released in 1960. Made for only $800,000, it eventually earned over $40 million. Hammer, so often the purveyor of cinematic vampires, was a vampire itself, and it quite happily fed on the trends of the time. Sir James famously quipped he would make Strauss waltzes if the public wanted them,[1] but it was Hitchcock, not Strauss, who provided the demand for suspense, and Hammer, ever on the lookout for what would appeal to the public, followed suit.

But Sir James' "mini–Hitchcocks" are just as much "mini–Clouzots," rooted, as they are, in Henri-Georges Clouzot's celebrated psychological thriller *Les Diaboliques* from 1955, which screenwriter Jimmy Sangster readily acknowledged as his inspiration for so many of the "mini–Hitchcock" screenplays he wrote for Hammer.[2] Such admissions should not overlook the fact that Hammer provided its own ancestor to such films back in the company's early days with Francis Searle's 1950 film based on the BBC's hit radio series *The Man in Black*.

Hammer's terror thrillers are very different from the company's more lurid Gothic shockers, and they are not always immediately recognizable as what most fans would nowadays regard as typical Hammer product. They have Gothic elements, to be sure, but they are predominantly set in the time they were made. They are also quite different in style (even though some of the directors who worked on them also directed Hammer's Gothic fare), and their subject matter is not lurid horror or the supernatural (though horrific things might be done, and the supernatural might be implied before being dispelled).

Just as Donald Spoto can claim that *Psycho* is more than a horror film, being an exploration of the past over the present, "an indictment of the viewer's capacity for voyeurism and his own potential for depravity" (surely something that applies to most horror films, in fact), as well as a "statement of the American dream turned nightmare,"[3] so Hammer's psychological thrillers can also be interpreted as more than catchpenny essays in suspense. They encompass many of the issues of the 1960s, such as greater affluence, material aspiration and social mobility, the family, domesticity, and what it meant to be British at that time, alongside more timeless psychological issues. As the titles of the films so blatantly proclaim, they are about paranoia, hysteria, fanaticism, fear, and the way in which such terrors often come to a crescendo in our nightmares. They address schizophrenia, duality, sadism, narcissism, isolation, insecurity, claustrophobia and agoraphobia and, like *Psycho,* the power of the past upon the present.

Robert Murphy has analyzed British fantastic-supernatural films of the 1960s according to Tzvetan Todorov's distinction between three distinct but related categories: the uncanny, the marvelous and the fantastic:

> In the uncanny, "events are related which may be readily accounted for by the laws of reason, but which are, in one way or another, incredible, extraordinary, shocking, singular, disturbing or unexpected.... It is uniquely linked to the sentiments of the characters and not to a material event defying reason." In the marvelous, events which we would think of as impossible (a man being made from dismembered corpses, a creature that sucks human blood and can only die by having a wooden stake driven into its heart) are accepted as part of the normal order of things. Thus [director Terrence] Fisher's films, where zombies, vampires and werewolves exist and only unenlightened fools question that brains and even souls can be transferred from body to body, can be classed as marvelous, and the Sangster-scripted thrillers like *Taste of Fear* and *Nightmare* as uncanny.
>
> Todorov's third category, the fantastic, poised uneasily between the marvelous and the uncanny, precisely describes Jacques Tourneur's 1940s films *Cat People* and *I Walked with a Zombie.* Here it is impossible to determine whether the bizarre events which occur are figments of a fevered imagination of manifestations of the supernatural.[4]

This tripartite categorization is useful as a means of distinguishing the various subgenres within British fantasy films of the 1960s, but I will also be referring to Freud's more specific use of the term "uncanny" with regard to the kind of films Murphy calls "uncanny" along Todorov's lines.

Murder Considered as One of the Fine Arts

If murder, as Thomas De Quincey once suggested, is one of the fine arts, conscience is surely its fiercest critic. As Hamlet knew all too well, conscience makes cowards us of all, and society is out to catch it. In a more popular arena, though still one based on Shakespeare (the film is loosely based on *The Tempest*), *Forbidden Planet* (dir. Fred M. Wilcox, 1956) has Commander J.J. Adams (played by Leslie Nielsen) point out to Walter Pidgeon's Dr. Morbius that we are all potential monsters. "That's why we have laws and religion," Nielsen says. It is also why we are allowed to indulge our fantasies through art—to let out Mr. Hyde in a safe place and know that we can lock him back again in our subconscious as soon as the fantasy is over. The safest and yet most visceral place to do this is in the cinema, where cocooned in anonymous, erotic darkness, and surrounded by light and sound, we have nothing to fear but what we discover about ourselves.

As all the films we are about to discuss are in one way or another about murder, we need first to work out why such a heinous crime has proved to be such a perennial money spinner—for there is no doubt that human beings are fascinated by murder while simultaneously preserving a censorious attitude towards it. Only in war, it would appear, or the prevention of crime do we seem to be happier about killing each other. Newspapers and television news programs largely depend on murder, handing out moral disapproval on one hand and prurient details on the other. Murder is the food of journalists and little old ladies. There is equally no doubt that the Mr. Hyde within all of us wants the murderer to get away with it. In Hitchcock's *Rope*, two (presumably gay) students murder another friend and serve dinner to his parents on the chest in which the dead body lies. Of course, they are not ultimately allowed to get away with it, but the moral indignation of James

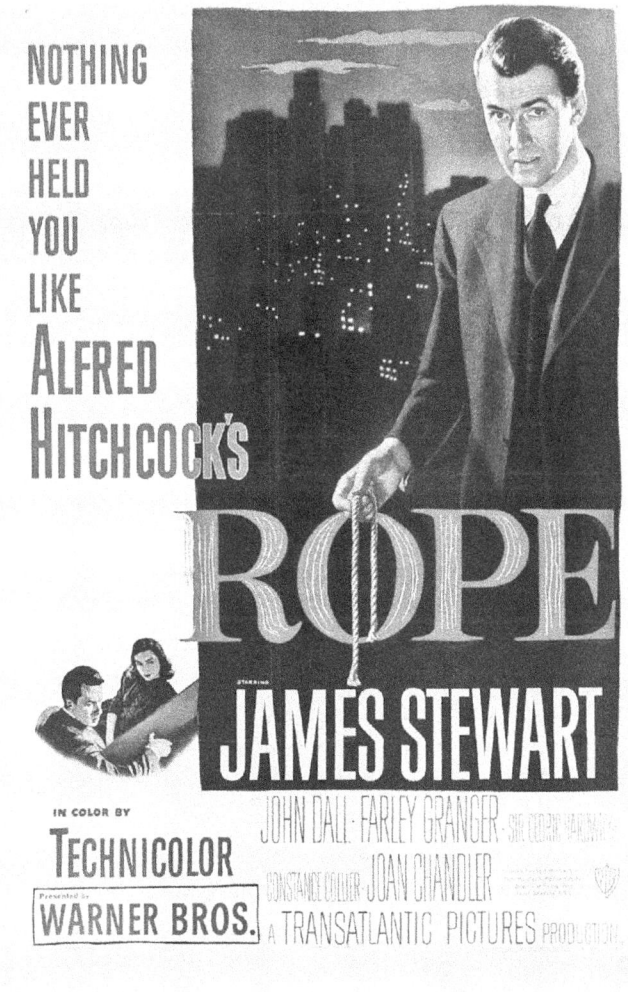

Poster for *Rope* (dir. Alfred Hitchcock, 1948), with a portrait of James Stewart holding the murderous cord.

Stewart at the end of the film, in which he points out the difference between *thinking* something and actually *doing* it, seems forced, as indeed it was. No Hollywood studio in 1948 would have tolerated an immoral or even an amoral ending. The consequence of this is that Stewart's character, Professor Cadell, becomes inconsistent. After a lifetime spent discussing murder as a fine art, his sudden *volte face* at the end is unconvincing to say the least; and is not the suspense of the film entirely due to our secret hope that the two students will actually get away with their crime? All the films in this book at some stage dangle that possibility before their audiences: Will the id get away with murder before it is locked back up by the superego? After the movie, we are returned to the bright light of civilization, or we turn off the DVD player and go to bed; but once we are asleep, who knows what crimes we will commit?

As one might expect, Count Dracula has something to say about this. "Ah, sir," he says to Jonathan Harker in Stoker's original novel, "you dwellers in the city cannot enter into the feelings of the hunter."[5] Or, to quote Count Zaroff, played so expertly by Leslie Banks in *The Most Dangerous Game* (dir. Irving Pichel, 1932), "Hunting has been the whip of all other passions. When I lost my love of hunting, I lost my love of life—of love.... What I needed was not a new weapon but a new animal." He means us, of course; but the exchange in *The Man with the Golden Gun* (dir. Guy Hamilton, 1974), between the assassin Francisco Scaramanga (played by that quintessential Count Dracula, Christopher Lee) and Roger Moore's James Bond, expresses the matter in the most elegantly concise terms of all:

SCARAMANGA: You get as much pleasure out of killing as I do, so why not admit it?
BOND: I admit killing you would be a pleasure.
SCARAMANGA: Then you should have done that when you first saw me. On the other hand, the British don't consider it sporting to kill in cold blood, do they?... You see, Mr. Bond, like all great artists I want to create one indisputable masterpiece: the death of 007.

Scaramanga's pretensions to genius in fact have a very respectable literary provenance. In 1827, Thomas De Quincey, author of *Confessions of an English Opium Eater*, published, in *Blackwood's Magazine*, an essay entitled "On Murder Considered as One of the Fine Arts." In it, he parades various examples of this crime of crimes in terms of their aesthetic ingenuity rather than of their moral depravity. Not that he denies the immorality of murder—he doesn't, but he adds, "Everything in this world has two handles. Murder, for instance, may be laid hold of by its moral handle (as it generally is in the pulpit, and at the Old Bailey); and that, I confess, is its weak side; or it may also be treated esthetically, as the Germans call it, that is, in relation to good taste."[6] De Quincey argues that it is possible to appreciate murder as one would criticize a picture, statue, or other work of art, and refers to the case of the brutal Ratcliffe Highway murders of 1811 in London, in which members of a hard-working, respectable family were killed for no apparent reason. The chief suspect was an Irish (or Scottish) seaman called John Williams, who protested his innocence and later committed suicide before going to trial. Like the much more sensational Jack the Ripper, Williams' motivation was never discovered—indeed, it was never proved that he had been responsible. This mystery added to the crime's aesthetic interest for De Quincey:

> Mr. Williams has exalted the ideal of murder to all of us; and to me, therefore, in particular, has deepened the arduousness of my task. Like Æschylus or Milton in poetry, like Michael Angelo in painting, he has carried his art to a point of colossal sublimity; and, as Mr. Wordsworth observes, has in a manner "created the taste by which he is to be enjoyed."[7]

Of course, De Quincey did not live long enough himself to witness the far more colossal sublimity of Jack the Ripper, but would no doubt have revised his essay accordingly if he had. As it was, he did write a second paper on the subject in which he claimed:

> A man is not bound to put his eyes, ears, and understanding into his breeches pocket when he meets with a murder. If he is not in a downright comatose state, I suppose he must see that one murder is better or worse than another in point of good taste. Murders have their little differences and shades of merit as well as statues, pictures, oratorios, cameos, intaglios, or what not.[8]

So if it was the mystery and sheer horror of the Ratcliffe Highway murders that gave them their appeal, it is ingenuity that offers an even greater aesthetic pleasure, the ingenuity we encounter in *Les Diaboliques*, *Vertigo* and *Hysteria* (dir. Freddie Francis, 1964). De Quincey was less satirical in tone in his other essay on the subject, "On the Knocking at the Gate in Macbeth," in which he explained what is perhaps the real attraction of such films:

> Murder in ordinary cases, where the sympathy is wholly directed to the case of the murdered person, is an incident of coarse and vulgar horror; and for this reason, that it flings the interest exclusively upon the natural but ignoble instinct by which we cleave to life; an instinct, which, as being indispensable to the primal law of self-preservation, is the same in kind (though different in degree), amongst all living creatures; this instinct therefore, because it annihilates all distinctions, and degrades the greatest of men to the level of "the poor beetle that we tread on," exhibits human nature in its most abject and humiliating attitude. Such an attitude would little suit the purposes of the poet. What then must he do? He must throw the interest on the murderer. Our sympathy must be with *him* (of course I mean a sympathy of comprehension, a sympathy by which we enter into his feelings, and are made to understand them, *not a sympathy of pity or approbation*). In the murdered person all strife of thought, all flux and reflux of passion and of purpose, are crushed by one overwhelming panic; the fear of instant death smites him "with its petrific mace." But in the murderer, such a murderer as a poet will condescend to, there must be raging some great storm of passion, *jealousy, ambition, vengeance, hatred*, which will create a hell within him; and into this hell we are to look.[9]

We are consequently faced with a conflict between aesthetics and ethics, which brings me briefly to *Either/Or*, the influential 1843 book by the Danish philosopher Søren Kierkegaard. In a variety of styles and forms, he discusses the options we have to choose from with regard to our behavior in life. He illuminates the argument with regard to our approach to love rather than murder, but in the most widely read section of the book, "A Seducer's Diary," the behavior of the seducer in question, Johannes Climacus, which also anticipates that more recent development of the stalker, demonstrates that "love," if approached purely aesthetically, can be almost as catastrophic as murder—indeed it can become a *form* of murder. Johannes goes about his seduction in a purely aesthetic manner.

He is not interested in the effect his deliberations will have on Cordelia, the object of his attentions. Indeed, like Mozart's Don Giovanni, he is not really interested in her as a person, only as the object of his aesthetic conceit. Don Giovanni never slept with the same woman twice as he is immediately bored with whoever he has seduced as soon as he has made his conquest. He is not really interested in the person but the idea. He is the ultimate aesthete. (This has led some psychological interpreters to suggest that Don Giovanni is actually homosexual, arguing that he doesn't actually like women. His relationship with his male servant Leporello is, after all, much more meaningful and affectionate. Whatever his sexual orientation, he is more significantly a narcissist.) Like Don Giovanni, Johannes plays with Cordelia in a purely aesthetic manner, as would a playwright with one of his characters, or an artist a figure in a landscape. He orchestrates other people as a composer would a symphony:

> One could think of several ways of surprising Cordelia. I might try to raise an erotic storm which was capable of tearing up trees by the roots. With its help I could see if I could sweep her off her feet, snatch her from her historic setting, and try in this agitation, by stealthy advances, to arouse her passion. It is not inconceivable that it could be done. A girl with her passion can be made to do anything at all. However, it would be wrong aesthetically. I am not fond of giddiness, and the condition is to be recommended only with girls for whom this is the only way of acquiring a poetic image.[10]

The ethical is entirely absent in his approach, and Cordelia herself points this out in one the letters that precede this diary. Indeed, she goes so far as to equate his behavior with that of a murderer:

> I do not call you "mine," I realize very well you never have been, and I am punished enough by this thought having once gladdened my soul; and yet I do call you "mine": my seducer, my deceiver, my foe, my murderer, source of my unhappiness, grave of my joy, abyss of my ruin. I call you "mine" and call myself "yours"; and as it once flattered your ear, which proudly bent down to my adoration, so shall it now sound like a curse upon you, a curse to all eternity.[11]

Johannes' purely aesthetic approach to love is indeed very similar to the way in which the criminals of Hammer's psychological thrillers operate. The relations of such characters with other people are entirely aesthetic, and they take particular pride in the elaborate "artistic" murder plots they have devised. Murder, here, is truly presented as one of the fine arts—indeed it *is* art, as it is the motivating element of the artistic experience of the movie as a whole: the sets, the lighting, the music, the photography and the acting. All these elements combine to present murder aesthetically rather than ethically (though ethics usually turn up at the end, as in *Rope*, to keep the superego and public opinion happy).

Method in His Madness

In Shakespeare's play, Polonius observes of Hamlet that there is "method in his madness." After his conversation with the ghost of his father, Hamlet admits to his friend

Horatio that he will assume an "antic disposition"—in other words, appear to be mad in order to find out the truth about his father's murder. But Polonius, at whom much of this charade is aimed, suspects that Hamlet's strange behavior is not quite as irrational as it appears. Hamlet uses madness to get at the truth, but the madmen and villains of Hammer's psychological thrillers are usually either after women or cash—or both.

Sometimes the characters in psychological thrillers are genuinely insane: think of Norman Bates (Anthony Perkins) in *Psycho* or Jacques, the brother of George Ryman (both played by James Olson), in Hammer's *Crescendo* (dir. Alan Gibson, 1970). These are genuine psychopaths, as are the Shane Briant characters Peter Clive in *Straight on Till Morning* (dir. Peter Collinson, 1972) and Emil in *Demons of the Mind* (dir. Peter Skyes, 1972). Sometimes a character is obsessed to the point of being deranged, such as Dr. David Prade (Claude Dauphin) in *The Full Treatment* (dir. Val Guest, 1960) and Kay Walsh's lesbian occultist Stephanie Bax in *The Witches* (dir. Cyril Frankel, 1966). Even James Stewart's Scottie in Hitchcock's *Vertigo* begins to crack up due to his obsessional infatuation with a woman who doesn't exist. Bette Davis' unnamed character in *The Nanny* (dir. Seth Holt, 1965) is driven mad by a guilty conscience. Oliver Reed's Simon Ashby in *Paranoiac* is more of an Othello type, driven mad through jealousy of his younger brother, whom he murdered when they were boys. Religious zeal causes Tallulah Bankhead's Mrs. Trefoil to live in denial and fully to live up to the title of the film in which she appears: *Fanatic* (dir. Silvio Narizzano, 1965). The appeal of such characters is similar to that of the inspired murderer. The Aristotelean explanation of the cathartic pleasure of being purged by pity and fear is surely part of the attraction but, like the inspired murderers admired by De Quincey, there is also a more ambivalent attraction, an identification perhaps, deep in the subconscious, with repressed impulses of our own. After all, the psychopath lives beyond the rules of convention, and is not afraid to transgress the limits imposed by society. He lives truly in his own imagination, to which he makes the world conform rather than the other way around. There is something at least momentarily liberating in such psychological freedom, though it is interesting that Norman Bates and Simon Ashby both suffer from guilty consciences, even though they try to repress their guilt. Paul Decker in *The Snorkel* is perhaps the only character in the films we will be exploring who can sing with Edith Piaf "Je ne regret rien." But even he is not allowed to get away with his crimes. These films were made at a time long before Hannibal Lecter appeared on the scene. Clouzot, Hammer and Hitchcock never permitted Mr. Hyde to triumph.

Human motivations are not always attractive, and we may prefer not to acknowledge any such blemish in our own psyche, but these movies do, and their fictional psychopaths, like the villains who attempt to induce insanity in their victims, must have something in common with their audiences, otherwise such films would have no commercial viability. The connection between them and us might well be that they, like us, are similarly motivated by the will to power. Friedrich Nietzsche, the first philosopher to reveal this important psychological drive, also asked three basic questions as well as offering three potential answers regarding it:

Introduction

> What is good?—All that heightens the feeling of power, the will to power, power itself in man.
> What is bad?—All that proceeded from weakness.
> What is happiness?—The feeling that power *increases*—that a resistance is overcome.[12]

Having said that, Nietzsche would have been the first to acknowledge that the robbery of a woman's estate by means of incarcerating her in an asylum for the insane (which is what happens in Hammer's *Nightmare*) is a very low manifestation of the will to power. For Nietzsche, the most powerful man is he who desires no power over others but has gained mastery over himself. Nonetheless, both are manifestations of the drive which is present in us all.

There is another kind of identification in such films which is far more benign. We may sympathize with those sane but vulnerable types whom the real villains attempt to *drive* mad. Such characters appear in *The Man in Black, Taste of Fear, Nightmare* and *Fear in the Night* (dir. Jimmy Sangster, 1972). Madness, real, imagined or induced, is therefore a key element in their plots. We are encouraged to doubt that Susan Strasberg's Penny Appleby *really* sees the corpse of her father in the lumber room in *Taste of Fear*. We are asked to question if she *really* hears a piano being played in an empty room. Does Jennie Linden's Janet *really* see a figure in white prowling through the corridors of the family home in *Nightmare*? Does Robert Webber's Chris Smith *really* hear people arguing in the unfinished adjacent flat in *Hysteria*? Has he *entirely* imagined the mysterious woman (played by Lelia Goldoni) whose photograph he was found holding after losing his memory in a car crash, and who *apparently* appears after she had been murdered?

Of course, we are all subject to doubting the evidence of our own senses, though usually on the more mundane level of mislaying an object which we had in hand only a short time before, or of waking up disoriented in a cold sweat after a nightmare. The method used by the insanity-inducing villains of these films is to amplify such commonplace self-doubts. The aim is to disorientate, confuse and contradict.

At some stage in our lives we all also suffer from anxiety and guilt, and can therefore, to some extent, sympathize with the predicament of Bette Davis' Nanny. Many people have also suffered from obsessional behavior in the pursuit of a lover (though not often to the same criminal extent as Dr. Prade in *The Full Treatment*). Fortunately, psychopaths are less common. In Evelyn Piper's original novel of *The Nanny*, which differs considerably from the film, a psychopath is defined as someone for whom "[a]ll the horror is in just this, that there is no horror."[13] Such people don't even feel what they have done to be wrong. In Piper's novel, Dr. Meducca's daughter Roberta is the psychopath, a character whom Jimmy Sangster completely cured in his screenplay, turning her into the benign and helpful Pamela Franklin character, Bobby, the daughter of Dr. Medman. But Piper's Roberta is a drug addict, selfish, completely callous and violent. Conversely, Simon Ashby in Josephine Tey's novel *Brat Farrar* is a murderer, certainly, but the character was transformed into a completely lunatic psychopath in Sangster's *Paranoiac*, and made even more frightening by Oliver Reed's hugely energetic and disturbing performance, which combined wild danger with apparently lucid, even charming reasonableness. Most infamous of all, Norman Bates in *Psycho* is horrified by his crimes, but doesn't really accept that it is he who committed them, having done so under the psychological and somewhat flimsy physical disguise of his own mother.

All these characters are presented as immature. They all, in some way or another, still live with their parents, or foster parents in the case of Simon Ashby, and are more or less under their control. Of course, living with one's parents after having come of age is by no means *necessarily* a sign of immaturity in itself, but it is nonetheless a popular cliché of immaturity and therefore a kind of shorthand for it in popular culture. Popular opinion decrees that one is supposed to have flown the nest, to have learned to stand on one's own feet, to have disassociated oneself emotionally and sexually from the parent, but none of these characters have achieved this. Roberta plagues her father with her insane misdemeanors, Oliver Reed's Simon gets drunk and harasses his devoted Aunt Harriet, and Norman Bates goes even further by absorbing the memory of his dead mother into his own psyche.

Freud suggested that, when we sleep, "men dream mostly of their father's death and women of their mother's" because "boys regarded their fathers and girls their mothers as their rivals in love."[14] We do not know what happened to Roberta's mother in Piper's novel. All we know is that Dr. Meducca is a widower, and he is at his wit's end to know what to do with his daughter for whom he is responsible and who is herself utterly irresponsible. Indeed, he even contemplates suicide as a way out of his predicament—surely something Roberta would be quite happy about. Jimmy Sangster no doubt felt that this was too extreme even for a Hammer thriller, but in *Paranoiac*, which Sangster also wrote, Simon's parents are dead, and Aunt Harriet, his substitute mother, protects him, though fully aware of his crime. Both relationships are a kind of marriage, as is Norman Bates' even more complicated "relationship" with his mother. Ernest Jones traced Hamlet's behavior to the apparently Oedipal relationship he has with his mother Queen Gertrude.[15] John Dover Wilson opposed this approach, arguing, "It is entirely misleading to attempt to describe Hamlet's state of mind in terms of modern psychology at all, not merely because Shakespeare did not think in these terms, but because—again—Hamlet is a character in a play, not in history,"[16] but I have chosen to differ with Wilson's view, at least with regard to the psychological thrillers under examination here, for not only were they made in the wake of Freud, and are sometimes *about* psycho-analysis (i.e., Hitchcock's *Spellbound* and Val Guest's *The Full Treatment*), but also because if a character in a film has psychological motivations, it must be possible to some extent at least to analyze them.

With the exception of Chapter 2, each of the chapters that follow is dedicated to a particular film in chronological order of their various releases, and each one is approached from the point of view of a particular topic: houses, sexual obsession, psychiatry, the Gothic, etc. Obviously, these topics will also be of relevance to the other films I will be exploring here, but each film strikes me as being concerned with one of these topics more than the others. I have also referred to all the Hammer films in question by their original British titles.

1

The Uncanny in *Les Diaboliques*
(dir. Henri-Georges Clouzot, 1955)

Jimmy Sangster referred to Clouzot's *Les Diaboliques* as "one of my favorite films of all time"[1] and also admitted that "most of my 'psycho' type movies ... were derivative of each other and they all went back to my original inspiration *Les Diaboliques*. I'm not the only one to follow that path. I guess I just did it more than most."[2] Hitchcock, who was certainly one of Sangster's competitors in this department, similarly reprised *Les Diaboliques*' bathroom imagery in *Psycho* and its duplicity plot in *Vertigo*, but Sangster was right: He did rework *Les Diaboliques* more than most. It's a load-bearing cornerstone of Hammer's temple to psychological terror, so we need to explore it in some depth before moving on to Sangster's variations upon Clouzot's theme.

When *Les Diaboliques* was first released in 1955 it caused a sensation, anticipating the even more sensational impact of Hammer Films' *The Curse of Frankenstein* in 1957 and *Dracula* the following year. Nineteen fifty-five was also the year of Christian Dior's A-line skirt and the re-release of the previous year's watershed in popular music, Bill Haley's "Rock Around the Clock," after that song's appearance in *Blackboard Jungle* (dir. Richard Brooks, 1955), which rocketed it to fame. Hammer also had their first significant hit in 1955 with *The Quatermass Xperiment* (aka *The Creeping Unknown*, dir. Val Guest), a film that laid the foundations of the company's subsequent House of Horror. The world was changing and with it the limits of popular culture. Ten years after the end of the Second World War, cinema audiences were not only younger and more fashion-conscious than before but also ready to be frightened in a more visceral and more psychologically unnerving manner. *Les Diaboliques* was aimed at this new audience. There had been horror films before, of course, but the idea of linking horror with the suspense genre was largely the creation of Clouzot, who had already refined his skills in that department with *Le Corbeau* (*The Raven*, 1943) and *Le Salaire de la Peur* (*The Wages of Fear*, 1953). *Le Corbeau* is concerned with poison pen letters, illegal abortion, suicide and insanity, while the huge success of *Le Salaire de la Peur*, with its high-tension plot about four men driving two trucks filled with nitro-glycerin over mountainous terrain, allowed Clouzot to make his most celebrated movie.

Clouzot (1907–1977) was born with appropriate multi-disciplinary skills for a career in film. The son of a middle class bookseller, young Henri-Georges played the piano and dreamed of becoming a writer before beginning his film apprenticeship in Germany (he worked as a translator at the famous Babelsberg film studios in Berlin). While there, he absorbed the expressionist techniques of directors F.W. Murnau and Fritz Lang, which certainly influenced his own directorial style. After being sacked by UFA because of his pro–Semitic friendships, he returned to France, succumbed to and recovered from tuberculosis, made films under the right-wing Vichy government and ultimately set up his own production company, named after his wife (Véra), to allow himself as much creative freedom as possible. This decision certainly paid off, and *The Wages of Fear*, the film for which the company had been set up, became France's second most popular film. In 1953, seven million people saw it just in France.

Most of Hammer's thrillers in the 1960s rejected color in favor of rather "artier" black and white, and one cannot help wondering if this was not a decision made out of purely financial considerations but was also an aesthetic choice, mirroring the expressionist but also grimy monochrome effects of Clouzot's film. Color was appropriate for Hammer's objective, theatrical and gory approach to Gothic horror, but it tends to flatten perspectives, inhibit lighting contrasts and in a curious way (at least with regard to Hammer's highly stylized approach to color) make things look more unrealistic. For the Gothic never-neverlands of Hammer's Dracula and Frankenstein pictures, this works well. Hammer's approach to color in such films emphasizes its corporeal, matter-of-fact approach to the Gothic, while simultaneously distancing audiences from the

Poster for *Les diaboliques* (dir. Henri-Georges Clouzot, 1954).

everyday world from which they had presumably come to the cinema to escape; but color would have seriously impaired Clouzot's vision even if he had been able to afford it at that time. (Hammer producer Anthony Hinds even spelled this out in response to director Silvio Narizzano's distaste at the amount of blood in the script of 1964's *Fanatic*: "Now that we're in colour, the audience seems to know it's not real blood." Narizzano observed that "horror and gore had been much more effective for the audience when they were in black and white."[3]) Black and white also facilitates the expressionist effects Clouzot had inherited from Murnau and Lang, which color would have contaminated. If color makes Hammer's Gothic horrors less realistic, Clouzot's use of black and white does just the opposite, despite—or perhaps *because* of—the expressionist effects, especially as his story is about grime, dullness and brutality. But black and white also serves Hammer's much more glamorous psychological thrillers, which similarly benefit from the expressionist effects that are best served by this palette. For this reason alone, *Taste of Fear*, *Hysteria*, *Paranoiac*, *The Nanny* and *Nightmare* are much more atmospheric than their color companions, excellent though *Fanatic*, *The Witches*, *Crescendo*, *Fear in the Night* and *Straight on Till Morning* undoubtedly are in their various ways.

The main titles of *Les Diaboliques* show us the stagnant, filthy water of a swimming pool (though on a first viewing we are not sure that this is what it is). The swimming pool is situated on the grounds of an equally grimy private boys' school in France, and it is the first of the film's series of watery motifs. Sangster was to reprise these, particularly in *Taste of Fear* and *Crescendo*, each of which have their own swimming pools. (The pool in *Crescendo* is kept clean, save for the occasional corpse floating upon it. In *Taste of Fear*, as in *Les Diaboliques*, the water is so dirty that a corpse is easily hidden beneath its scummy surface.)

Water is a powerful symbol. It is the *fons et origo* of life, an agent of cleansing. It extinguishes fire, and it sustains life; but in Clouzot's film, all these positive connotations of water are inverted. Water becomes a place of burial. It is dirty. It is the means by which the crimes of fiery passion are committed, and it kills. To emphasize the sinister nature of this opening shot of dark and troubling water, composer Georges van Parys suggests, in the strident theme that accompanies the main titles, the "Dies Irae" chant, which Berlioz had first demonized in the fifth movement of his *Symphonie fantastique* of 1830. "Day of wrath and doom impending," as this famous thirteenth-century sequence begins:

> Oh, what fear man's bosom rendeth, ...
> Death is struck, and nature quaking,
> All creation is awaking,
> To its Judge an answer making.
> ...Guilty, now I pour my moaning.

Though van Parys only *suggests* the music that accompanies the opening words of this plainchant sequence, the lines I have selected from the translation of the Latin original (in the version approved by the Catholic Church) certainly apply to this film. A day of wrath and doom is certainly at hand. Death does indeed appear to awaken and judge those who have perpetrated murder, and the guilty do indeed moan, before dying themselves (though Clouzot's famous double-twist at the end of the film suggests that no one in fact has actually died—more of which anon.)

Van Parys then introduces the even more terrifying timbre of the organ, emphasizing the atmosphere of deistic doom, but ironically so, for in this film the idea of God and the Devil, let alone religion, are singularly absent. Clouzot's universe in *Les Diaboliques* is a particularly existential one. (Significantly, Clouzot was an almost exact contemporary of France's most famous existentialist, Jean-Paul Sartre [1905–1980], who had defended the filmmaker from accusation of collaboration with the Germans during the days of the Vichy government and who actively supported Clouzot's controversial indictment of that period in *Le Corbeau*.)

Next, we are shown the grand, rather Gothic gates of the school in which most of the action is set. Hammer's *The Man in Black* anticipated (and *Nightmare* echoed) this image. The gate is an entrance not just to the location but also to the story. It also suggests that once we pass through it, we are somehow trapped, or at least enclosed, in a sequence of events from which there is no escape until the end of the film. It suggests a sense of inevitability to which we must submit and from which there will be no going back. A grocery van drives through the gateway, running over a paper boat that floats forlornly in a dirty puddle, and this image gives us an idea what kind of film *Les Diaboliques* is going to be. There is nothing refined, civilized or compassionate about this place: Cruelty, brutality and crudity is the norm. The van pulls up before the school building, but whatever elegance it may have had is now lost to its grubby institutionalization. There are no rose beds or well-tended lawns around it. All is mud, and the building itself is tired, worn-out, its architecture abused by disillusioned staff and careless, rowdy boys. (Sangster would blatantly, though less grimily, reprise Clouzot's solitary scholastic location in the similar setting of *Fear in the Night*.)

Such meticulous attention to the *mise-en-scène* raises the important element of *location* in all the films explored in this book. A Brechtian approach to a psychological thriller would fail miserably, as psychological thrillers are largely about the claustrophobia of environment. The human beings who populate the various houses featured in them are trapped—not just physically but, more significantly, psychologically, either as victims of psychopaths and murderers or, perhaps even more worryingly, of their own neuroses and obsessions. The environments in which these dramas are enacted therefore provide us with a vital visual and dramatic symbol of the characters' *emotional* situation.

Everyone is *Les Diaboliques* is unhappy. As *Sight and Sound*'s Derek Prouse, in his original 1955 review of the film, put it, "[T]he atmosphere of the school, soggy with sexual perversion as it is, remains passionless—and, ironically, immature in its all-too-knowing Frenchness."[4] We are introduced to the tired, cynical and downtrodden staff members (one of whom, played by Pierre Larquey, has the appropriate name of Monsieur Drain). It is a very male establishment but the two protagonists are women, played by Simone Signoret as teacher Nicole Horner, and Clouzot's wife Véra as Christina Delassalle. Christina, the wife of the headmaster Michel (Paul Meurisse), loathes her brutal, unfeeling and cynical husband. Nicole is his mistress—a fact of which Christina is well aware. In fact, she and Nicole are allies against Michel, who treats them with equal contempt. Nicole even has a black eye to prove it.

Everyone is looking forward to the weekend and a break from the routine of school life. As it is Friday afternoon, lunch consists of fish pie, but the fish is old and stinks, and the vegetables delivered earlier by the van are rotten. The headmaster uses lunchtime to humiliate his wife in public. She cannot bring herself to swallow the disgusting meal, but Michel, keen to save money, eats it with gusto and shouts, "Swallow!" to his gagging wife. Christina has a weak heart, but she is also the one who has the money. Her husband may be the headmaster, but she owns the building, she pays for the food. Everything, in fact, is hers, but she has allowed her husband to dominate her. The subsequent plot is gradually made clear. Nicole and Christina plan to murder Michel during the weekend, but before that happens we witness their elaborate preparations. They meet in Christina's bedroom (which, incidentally, features room partitions similar to those in Hammer's *Paranoiac* and *Nightmare*). The idea is to lure Michel to a lodging house where Christina will ask for a divorce. They then drug him, drown him in a bathtub, wrap his body in a plastic sheet, bundle it into a wicker trunk brought along especially for the purpose, and throw it in the school swimming pool. All these preparations are shown in a commonplace, practical manner, though Christina expresses a degree of disquietude about their crime. Nicole, however, is quite confident and determined.

Clouzot's main concern is to show the brutality of what the women are doing in a gruesomely realistic manner. There is nothing glamorous about this murder. Having submerged Michel, the two women weigh him down with an ungainly bronze sculpture of a lion rampant. But this sequence of events is not without some powerful cinematic techniques, principal of which is the manner in which Clouzot monumentalizes mundane objects and events. The mere sound of water, which Nicole runs in the bath in preparation for the grisly deed, here acquires a sinister frisson. The drugged whiskey bottle is then placed on the plastic tablecloth after Christine munches some bread while waiting for her husband to arrive. Clouzot shows the bottle in close-up, an image which may have been inspired by the equally atmospheric yet poignantly mundane close-up of a table setting in Fritz Lang's *M* (1931). In *M*, the table-setting implies that the child for whom it has been prepared has already been killed by the film's psychopathic child-murderer (played by Peter Lorre). The close-up of whiskey bottle in *Les Diaboliques* serves a similar premonitory function.

Soon after this shot, Clouzot again exploits the dramatic effect of an exaggerated close-up to invest a prosaic action with foreboding, showing the advancing footsteps of Christine's husband on the damp cobblestones in the street outside, but he does not show the whole figure, restricting the shot to the legs and feet. We of course know to whom the legs and feet belong, but by restricting the field of vision and also showing us the damp cobblestones we experience the intended *frisson* of ambiguity along with the atmospheric element of the wet stones. This technique owes much to Leni Riefenstahl's pioneering exploitation of close-ups in *Triumph des Willens* (*Triumph of the Will*, 1935) and

Olympiade (1938). Lotte H. Eisner claims that this was already a "well-worn technique," but Riefenstahl's application of them to Nazi propaganda invested them with an apparently novel power, which could not fail to make an impact on all who saw these films. Eisner gives various examples of Riefenstahl's "frequent use of the close-up to confer gigantic proportion on the meanest of object; the policeman's hands linking against their cartridge belts take on the appearance of some giant-stopping palisade. Here man becomes statue.... The faces in close-up seem like granite, with their vast strongly modelled surfaces and inhumanly sculptural chins."[5]

Though Clouzot is not being overtly political in *Les Diaboliques*, his use of close-ups achieves a comparable dramatic impact. Another monumentalizing close-up follows when Michel is shown drinking the drugged whiskey. Clouzot's camera stares at the motion of his throat, articulating the horror of what is happening; but before that, we are given another image which was profoundly to affect Hitchcock (in *Psycho*) and various of Hammer's subsequent thrillers: As the husband and wife have their uncomfortable discussion about divorce, Christine is reflected in a mirror. Michel addresses her in the room, thus facilitating a single shot that captures both their facial reactions simultaneously but, more symbolically speaking, the use of a reflection here suggests a psychological truth about Christine's behavior. She is, after all, disguising her true motivation—projecting a deception. Like a conjuror who uses smoke and mirrors, she is creating a convincing *illusion*, and we will be encountering mirrors as symbols of deception and of psychosis, split personalities and doppelgängers in several later films.

Clouzot also uses sound effects very effectively, having experienced their potential in the work of German directors such as Lang, who famously used sound as an integral part of his *Das Testament des Dr. Mabuse* (*The Testament of Dr. Mabuse*, 1933). In the opening scenes of that film, Lang rejected all dialogue and music (apart from the brief appearance of music during the titles, which sets up the rhythm of the machinery in the first scene). Instead, he used sound effects to fulfill the emotional function of an underscore as well as to aid naturalism. The ostinato of the machinery reflects the anxiety of the spy who is in hiding, as well as informing us that he is in a factory of some kind. The sudden silence as he emerges from the building, followed by the rolling of a metal barrel along the pavement, which then explodes, are similarly dualistic in their function. In *Les Diaboliques*, Clouzot's use of the sound of water running into the bath follows Lang's example. We do not see Nicole running the bath at first, we only hear the sound and see Michel's reaction to it as he sits up in bed and asks, "Qu'est-ce que c'est?" Indeed, we do not even realize at this point that the two women are planning to drown Michel, who by this stage is merely drugged by the whiskey. The sound of water consequently becomes a leitmotif, an aural symbol of horror, and because it is initially isolated from its source, it is monumentalized in a manner comparable to the use of a visual close-up.

The ancient plumbing of the building then creates a grotesque series of almost abstract noises, which Clouzot again exaggerates to heighten their emotional impact. An element of black humor results when we are shown how the sound disturbs the eccentric couple trying to listen to a quiz show on their radio in the room below. A similar effect is achieved in Alexander Mackendrick's British black comedy *The Ladykillers*, which was released in the same year as *Les Diaboliques*. In it the little old lady, played by Katie Johnson, runs the tap in her antiquated kitchen and has to knock on the pipe to set the water flowing. The comic effect is greater in *The Ladykillers*, but its grotesque quality is certainly related to the noisy plumbing in *Les Diaboliques*. In Clouzot's film, the eccentric couple also have a role to play in the plot, for Nicole and Christine need them to secure their alibi. The two women were seen to leave the school by the rest of the staff. They were also seen to enter the flat by the eccentric couple. No one knows that they have lured Michel to the flat, or that they intend to take his corpse back to the school. They therefore hope that when Michel's body is eventually discovered in the school swimming pool, they will not appear to be connected with the crime.

After Michel's murder, Clouzot again uses the sound of water—this time a close-up of water dripping from a faucet on the plastic sheet over the corpse—as a signifier of death. The sound of the dripping water once more masterfully monumentalizes the mundane, transforming the ordinary into the extraordinary. A later shot of the water gurgling down the plughole of the tub just before the women remove the corpse undoubtedly influenced the comparable scene in *Psycho* after the murder of Janet Leigh's Marion in the shower. Clouzot varies the gurgling sounds here. At first there is a rush of water, which is heard by the tenants. This is then subdued as Christine drags the empty trunk into the bathroom, and we are shown the dead body. Then, as we focus on the plughole between Michel's legs, Clouzot increases the intensity and rush of the sound to underline the impact of the visual horror.

When the women return to the school with the body they set about depositing it in the stagnant swimming pool, thus explaining the opening shot of the main titles and also continuing the predominant water symbolism. The following day, they arrange to have the pool drained to reveal the body. While waiting for this to happen, Christina resumes her teaching duties. Her mind is obviously not on the job, and she anxiously watches the clock, which Clouzot shows in another monumentalizing close-up to evoke the agonizingly slow passing of time. But to Christine's horror, when the pool is finally drained, the body is nowhere to be seen. Some time later, Michel's suit is returned from the cleaners. The women visit the cleaners, where a worker gives them a hotel key found in one of the pockets. Christine visits the hotel and walks down the corridor to the appropriate room where a door swings open; another mirror throws back Christine's duplicitous, accusing reflection. Exploiting a classic shock tactic of reversed expectation, a cleaner now emerges from behind the door and explains that the bed is always neat and that there is no evidence of anyone's having slept in the room.

The newspaper report of a suicide compels Christine to visit the morgue to find out if this is where Michel has ended up. Clouzot dwells some considerable time on the process of bringing the corpse from the refrigeration chamber to the examination room, luxuriating in the cold, bureaucratic impersonality of dealing with the dead, but the corpse in question has nothing to do with Michel. More importantly, a new character is introduced during this scene. This is the retired police inspector, Alfred Fichet. He may well have informed the character of Peter Falk's famous cigar-chewing TV detective Columbo, who shares Fichet's annoyingly friendly persistence and general shabbiness. Charles Vanel's performance as Fichet suggests to the audience that he is already fully aware of what has been going on, the facts of which are finally revealed to the audience in the famous sequence in which Christine is terrorized by various inexplicable happenings—and it was this sequence in particular that made such an impact on Jimmy Sangster's imagination.

A door opens at the end of a corridor in the darkened school. A gloved hand (in close-up) is shown resting on a banister rail. Christine wakes up and gets out of bed. She looks out of the window to see a figure walking about and switching on lights in the opposite wing of the building. Clouzot exploits corridors and lighting effects to summon an intensity of terror and claustrophobia, which Freddie Francis attempted to emulate in the opening sequence of Hammer's *Nightmare*. We hear the sound of advancing footsteps and doors creaking as Christine shouts, "Qui est là?" Shafts of light emerge from the threshold of the corridor's terminating door and, as was the case in the hotel room earlier, light and shadows from Venetian blinds or shutters disorientate the perspective. Crucially, Clouzot once more exploits the terror of *sound:* We hear a typewriter clattering, but when the door is opened, the room behind it is shown to be deserted. This apparent emptiness is then contradicted by the shadow of a hand on the wall. In another close-up we are shown a pair of gloves resting on the typewriter keyboard as though they have somehow typed the message that is left in the roller of the machine. The paper is covered with the name of Christine's husband.

Then, in the ultimate cliché, but still the ultimate shock, we are plunged into a blackout. Christina runs down the corridor and locks herself in the bathroom where, in the filled bathtub, lies Michel's corpse. He rises from the water with white, iris-less eyes and Christine collapses from a heart attack, emitting a terrifying gurgling gasp as she dies. Michel's hand rises from the bathtub in the same way as would Dracula's from his tomb after the grisly resurrection sequence in *Dracula—Prince of Darkness* (another film scripted by Sangster but directed by Terence Fisher in 1966). He removes the white contact lenses from his eyes, steps out of the bath, his shoes squishing from the water, and at this moment, Nicole arrives. They embrace and reveal themselves to be genuine lovers. Their plan to kill Christine and make her death look like heart failure has worked perfectly— or so they think, not having counted on Inspector Fichet, who promptly emerges from the shadows to arrest them.

There is another twist to come, but before we deal with this, we need to address why this final sequence has such power, not only because it is so powerful in its own right but also because it influenced so many other films. Although Clouzot was not afraid of using the kind of terror clichés that have their origin in the Gothic novels of Ann Radcliffe, their power here is rather greater than a straightforward Gothic effect. Of course, the sight of a man with white eyes is frightening because it is grotesque. Also, eyes are said to be the windows of the soul, and a man with no eyes might well be regarded as soulless in a symbolic sense. In E.F. Benson's horror story "At Abdul Ali's Grave," one of the characters describes the eyes of the Spirit of Black Magic as being "white all over" and "as big as the eyes of a horse,"[6] which is a fairly accurate description of Clouzot's effect. But there is more.

In his essay on "The Uncanny," Sigmund Freud suggests at least a psychological approach to the deconstruction of this final sequence. He asks what it is that creates an "uncanny" (or, in German, "unheimlich") effect, and quotes Friedrich Schelling (1775–1854), who intuitively arrived at this explanation: "Unheimlich is the name for everything that ought to have remained ... secret and hidden but has come to light."[7] Freud eventually interprets this as phenomena which trigger an unconscious memory of infantile anxieties:

> It seems as if each one of us has been through a phase of individual development corresponding to this animistic stage in primitive men, that none of us has passed through without preserving certain residues and traces of it which are still capable of manifesting themselves, and that everything which now strikes us as "uncanny" fulfills the condition of touching those residues of animistic mental activity within us and bringing them to expression.[8]

He adds that "this uncanny is in reality nothing new or alien, but something which is familiar and old-established in the mind and which has become alienated from it only through the process of repression."[9]

Freud also cites various examples that have a specific relevance to the imagery of the final sequence in *Les Diaboliques*. The first of these is the uncanny effect of E.T.A. Hoffmann's story "The Sandman" (1816), which formed the basis for the very sanitized version of it in Delibes' comic ballet *Coppélia* (1870). In Hoffmann's highly disturbing tale, the narrator, Nathaniel, is terrified by the idea of the Sandman who steals children's eyes. He is convinced that the lawyer Coppelius (a strange man who visits his father when Nathaniel is in bed) is in fact the Sandman; in later life he is convinced that an Italian occultist called Coppola is one and the same. He has a terrible attack of anxiety when he is told that Coppola stole Nathaniel's eyes to put in the sockets of an automaton called Olympia, which has been constructed by a Professor Spalanzani. When the doll's eyes are thrown at him, Nathaniel suffers an attack of madness. More things happen in Hoffmann's story, but its basic theme of a fear of losing one's eyes is the key element. Freud interprets such an anxiety as a substitute of the even greater fear of castration. The "uncanny" effect of Hoffmann's tale therefore results from Schelling's instinctive definition of it as something that ought to have remained secret and hidden but has come to light. The "uncanny" effect is always an echo of something else, otherwise it would be merely "horrific" or "terrifying," and the highly stylized way in which Clouzot presents the white-eyed Michel emerging from the bath at the end of *Les Diaboliques* displays the image as a symbol, much as Hoffmann's story had done. Michel has certainly done his best to castrate his wife in all but the physical sense by humiliating her, exploiting her, undermining her confidence, abusing her emotionally and flaunting his infidelity before her. For the audience, the ocular imagery also resonates independently of the narrative context in which it occurs. It is an uncanny effect in its own right. If Freud's theory is correct, and this imagery does indeed symbolize a castration complex, this in turn feeds into our shared response to the imagery, *investing* it with its uncanny resonance. In addition, the uncanny effect of a dead body coming back to life simultaneously articulates Freud's argument that our fear of death is the most powerful repression of all, which bubbles to the surface despite the manifold repressions of reason:

> [O]ur unconscious has as little use now as it ever had for the idea of its own mortality.... Most likely our fear still implies the old belief that the dead man becomes the enemy of its survivor and seeks to carry him off to share his new life with him.[10]

This is the reason why Michel rising from the bath in *Les Diaboliques* is so *uncanny* in its effect, for it releases a *repressed* unconscious fear. It is not merely our rational fear of death but our irrational fear that the dead will return and have their revenge upon us. A person finds something "uncanny" when he recognizes in it something of which he is "dimly aware ... in the remote corners of his own being"[11] Also, "an uncanny effect is often and easily produced when the distinction between imagination and reality is effaced, as when something that we have hitherto regarded as imaginary appears before us in reality."[12] Like Hoffmann, Clouzot realized that uncanny effects succeed most powerfully in a realistic context. As Freud observes, equally strange and magical things happen in fairy tales but the imaginary, fantasy context in which they occur removes the uncanny element:

> The contrast between what has been repressed and what has been surmounted cannot be transposed on to the uncanny in fiction [by which Freud means fantasy, non-naturalistic fictional contexts] without profound modification; for the realm of phantasy depends for its effect on the fact that its context is not submitted to reality-testing. The somewhat paradoxical result is that *in the first place a great deal that is not uncanny in fiction would be so if it happened in real life....*
> In fairy tales, for instance, the world of reality is left behind from the very start, and the animistic system of beliefs is frankly adopted. Wish-fulfillments, secret powers, omnipotence of thoughts, animation of inanimate objects, all the elements so common in fairy stories, can exert no uncanny influence here; for, as we have learned, that feeling cannot arise unless there is a conflict of judgment as to whether things may not, after all, be possible; and this problem is eliminated from the outset by the postulates of the world of fairy tales.[13]

Hoffmann made sure to set the "uncanny" effects of "The Sandman" in the real world. Similarly, Clouzot's careful creation of a grimy real world makes the effect of Michel rising out of the bath "uncanny" and terrifying, whereas the image of Dracula's hand clutching the side of his coffin in *Dracula—Prince of Darkness* is merely "Gothic" and supernatural. Dracula's fantasy context strips this image of anything "uncanny" and consequently reduces its terror. This, I think, is the reason why Hammer's psychological thrillers are more frightening than their Gothic horrors, and why they were filmed in contemporary settings in a much more realistic manner.

But, as mentioned earlier, there is a final twist to *Les Diaboliques* which, though dramatically stunning is, on reflection, implausible. After the lovers have been taken

1. The Uncanny in Les Diaboliques

away, we are shown the staff and pupils of the school being sent away, as the school is to close. Earlier in the film, one of the boys claimed to have spoken to the headmaster, even though he was by that stage supposedly dead. This, we eventually surmise, is part of Michel and Nicole's plot to convince Christine that her husband has indeed come back from the dead. It seems to be confirmed when a school photograph is taken and a shadowy figure, which could be Michel, can be seen in the background. However, at the very end of the film, the same boy claims also to have seen the apparently dead Christine. Is he lying? If he is telling the truth, does this mean that Christine was aware of the whole plot from the beginning and merely pretended to die of a heart attack? Such a complex double bluff is hard to swallow, though the shock of the revelation is administered like a pill to a child before he has properly woken up, and we swallow it obediently. Only later do we perhaps regurgitate it.

Such reversals were integral to Sangster's later Hammer thrillers, and they became ever more complex as the series progressed, stretching credulity even further than Clouzot had done, but they are similarly administered in such a stylish manner that we accept everything, at least until the final credits roll.

2

Echoes and Inspirations in Four Hitchcock Classics

Alfred Hitchcock very nearly acquired the rights to the original novel on which *Les Diaboliques* was based (he made sure to snap up the rights to the authors' next novel, which became *Vertigo*). His failure to do so did not stop him from exploiting some of the themes of *Les Diaboliques* in his own movies. The bathroom imagery and the mirrors went straight into *Psycho*, the double-cross plot cross-fertilized *Vertigo*, and Clouzot's demonstration of the brutality (and difficulty) of killing someone was amplified by Hitchcock in *Torn Curtain* (1966). On the other side of the equation, Hitchcock had developed techniques of his own which no doubt influenced Clouzot. The idea of a body in a trunk was prefigured by *Rope* (1948). Clouzot's use of the sound effects as harbingers of doom (the gurgling water of the bath) had been used by Hitchcock as early as *Blackmail* (1929) where the sound of bird calls, traffic noise, doorbells and Morse code were all manipulated to increase dramatic tension. Shadows were no one's particular trademark, but Hitchcock shared Clouzot's use of them in *Rebecca* (1940), a film which also demonstrated the immense psychological power of the monumentalizing close-up. (The zoom into the door handle that leads to Rebecca's bedroom is a particularly effective example. The close up of the door handle condenses all the accumulated anxiety of Joan Fontaine's unnamed character as she summons courage to penetrate the inner sanctum of her predecessor's domain.) *Spellbound* also used the close-up in this way. (The *coup de cinéma* of a gun being turned on the camera at the end to suggest the suicide of the villain was unprecedented in its impact at the time.) Similarly, the various close-ups of the shower scene in *Psycho* turn the seemingly benign environment of a bathroom into a veritable Auschwitz of anxiety and dread.

Because several of the motifs from Hitchcock's films recur in or at least inspire some of Hammer's subsequent forays into the suspense genre, it will be useful to give an outline of *Rebecca*, *Spellbound*, *Vertigo* and *Psycho* before we go any further.

Rebecca *(1940)*

Faithfully adapted from Daphne du Maurier's 1938 novel, *Rebecca* is almost pure Gothic, and bears most resemblance to Hammer's *Taste of Fear*. Rebecca is noticeable by her absence—a physical absence memorably filled by Franz Waxman's magical score, the ghostly timbre of the novachord providing a musical symbol of the dead woman's spirit. As Rebecca is dead before the action commences, the narrative is in some respects an extended flashback. We are encouraged to speculate about the manner of her death, to ask what she was really like, and to wonder if Maxim de Winter, her husband, really loved her as everyone claims. Maxim (played with Hamlet-like melancholy and detachment by Laurence Olivier) meets, in Monte Carlo, a vulnerable "plain Jane" (Joan Fontaine) whose name is never mentioned in the movie. She is the companion to the ghastly Mrs. Van Hopper (Florence Bates). Maxim marries the girl and takes her back to Manderley, his ancestral seat, without telling her about the jealous housekeeper, Mrs. Danvers (Judith Anderson). Mrs. Danvers loved Rebecca far more than any man ever could, for Rebecca hated men. (Such lesbian undertones, which Hitchcock emphasized far more than du Maurier had herself, resurfaces in Hammer's *The Witches.*) Rebecca and Mrs. Danvers were well-suited to each other in their man-hating egocentricity. In Jungian terms, they both personify the anima—the destructive feminine aspect of the psyche, of which Lady Macbeth, H. Rider Haggard's immortal Ayesha—"She-Who-Must-Be-Obeyed"—and several of Hammer's leading ladies offer other excellent examples. Maxim consequently loathed rather than loved this apparent paramour, and when he could bear her cruelty and duplicity no longer he thought of killing her. In the novel he does indeed shoot her, but Hollywood morality of the time insisted that if a husband kills his wife he must be punished for it, so Hitchcock has Maxim initiate a confrontation during which Rebecca stumbles and fatally hits her head. Maxim then dumps her body in a small boat and sinks it. When a body is washed

Poster for *Rebecca* (dir. Alfred Hitchcock, 1940) showing Joan Fontaine and Laurence Olivier.

up some time after his return to Manderley, questions are raised and the truth very nearly also surfaces. Maxim is saved, however, by the eventual revelation that Rebecca was suffering from incurable cancer and had arranged things so that Maxim would indeed kill her, thus releasing her from her suffering and incriminating himself at the same time. There is no need for this last detail to be revealed to the powers of the law and Maxim gets away with it. Mrs. Danvers, though, has different ideas. Unable to cope with the smear on Rebecca's glittering image, she sets fire to Manderley as Mrs. and Mrs. de Winter return from the court hearing. In the novel this final conflagration takes only half a page to describe, and it is left to the reader to realize Mrs. Danvers' responsibility for it. Hitchcock leaves us in no doubt with regard to the cause, and shows us the conflagration in all its cathartic (not to mention Wagnerian) sublimity.

Donald Spoto called *Rebecca* Hitchcock's most straightforward film,[1] but it would be more appropriate to call it his most Gothic film. What makes it particularly Gothic is the emphasis Hitchcock placed on Manderley itself. The masterly opening shots of the camera wandering down the overgrown drive towards the ruins of the mansion (a model) would certainly not be out of place in a later Hammer horror film. Hammer was always very careful to create the right atmosphere in their domestic settings, though none of their psychological thrillers featured a house quite as Gothic and overgrown as Manderley. It is an image that informs all of Hammer's subsequent venerable piles, whether they are villas in the south of France or more traditional English affairs.

Another thing that *Rebecca* shares with the Gothic tradition is its relatively slow pace. This is a mystery story, of course, and the whole point is the delay of its revelation, but the leisurely pace echoes the traditionally expansive style of Ann Radcliffe, for whom description and mood were just as important as plot, if not even more important. Similarly, the opening scenes set in Monte Carlo have nothing much to do with the story but they provide an opportunity for light comedy and romantic attraction, mirroring Radcliffe's comic maidservants and sentimental love scenes. The same technique was used by Michael Carreras in Jimmy Sangster's carefully constructed screenplay for *Maniac*, which similarly starts off at a very slow pace indeed.

As Rebecca is dead, it is up to Manderley itself (and Waxman's score) to suggest her presence. Manderley is the empty shell of her departed spirit. Everywhere the hapless Joan Fontaine character goes, she is pursued by reminders of Rebecca's past—Mrs. Danvers makes sure of that. From ordering the menus to being shown her predecessor's underwear (in one of the kinkiest scenes in any Hitchcock film, made even more sensual by Waxman's shimmering vibraphone and muted strings), Rebecca pursues her. Key scenes show her wandering about the house, just as Jennie Linden will wander around High Towers in *Nightmare*. The bedroom scene is in many ways the climax of the film. Obviously, it appears long before the dénouement of Maxim's trial, but as this film is really about Rebecca's relationship with Mrs. Danvers, the moment when the housekeeper gives the unfortunate girl a guided tour of this shrine to her former mistress is central to the drama.

One of the things this scene does is to transform domestic comfort into an environment of distinct alienation and anxiety. The new Mrs. de Winter enters the room in darkness, but ironically the place becomes even more frightening after Mrs. Danvers appears and opens the curtains. The luxurious setting becomes repellent—the silks, the satins, the monogrammed bedclothes, the fact that Mrs. Danvers has kept the place exactly as it was since Rebecca's death causes the heroine's flesh to creep (and that of the audience as well). It is one of Hitchcock's most unnervingly sensuous scenes, as he invites us to imagine even the texture of erotic fabrics.

Waxman articulates the emotional state of the unfortunate young woman in immense detail. As she climbs the stairs to the entrance, a rising scale for the harp synchronizes with her ascent, the novachord oscillating throughout as an ominous invocation to the dead woman's spirit. As the door opens, a tam-tam is lightly struck against tremolo strings, suggesting the sound of air rushing from the dead woman's room. We cut to the darkened space, which is full of shadows, as a flute in its low chalumeau register intones the "Rebecca" theme. A solo string then plays in counterpoint to the novachord's statement of the theme, as the girl parts a gauze curtain. The intimacy of the sound suggests that she is now ensnared in Rebecca's web. As she partly opens a curtain, a harp glissando and tuned percussion imitate the light that now penetrates the gloom. She flinches from touching Rebecca's hair brush on the dressing table as the theme returns again on muted strings. Waxman then fades the music to nothing to allow for the sudden noise of a window casement banging in the breeze—a classic shock tactic, which announces Mrs. Danvers' entrance: "Do you wish anything, madam?" She appears in silhouette at first, accompanied by the similarly dark timbre of the low-pitched flute. A truly Wagnerian moment follows when Mrs. Danvers opens the curtains fully, and the music echoes the technique of crescendo, rising pitch contour and the angelic (hence light-associated) timbre of the harp, by which Wagner suggested the sunrise in the prelude to *Götterdämmerung*. The windows flood the room with light. Again, solo string textures accompany the intimate examination of Rebecca's clothes, and Waxman's use of the celesta's sugarplum timbre as Mrs. Danvers brushes a fur against Mrs. de Winter's cheek creates an almost tactile sensation, which is repeated as the underwear drawers swing open, synchronized with similar musical accompaniment.

Mrs. Danvers' recreation of the ritual in which she nightly brushed Rebecca's hair was specifically echoed in Hammer's *The Nanny* when Wendy Craig's Virgie Fane asks Bette Davis' Nanny similarly to brush her hair. Richard Rodney Bennett's music for that scene suggests the immature dependency of Virgie on Nanny, along with the ambivalence of Nanny herself, but Waxman's score helps to articulate Mrs. de Winter's cringing response to Mrs. Danver's insistence. The sense of her being compelled to submit to this sadistic little drama against her will is musically suggested by stressing the first note of each small phrase for the solo viola, before immediately reducing the dynamic—a musical equivalent of Fontaine being almost magnetically pulled into position on the dressing table seat. Fontaine has no dialogue during this exchange, but the music fully expresses her state of mind. After Mrs. Danvers displays Rebecca's negligee (previously folded away in a silk case embroidered by the crazed housekeeper herself), it grows increasingly agitated, as the girl walks tremulously away. As she parts the gauze curtain (the hapless "fly" escaping the "web," so to speak), a very light roll on a drum supports the movement, enhancing its significance. Waxman even suggests the action of Rebecca's "quick, light step" spoken of by Mrs. Danvers just before the end of the scene.

The second half of the film is dominated by the legal proceedings, a narrative device Hammer avoided in its own thrillers (if we reject Cyril Frankel's 1960 *Never Take Sweets from a Stranger* from the company's psychological canon), and though the final fiery dénouement indeed anticipates the equally flammable climaxes of Hammer's Gothic horrors (not to mention those of Roger Corman's Poe adaptations), Hammer's thrillers avoided these (though a garage does go up in smoke at the end of *Maniac*). But the presence of the House—of Manderley—is always there. *Rebecca* is about Manderley, because Manderley *was* Rebecca. Similarly, when Roger Corman first suggested a movie adaptation of "The Fall of the House of Usher" in 1960, his studio bosses were doubtful about the lack of monsters. But Corman replied, "The house is the monster."[2] And so is Manderley.

Spellbound *(1945)*

Spellbound is Hitchcock's most overtly psychoanalytical film. In it we actually see the protagonist's dreams (stylishly designed by Salvador Dali), which are then analyzed on screen by two psychiatrists. The hero, Dr. Edwardes (Gregory Peck), is also apparently a psychiatrist, but he is suffering from severe amnesia and is laboring under the delusion that he is an impostor who has murdered the real Dr. Edwardes. Dr. Petersen (played by Ingrid Bergman), with whom Edwardes falls in love, applies psychoanalytical methods to help him sort out the mystery, and together with her old professor Dr. Brulov (Michael Chekhov) they discover that the fake Edwardes is suffering from a repressed guilt complex caused by the death of the real Dr. Edwardes, with whom he had been skiing and who had fallen over a precipice. They also discover that the fake Dr. Edwardes also traumatically observed the death of his own brother, who was accidentally impaled on the points of a railing. The sense of guilt over that tragedy informs and enforces the other, and at the moment of revelation, Edwardes also remembers his real name: John Ballantyne. In the end we discover that real villain of the piece is Dr. Murchison (Leo G. Carroll), the director of the psychiatric hospital at which Edwardes-Ballantyne is employed. Murchison shot the real Dr. Edwardes while he was skiing with Ballantyne, in an attempt to save his own job. This revelation leads to that stunning close-up of the revolver mentioned above.

Spellbound also uses close-ups to signify Ballantyne's guilt complex: The marks made by a fork that Dr. Petersen draws over a white table cloth suggest to Ballantyne the marks of skis in snow, which stir the repressed memory of the death of the real Dr. Edwardes. The repressed memory of snow is also activated by the shaving mug with its white frothing foam, the white bathroom wash basin, the white bathroom chair, the white enamel of the bath—all serve as metaphors for the snow in which Ballantyne witnessed the killing

Poster for *Spellbound* (dir. Alfred Hitchcock, 1945) with portraits of Gregory Peck and Ingrid Bergman.

of the real Edwardes. Once again mundane objects, due to the way they are lit and the angle at which they are photographed, are made into numinous psychological symbols.

More pertinent to Hammer's later films, such as *The Full Treatment* and *Hysteria*, is the subject of amnesia. Both these films concern victims of that condition, who are exploited by the villains of the piece to further their own ends; and amnesia is related to that other important topic of psychological thrillers: the doppelgänger. Someone with amnesia is someone else (i.e., someone they themselves have forgotten) who looks just like them. The crisis of identity is so resonant in such films because it is a danger we all face from time to time. We have all awoken from dreams and been momentarily disoriented or even unsure of our own identity. On a more prosaic level, our social identity can collapse if we lose our job, for example, or suffer a divorce; even during an illness, reality is rearranged for us. Someone without a past has no future, scarcely a present. Identity is in fact a fragile thing. But the idea of the doppelgänger also has a more straightforward though perhaps more terrifying manifestation. It suggests that there is indeed someone else out there who looks, sounds and behaves exactly like ourselves. He is our equal and opposite. Indeed, Gerry Anderson's feature film *Journey to the Far Side of the Sun* (dir. Robert Parish, 1969) was originally entitled *Doppelgänger* and explored this very theme, just as had E.T.A. Hoffmann considerably earlier in his 1821 story of that name (which we will be exploring later), along with Edgar Allan Poe in "William Wilson" (1839).

One aspect of *Spellbound* that makes it very different from Hammer's equivalents is its musical score by Miklós Rózsa, which is very much to the fore. It is so dominant, in fact, that Rózsa was unable to resist the temptation to transform it into a full-fledged concert piece in piano concerto idiom. The Romantic nature of this music is appropriate for a film that is fundamentally a romantic drama but it does tend to dominant the proceedings at the expense of the drama. Not even Hammer's *Crescendo*, a film with an overtly musical subject, featured so much intrusive music, evocative though Rósza's contribution is, especially in its use of the theremin as an electronically generated signifier of psychosis. So successful was this timbre in such a context that Rósza became associated with it by Hollywood directors of psychological dramas such as *The Lost Weekend* (dir. Billy Wilder, 1945) and *The Red House* (dir. Delmer Daves, 1947). Hammer, on the contrary, used music relatively sparsely in its own thrillers, and when it did decide to move the music center stage it was far more adventurous than Hollywood's more conservative approach to music in general. Hammer's film scores range from the advanced noteclusters and avant garde techniques of Richard Rodney Bennett in *The Nanny* to the highly integrated up-to-date jazz style of Don Banks and Stanley Black in, variously, *Hysteria*, *Maniac* and *The Full Treatment*.

The love story of *Spellbound* is also reflected in *The Full Treatment*, *Maniac* and even (in a more troubling way) *Straight on Till Morning*, but Hammer never resorted to the stylization of *Spellbound's* Dali dream sequences or the magical imagery of opening doors, which suggests that an emotional breakthrough has been achieved by Edwardes regarding his feelings for Dr. Petersen. Hammer had no aspirations towards this kind of cinematic poetry, taking a much more literal approach to their subjects. This, as we shall see, has its own rewards.

Vertigo *(1958)*

Visual poetry informs Hitchcock's *Vertigo* to an even greater extent. Donald Spoto refers to the work's "astonishing purity and formal perfection in every element. Each line of dialogue, each color, each piece of decoration, each article of wardrobe, each music cue, camera angle and gesture, each glance—everything in this motion picture has an organic relationship contributing to the whole"[3] Indeed, Hitchcock's favorite scene was the one in which Madeleine (Kim Novak) visits the grave of Carlotta Valdes, the ancestor by whose spirit she is supposed to be possessed; this scene does encapsulate the stylization of the whole film and reflects the description of it in Boileau and Narcejac's novel, which describes how "the roar and clatter of the town seemed to come, filtered, from far away."[4]

Boileau and Narcejac reprised this sense of dream-like alienation when the hero, Flavières, has "the impression he was living in an aquarium, that other people past him noiselessly as fish."[5]

The Madeleine of the novel also confesses, "When I was little, I thought colors had mystical properties,"[6] and this perhaps gave Hitchcock the idea of the color symbolism in his film, in which Flavières becomes the detective Scottie (played by James Stewart). As he emerges from the Mission building, we observe him walking down a path that is flanked on our right by two yellow iris-like flowers and a group of dark red flowers lower down. The golden section of the frame is occupied by a white column, the whole ensemble resembling a carefully arranged still life painting. The tall yellow flowers (yellow being the traditional symbol of caution) recur in subsequent shots, as do the red flowers, which are presented *en masse* just after Scottie glimpses Madeleine by a grave in the distance. These flowers flare forth the color of passion, but also of danger (Hitchcock consciously exploited the symbolism of red and green throughout the film (passion and fantasy, danger and tranquility, stop and go). The mood of romantic but also sinister fantasy in the cemetery scene is partly created by this stylized use of color, which makes the scene seem much less real than would have been the case in monochrome. Also, the location (a walled cemetery garden) encloses Scottie from the outside world; but the most powerful

Saul Bass' poster for *Vertigo* (dir. Alfred Hitchcock, 1958) with its highly influential spiral imagery.

element of all, perhaps, is Bernard Herrmann's music, which echoes the high-pitched strings in the Act III prelude of Wagner's *Tristan und Isolde*—another tale of romantic love flying in the face of reality. As Spoto records, Hitchcock "diffused" this scene and "gave it a kind of undefined outline"[7] by means of filtering the light. The whole is virtually surreal in its effect.

Hammer rarely indulged in such diffusion and undefined outlines, an exception to this general rule being the dream sequences of *Crescendo* which are deliberately confusing and visually "diffused" in Hitchcock's meaning of the term; but the dream that opens *Nightmare* is far more corporeal, as are that film's later apparent visions of a mysterious woman in white (imperiously played by Clytie Jessop). Hammer's other films in this genre are singularly naturalistic. Such an approach enhances the reality of the apparently "inexplicable" events in their thrillers and helps objectify the psychological content. Artistry is obviously used by Hammer but the results are not self-consciously "artistic." Though Hammer's thrillers play with ambiguity, the ambiguity is always resolved in the end. *Vertigo*, by contrast, is a highly subjective affair, mainly concerned with Scottie's own perception. Although the narrative ambiguity is resolved in the end (the plot is "explained"), the real point of the film is the ambiguity itself. *Vertigo* is concerned with illusion and reality, and the nature of what Luis Buñuel called, in the title of his 1977 film, *That Obscure Object of Desire*. Hammer's narratives exploit ambiguity to further the ends of the plot, where for Hitchcock, the plot provides a structure on which to explore the nature of ambiguity.

The plot of *Vertigo* is, however, exactly the kind of thing that Hammer would have found attractive. For a start, it features the concept of the double. A policeman, who discovers he suffers from vertigo, is employed by an old friend, Gavin Elster (played by Tom Helmore), to follow his wife Madeleine. Madeleine apparently believes herself to be possessed by the spirit of an ancestor who is compelling her to re-enact her suicide. Scottie saves Madeleine from drowning and begins to fall in love with her, but due to his vertigo he is unable to save her when she hurls herself from a church tower. This suicide causes Scottie to suffer a mental breakdown, but once he is back on his feet, he observes a woman who strongly resembles Madeleine. This is Judy Barton, a shop assistant, who had been employed by Elster to impersonate his wife so that an elaborate murder could be made to look like suicide. Judy was Gavin's mistress. Elster strangles the real Madeleine, and Judy's role in the proceedings gives Scottie the impression she has committed suicide. In fact, Elster has thrown his wife's body from the tower, realizing that Scottie's vertigo would prevent him from following Judy up the stairs.

The central scenes in the film, however, are those which show us Scottie's increasing infatuation with Judy, whom he dresses like a doll, in an attempt to resurrect the lost Madeleine. He is shown to be falling in love with the ghost of an impostor—an impostor who is with him in the room as he succumbs to his own fantasy. Like Berlioz's infatuation with the actress Harriet Smithson, for whom he composed his famous *Symphonie fantastique*, Scottie is not falling in love with Judy but with Judy's impersonation of Madeleine. Similarly, Berlioz fell in love with Harriet's Ophelia. The failure of both relationships was inevitable. Disillusioned to discover that his romantic love has proved to be nothing more than an illusion, Scottie drags Judy back to the church tower and compels her to tell him the truth, but she trips and falls to her death. Thus, Hitchcock informs his audience, is the fate of all who allow themselves to be seduced by illusion and the ideal of romantic love. In many ways, *Vertigo* is an indictment of the cinema itself.

The main titles of *Vertigo* foreshadow the elaborate James Bond title sequences by Maurice Binder, and they also made their impact on Hammer's *Hysteria*, but in the latter case the symbolism has less to do with the plot or style of the film than with their association with the genre of the psychological thriller, with which the success of *Vertigo* had invested them. The multicolored spirals that accompany the credits of *Vertigo* refer to the spiral imagery employed throughout the film (such as the spiral staircases, the curl in Madeleine's hair, the sensation of spiraling out of physical control during an attack of vertigo—and also spiraling out of mental control into a fantasy world). Herrmann's music echoes this interpretation, with a spiraling theme of two superimposed arpeggios, rising and falling in contrary motion, their diminished seventh harmonies unresolved and unending. Together, these elements created a subsequent cliché which, when combined with the op-art of Bridget Riley later in the sixties, made spirals and concentric circles and instant symbol of psychosis. (The film poster for Mel Brooks' 1977 Hitchcockian satire *High Anxiety* shows Brooks in free fall against just such concentric circles.) Boileau and Narcejac refer to "the giddy nausea of the soul."[8]

But spirals also have a more mystical interpretation, as Jill Purce has explained: "This symbol, which is perpetually turning in on itself, expanding and contracting, has an interchangeable center and circumference, and has neither beginning nor end.... [The] spiral may be imagined either as the aspiring upward spiral or as the downward vortex...: the choice of travelling with or against the sun. That the latter, widdershins or 'sinister' direction has the associations it does is an indication of man's close relationship with the movement of the heavens: it is said to be the entropic, unwinding movement from order into chaos, or, according to C.G. Jung, away from the conscious and towards the unconscious."[9] In the context of *Vertigo*, this mystical interpretation suggests the boundless realm of human imagination, wherein nothing is impossible.

Psycho *(1960)*

Spoto refers to *Vertigo* as a "slow chase."[10] Indeed, Scottie drives his car very slowly around the streets of San Francisco, and the deliberate slowness of Hitchcock's approach to this film is appropriate for a story about romantic love with Gothic elements, even if in a suspense thriller milieu. Romance certainly features in Hammer's thrillers, but it was never the main subject, and Hammer often preferred the imagery of visual speed even if the plots themselves took some time to unfold. Speed was perhaps inevitable in *The Full Treatment*, which concerns a racing driver, but fast cars also feature in *Hysteria*, *Taste of Fear*, and *Paranoiac*.

Hitchcock's pace speeded up in *Psycho*, though it is interesting to observe that the scenes featuring Janet Leigh as Marion Crane driving her car only give the impression of speed thanks to Bernard Herrmann's ostinato score. Take the music away and Leigh's car is revealed to be moving remarkably slowly. Herrmann's music also makes the infamous shower scene far more frightening than its visual imagery alone, and it is there that I would like to begin.

Bathrooms

Bathrooms are places of extreme vulnerability. If a character enters a bathroom in a psychological thriller, we expect the worst. There is, after all, no point in anyone entering such a place if the vulnerability he exposes by so doing is not exploited in some way. Merely to observe someone washing serves no useful dramatic purpose in itself. In fact, the only other reasons why any dramatic character should enter a bathroom is either to take their clothes off for erotic reasons (as happened in Hammer's *The Vampire Lovers* [dir. Roy Ward Baker, 1970] or to eliminate the possibility of being overheard by the sound of running water (an eventuality that often occurs in spy dramas). In psychological thrillers, to enter a bathroom is to dance with death. Stripped of one's clothing, one has no protection and no social identity. One can, of course, be killed with one's clothes on, but when naked the likelihood is all the greater.

Psycho was not the first

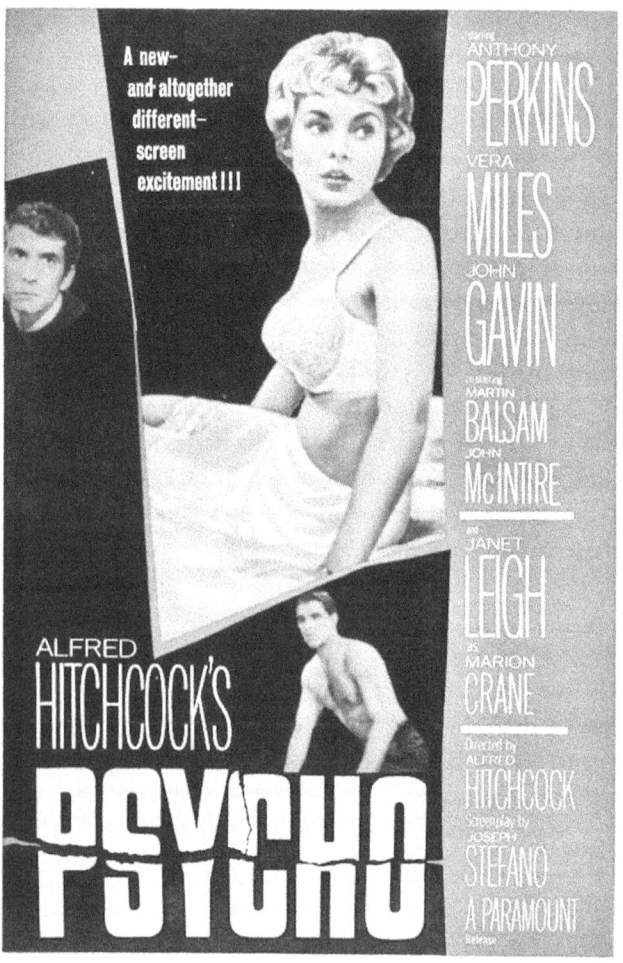

The classic poster for *Psycho* (dir. Alfred Hitchcock, 1960), featuring Anthony Perkins (top left), Janet Leigh, and John Gavin.

artwork to associate bathing with murder. Jean-Paul Marat (1743–1793) was, after all, stabbed in his bath by Charlotte Corday during the French Revolution, though Marat was not so much washing as alleviating a skin condition, which forced him to work in the bath. Nonetheless, the vulnerability of his situation perhaps made his murder in the bath all the more likely, and this event no doubt affected our response to later hydro-psychotic assassinations. Hitchcock certainly tapped a well-spring of anxiety here, exploiting it in such a complex way that no subsequent murder in such an environment can avoid comparison with it, and a large part of the shower scene's impact is the element of eroticism which he combines with it. There is nothing erotic about the death of Marat—particularly so in Jacques-Louis David's chilly, neoclassical painting of the event, which exploits the iconography of the Christian *pietà* rather than a nude, erotic or otherwise; but Hitchcock dwells on the body of his star Janet Leigh in a particularly voyeuristic way. We watch her walk to the shower in a silk dressing robe which clings to her buttocks; she closes the door of the bathroom, turns and removes the robe exposing the back of her shoulders. The camera follows the descent of the robe as it drops to the floor, brushing against her bare legs as she steps into the bath. The shower curtain is then pulled across the audience's field of vision, tantalizing us with the silhouette of her naked figure behind.

We then cut to Leigh's torso inside the shower. We watch her unwrap the soap and, as in the rest of the scene, *sound* is used in a vividly sensual manner: the *sound* of the paper being taken off the soap, the *sound* of the shower curtain, the *sound* of the shower itself. Indeed, the scene would be nowhere near as dynamic and sensual if Leigh had taken a bath instead. The running water of *Les Diaboliques* is ponderous and threatening, as it should be, but the shower in *Psycho* is altogether more dynamic with its brighter, more staccato and penetrative timbre, the jets of water anticipating and complementing Norman Bates' sharp, penetrative knife thrusts. For these shots before the murder, Hitchcock exploits only naturalistic sound effects, creating an almost *musique concrète* collage of anticipation. In sexual terms, the scene is really a kind of foreplay, and Hitchcock sensibly leaves Herrmann's orgasmic string shrieks for the stabbing sequence. The sexual excitement begins for Marion Crane when she looks up to the shower-head and opens her mouth orgasmically as the water showers upon her like a lover's kisses on her neck.

Sex is central to the film. It begins with a lunchtime assignation, showing Leigh wearing a bra. Even though we do not see her naked breasts in the motel shower, that scene is actually made more erotic by implication and suggestion. It too becomes part of the implied violence, for the way in which Hitchcock films the chrome shower head itself is intensely erotic and sinister, his imagery here recalling the legend of Danäe who was raped by Zeus in a shower of gold. We see the shower head ejaculating water from Marion's point of view, looking up at it. We also see it in profile, following several shots of Leigh soaping her arms—shots, incidentally, that take us closer towards her body. The profile shot of the shower is alternately photographed from below and later in profile at a diagonal. It thus becomes predatory, like a snake, and it doesn't take too much understanding of Freudian psychoanalysis to interpret it as a phallic symbol, especially when it is juxtaposed with Leigh's coital expressions of pleasure in the next shots.

The knife is also phallic, and it penetrates Marion's body (or is suggested so to do by Hitchcock) in a compulsive and sexually repetitive manner. Initially, it rips through the shower curtain as a rapist would rip a woman's clothing (an image, incidentally, which would be graphically enacted in Hammer's *Maniac* three years later). Many of the shots of Leigh's face during the attack could be interpreted entirely sexually if taken out of context, and there is no doubt about the post-coital imagery of the blood and water mingling as it swirls down a plug hole later, the eye of the corpse staring back at us in accusatory horror but also in lethargy. Hitchcock present us with a literal interpretation of the French term for sexual climax: *petite mort*. Here, we have *grande mort* with a vengeance.

Herrmann's music, more than anything, expresses this sense of emotional release—the shrill, explosive violence of repressed libidinous energy, which is always so close to violence and domination. Hitchcock's technique of suggestion also comments on the voyeurism of the audience's imagination. As the music hall star Marie Lloyd once demonstrated, it is possible to make anything appear lewd by means of innuendo. When criticized for offending public morals, she replied by injecting innuendo into a performance of "Come into the Garden, Maud," thus demonstrating that the obscenity was in the minds of the audience rather than the material she was singing. Similarly, Hitchcock lays accusations of depravity at the feet of his audience. He leaves us to assemble and interpret the imagery but refrains from graphic violence. We never see the knife enter the body and that is why the shot of Leigh's staring eyes at the end of the sequence is so powerful. They are staring at us and accusing us. We have watched this crime and been complicit in it, just as earlier we had conspired with Norman Bates and looked with him through the peep hole into Marion's room, watching her go about her private business.

The lengths to which Hitchcock goes in this scene to expose us to Marion's sensual enjoyment of the shower and the highly stylized, complex choreography of the killing sequence is disturbing in itself—and deliberately so. When watching a film like *Psycho*, intelligent viewers will inevitably ask themselves why they are watching this film. Are we enjoying it? And if we are, what is the nature of our pleasure? Is it, in some brutalized way (brutalized because, ironically, so highly sophisticated and manipulated) a kind of Liebestod?—a motel Liebestod with a corrupt Isolde and a psychopathic Tristan, combining the psychological drives that Freud labeled Eros and Thanatos: the pleasure-principle and the death wish that lies beyond it. Hitchcock seems to be paraphrasing Baudelaire's famous accusation, "Hypocrite lecteur—mon semblable—mon frère!" from *Les Fleurs du Mal*.

Hammer reprised *Psycho*'s shower scene in *The Nanny* and *Hysteria*, and these films obviously depend on Hitchcock's example. By calling upon *Psycho* in this derivative manner, they drew strength from the echo in much the same way that the evocation of an ancient myth adds resonance to a dramatic event in a more contemporary setting. Hammer evokes Hitchcock as a modern myth, not that the scenes in question in *The Nanny* and *Hysteria* do not have their own power (*The Nanny* in particular, even though that film features a bath rather than a shower), but they cannot be interpreted without reference to Hitchcock.

Hitchcock's use of the close-up again exerts a monumentalizing power that Hammer's directors were careful to apply to their own films. The close-up image of Leigh screaming was very deliberately reprised by Hammer the following year in the only pre-release still for *Taste of Fear*. It shows the star, Susan Strasberg, in a similar pose, and had a considerable impact, but Hammer had to wait until *The Nanny* for a bathroom montage that approached the 78 different camera angles of Hitchcock's shower scene, which took seven days to film. The complexity of Hitchcock's sequence, combined with the vital momentum and corporeity of Herrmann's music (to use a terms used by Hanns Eisler and Theodor Adorno[11]), is what creates its astonishing impact, transcending what would otherwise be a perfunctory killing in a motel shower. It is also what transforms mere *narrative* into visual poetry. Hammer rarely indulged in such complex montages, but they did employ music of comparable ingenuity (such as the advanced atonality of Richard Rodney Bennett for *The Nanny* and the driving rhythms of Don Banks' jazz-inspired score for *Hysteria*). By means of simpler, though no less effective techniques (such as distorted camera angles in *Taste of Fear*), Hammer achieved a heightened prose of its own.

BIRDS

Throughout Hitchcock's oeuvre, birds recur as symbols of unrest, discord, disruption and violence. Most obviously this is the case with *The Birds* (1963), but we also encounter them in *Spellbound* (where, in the dream sequence, giant wings pursue Gregory Peck) and *Psycho*. Norman Bates' stuffed birds (a euphemism that Donald Spoto points out also has a sexual connotation[12]) are harbingers of Bates' psychosis. Spoto also observes that Marion Crane is not only named after a bird but also comes from Phoenix, though in her case she will not be resurrected from a funeral pyre. Her irreversible death takes place in a quite different element.

Hammer referenced Hitchcock's use of avian symbolism only twice, in *Hysteria* and at the end of *The Kiss of the Vampire*, the company's most overt reference to *The Birds*. As we shall see in Chapter 10, *The Kiss of the Vampire* is indebted to Hitchcock in other ways, as well as being a vampiric reworking of Terence Fisher's *So Long at the Fair*, which he directed in 1950, seven years before his association with Hammer horror began. These uses of avian imagery are significant, however, not only because they highlight the impact of Hitchcock on Hammer but also because they help consolidate the use of an ancient symbol in terms of twentieth-century popular culture. Birds have long been regarded as omens of misfortune, evil or destiny. The magpie, because of its black and white markings and the fact that it was the only bird that refused to enter Noah's ark, is traditionally a bird of ill omen. Ravens are even more baleful in reputation. Wotan's two ravens, Huginn and Muginn, whom Wagner includes in the cast list of *Der Ring des Nibelungen*, are eloquent examples of this association. "Fliegt heim, ihr Raben!" Brünnhilde sings at the end of *Götterdämmerung*, "Raunt es eurem Herren, was hier am Rhein ihr gehört!" ("Fly home, you ravens! Recount to your master what you have heard here by the Rhine!") She then sets fire to Siegfried's funeral pyre, rides into it and the world ends. A raven also appears in Hoffmann's story "Die Doppelgänger" ("The Doubles," 1821). It says "'Murder! Murder!' in a hideous croak"[13] in a manner which Poe no doubt remembered when he made the raven of his famous poem croak "Nevermore!" The ambiguity of the raven's replies to the poet's questions suggest a supernatural element at work. As his essay on the technicalities of the poem explains, Poe assembled the elements of the text in a methodical, highly rational manner, but the effect is highly irrational. Presumably the bird has learned the word "Nevermore" without any understanding of its meaning, and yet in response to the poet's questions about the afterlife and the spirit of his dead beloved, Lenore, the word, reiterated by the bird, suggests otherwise. The graveyard imagery assists the impression, and this is also quite logical given the diet of the creature, its coloration and boldness, which, along with the owl's crepuscular and predatory lifestyle, creates the ill-omened reputation of both birds. Similarly, a raven is used as both a "character" in and an advertising image for *Damien: Omen II* (dir. Don Taylor, 1978).

Norman Bates stuffs both ravens and owls, thus furnishing the film with echoes of a Romantic Gothic tradition, which Hitchcock was keen both to exploit and invert by means of a contemporary setting and reversing the expected narrative conventions. In *Psycho*, the heroine is not rescued and order is not restored at the end. Herrmann also assisted in this process by using serial techniques in the final music cue to suggest Bates' now irredeemable insanity. Herrmann was not an admirer of Arnold Schoenberg's radical twelve-tone style, which he regarded as soulless and narcissistic, but this attitude made serialism the perfect symbol for Bates' insanity. Just as tonal stability is overthrown by serialism, so is Bates' mind overwhelmed by his psychosis. Claude Chabrol has also suggested that the sound of Herrmann's shrieking strings during the shower scene murder also imitates the sound of bird calls, thus indicating that Bates is indeed the killer.[14] Such an interpretation is debatable but worth considering even though Herrmann made no such claim for the music, which is much more likely to have been inspired by the kinetic movements on screen at the time.

As we shall see, Hammer's use of bird imagery in *Hysteria* is a highly effective detail, but it is hardly integral to what the film is about, being imposed onto the narrative to create a sense of the grotesque rather than to imply any narrative or psychological meaning. Having said that, *Hysteria* as a whole is about little more than the creation of an uncanny mood. In this sense, it represents the triumph of style over content—a style indebted to Hitchcock's example, and consequently an excellent example of exploitation cinema. *Psycho* is quite the opposite state of affairs, and, indeed, an indictment of exploitation cinema, as we have seen.

The imagery in *The Birds* is even more symbolic, representing the complete breakdown of human relationships. To many viewers, the preliminary scenes, prior to the attack of the birds themselves, might seem somewhat of a longueur, even irrelevant, but this is, of course, to miss the point, as the film is not about horror or even the uncanny, but rather the way in which human beings attack each other emotionally on a daily basis by means of small cruelties and selfishness. The attack of the birds upon humanity is "merely" a symbolic—even surrealistic—expression of this very human state of affairs. Thus we might refer to the bird scenes as representations of the film's own "unconsciousness," which, as in a dream, works out in symbolic form the emotional implications of the film's earlier "conscious" reality. Norman Bates' stuffed birds similarly express the psychotic, necrophiliac aspect of his personality.

Mirrors

Spoto has written at length about the mirror symbolism of *Psycho*. He draws our attention to the fact that Marion stands in front of a mirror two times in the opening scene set in a hotel.[15] She looks at herself in the mirror of her powder compact. She looks in the mirror in her hotel room as she counts her stolen cash. She is seen thinking before a mirror. She glances at the police car in her rear view mirror, her reflected eyes expressing the guilty conscience she is trying to hide. In Robert Bloch's novel on which the film is based, Marion (or Mary, as she is there) remembers throwing something at a mirror, "and then the mirror broke into a thousand pieces and she knew that wasn't all; *she* was breaking into a thousand pieces too."[16] The Bates Motel is also filled with mirrors. These images have dual functions, suggesting not only duality and split personality but also the nature of illusion and reality. Hitchcock is almost obsessed by showing his characters looking in mirrors, and he reflects this back at his audience, exposing the duality in all of us—the Jekyll and Hyde who make such an entertainment as *Psycho* a commercial viability in the first place. Cinema is itself a mirror, reflecting and distorting reality.

Even the main title sequence suggests the broken shards of a mirror, a disrupted, shattered sense of self; not only is Norman Bates disassociated from himself, so too, in different, less overtly worrying ways, are the other characters disassociated from themselves. Trapped as they are in the superficial materialism of modern urban life, they are, to quote the title of a paper by Jung, examples of modern man in search of a soul. In the dominant ideology of 1960s America, materialism was deemed to be the answer to the meaning of life, and money represented the American Dream come true; but *Psycho* demonstrates the meaninglessness of money when there is nothing of value to purchase with it—when society offers nothing but spiritual death (symbolized here by physical death). The mirrors of *Psycho* reflect this duality and suggest that what such a society offers is nothing but an illusion, a mere reflection of an ideal, without any substance to it. As in *The Birds*, Hitchcock argues that there is no real love shared between his characters, who labor under the corrupting influence of modern capitalism with its false idols and empty values. Hammer's use of mirrors was perhaps less complex, but no less psychologically revealing.

Mothers

The archetype of the devouring mother is central to *Psycho*. In Bloch's original novel, the unreliable narrator is able to sustain rather longer than a filmmaker can, the illusion that Norman Bates' mother is still alive and not merely a figment of his own disturbed imagination; but in both the film and the novel Mrs. Bates is presented as a malevolent, baleful influence. Bloch gives her a very revealing speech early on in the book:

> I know what you're thinking, Norman. I know all about you, boy. More than your dream. But I know that, too—what you dream. You're thinking that you'd like to kill me, aren't you, Norman? But you can't. Because you haven't the gumption. I'm the one who has the strength. I've always had it. Enough for both of us. That's why you'll never get rid of me, even if you really wanted to.
>
> Of course, deep down, you *don't* want to. You need me, boy. That's the truth, isn't it?[17]

As Norman is thinking up Mother's dialogue for himself all the time, he is obviously psychoanalyzing himself fairly accurately here. The classic Freudian theory of the Oepidus complex will concern us in several of Hammer's thrillers but it surely receives its most notorious cinematic manifestation in *Psycho*. Freud, however, was not the first person to be interested by mother-son relations. Edgar Allan Poe was similarly intrigued by the dynamic, particularly as expressed in what he regarded as his best tale, "Ligeia" (1838). In this story, Poe's obsessive love for his own mother, lost in infancy, is expressed in the narrator's equally obsessive love for Ligeia. He explains that "her rare learning, her singular yet placid cast of beauty, and the thrilling and enthralling eloquence of her low musical language, made their way into my heart by paces so steadily and stealthily progressive that they have been unnoticed and unknown"[18]; and when Ligeia dies, the narrator, reflecting Poe's own devastation at his mother's death, is "crushed into the very dust with sorrow."[19] But Ligeia's spirit eventually returns from the grave, actually to inhabit the body and displace the personality of the narrator's new wife, Lady Rowena Trevanian of Tremaine. The implication here is that devouring mother, represented by Ligeia, prevents the narrator from living an independent life with a wife of his own, much as Norman Bates' mother stunted her own son's development and turned him into a psychopath. (Indeed, in a psychological parallel to the fate of Lady Rowena, Norman Bates "becomes" Mother at the end of the story, as he abandons his own personality in favor of what he believes to be hers.) Goethe had expressed a similar meaning in *Faust* in the scene in which Faust goes in search of Helen of Troy. Before he can find her, he must encounter "The Mothers," who represent both the devouring mother archetype and the powers of the unconscious mind. The legend of St. George and the Dragon may also be interpreted in this fashion. Indeed, in *Siegfried*, the third of Wagner's *Ring* operas, Siegfried has to slay the dragon, Fafner, before he can bond meaningfully with his future wife, Brünnhilde. As Wagner's Jungian interpreter, Robert Donnington, suggests, "In Fafner the Dragon, Siegfried the hero meets the Terrible Mother. Being, however, the true hero that he is, he meets her on terms not of seduction but of mortal combat.... The dragon symbolizes a terrible danger from our mother-image."[20]

Significantly, the Dragon motif accompanies Brünnhilde's challenge to Siegfried:

> Are you not blinded by my blazing eyes, she cries, burned by the fire in my blood? Are you not afraid of the wild raging girl? And we hear, unexpectedly but logically enough, Fafner's growling motive in the bass, a clear reminder that even the most desirable of women still has an animus which can display a devouring and destructive aspect."[21]

Poster for *Psycho* (dir. Alfred Hitchcock, 1960), with Hitchcock himself pointing out the necessity of arriving at the cinema on time.

Hammer was similarly interested in this devouring, Black Widow spider aspect of the Mother archetype. As early as 1950, Francis Searle's *The Man in Black* featured an avaricious and ruthless stepmother who does her best to drive her stepdaughter insane to get what she wants, which is, predictably, a large amount of money. The same sort of thing happens in the rather more conventional *film noir* premise of Terence Fisher's *Murder by Proxy* (1955), in which Ann Davies' mother is quite ready to sacrifice her own flesh-and-blood daughter for similar gain. Rather more interesting Terrible Mothers appear in Hammer's later psychological thrillers, and they include Ann Todd's wicked stepmother in *Taste of Fear*; Nadia Gray's scheming and appropriately named Eve in *Maniac*, who quite happily drives her daughter to the maniac in question with the cold-blooded intention of having her killed by him; the psychopathic and incarcerated mother of Freddie Francis' *Nightmare*; Tallulah Bankhead's crazed mother in *Fanatic*, who wants to kill her dead son's ex-fiancé; Bette Davis' murderous mother substitute figure in *The Nanny*; Kay Walsh's lesbian dominatrix in *The Witches*, who plans to transplant her own personality into the body of a schoolgirl; and Margaretta Scott's Danielle Ryman in *Crescendo*, who feeds the heroin addiction of her disabled son and eventually shoots his psychopathic identical twin. Both *The Full Treatment* and *Paranoiac* feature overly protective mother figures, who shield their respective psychopathic charges. If Roy Ward Baker's *The Anniversary* (1963) belonged to the genre of psychological thriller rather than that of grotesque black comedy, Bette Davis' performance in it as the appalling Mrs. Taggart would certainly qualify for inclusion here. Alas, it does not, but in all conscience, the list is already long enough to entertain us for some considerable time.

3

Houses in *The Man in Black*
(dir. Francis Searle, 1950)

Hammer's most celebrated location, Oakley Court, stands on the banks of the river Thames near Bray in Berkshire. Now a luxury hotel, it was built by Sir Richard Hall-Say in 1857 after his marriage to Ellen Evans. Legend has it that he chose to build in a French style to help his wife feel less homesick for her native land, but the architecture, with its Anglo-Saxon castellations, brickwork and Tudor Gothic arches, is not particularly French, and the legend has little other evidence to support it. During the Second World War, the Court was apparently used by the French Resistance movement, and Charles de Gaule is even said to have slept in one of the bedrooms; but very little is known beyond these suppositions and the roll-call of its past owners. The house, it would appear, has decided to keep its private history to itself, but with such a mysterious past, its imposing Victorian Gothic style, complete with castellated tower, and its close proximity to Bray Studios, it was inevitable that it should eventually have served as the backdrop to so many Gothic horror films and psychological thrillers.

Oakley Court is well furnished with brooding architectural details that make it the perfect location for such entertainments. Its main entrance is flanked by two stone griffins wearing chained collars and grasping shields. There is a balustraded *porte-corchère* as well, adding further gravitas. Well-known of all to aficionados of Hammer films are the three stone dolphins whose intertwined tails support the basin of a nearby fountain. (Hammer's most celebrated shot of this occurs in *The Plague of the Zombies* [dir. John Gilling, 1966]). The roofline is punctuated by numerous heraldic and grotesque creatures mounted on tall pedestals, a motif which is continued inside where the Gothic oak bookcases of the library are similarly adorned. Also inside is a grand staircase, highly suitable for sweeping entrances, though the interior of the building has in fact been exploited by filmmakers to a much lesser extent than the exterior.

One film that made full use of all these aspects of Oakley Court was Hammer's early feature *The Man in Black*, which was released some seven years before the company's emergence as the world-famous House of Horror. The title was derived from a successful BBC radio series in which different mystery stories were introduced and narrated by the actor Valentine Dyall as "The Man in Black." He has nothing to do with the main story of Searle's film, and so the title is something of a misnomer, though given the popularity of the original radio series it was obviously deemed to be a crowd-puller at the time. The story itself anticipated many of the themes of Hammer's later psychological thrillers, the most significant of which was the setting itself. Virtually all of Hammer's thrillers are domestic in nature as they usually concern inheritance, the most visible element of which is the inheritance of property, and this is very much the case with *The Man in Black*.

But there is more to such stories than mere acquisition, surely the dullest of subjects, and really only useful as a plot motivation (or "MacGuffin," as Hitchcock frequently called it). Working alongside such plot motivations, and far more significantly from a dramatic point of view, is the motif of the house itself as a symbol of the mind and personality. After all, there is a particular resonance to the phrase "Hammer House of Horror," which cannot be explained merely by its alliteration. The word "house" has many layers of meaning, making it suitable to express both horror and the comforts of hearth and home. One of the most compelling writers to exploit the complex connotations of the word is Edgar Allan Poe. Poe took the established Gothic conventions of the creepy mansion and made its psychological symbolism explicit in his poem "The Haunted Palace," which first appeared as part of his tale about congenital madness, "The Fall of the House of Usher" in 1839. In "The Haunted Palace," the mind is described as a "fair and stately palace," which is originally ruled over by the "monarch Thought." But Poe then extends the metaphor to suggest the physical head in which the brain or mind is housed. The hair is described as "[b]anners yel-

Poster for *The Man in Black* (dir. Francis Searle, 1950).

low, glorious, golden," and these flutter over the roof. The eyes are "two luminous windows," and the teeth are the "fair palace door." "But evil things, in robes of sorrow/Assailed the monarch's high estate," and with the descent of the mind into madness, the "red-litten windows" suggest the madman's bloodshot eyes. Finally, the "pale door" of the madman's mouth emits insane laughter but no longer smiles.

This is a highly appropriate poem for the unstable melancholic Roderick Usher to write and recite to his unnamed guest, for he is a man who has buried his sister alive to prevent the inherited madness of the Usher line from endangering future generations. Poe further emphasizes the correlation between the house and Usher's insanity by remarking twice on the "eye-like" windows of the House of Usher. He also comments variously on the building's excessive decay and mentions the confusion of the local peasantry who used the term "House of Usher" as "an appellation which seemed to include ... both the family and the family mansion."[1]

Jung went one step further than Poe by equating the symbol of the house (statistically the most common motif of all dreams) with his theory of archetypes and the collective unconscious. In his autobiography, Jung explains how he once dreamed about a house, which he was quite certain was "my house":

> I found myself in the upper storey, where there was a kind of salon furnished with fine old pieces in rococo style. On the walls hung a number of precious old paintings. I wondered that this should be my house, and thought, "Not bad." But then it occurred to me that I did not know what the lower floor looked like. Descending the stairs, I reached the ground floor. There everything was much older, and I realized that this part of the house must date from about the fifteenth or sixteenth century.... I went from one room to another, thinking, "Now I really must explore the whole house." I came upon a heavy door, and opened it. Beyond it, I discovered a stone stairway that led down into the cellar.

After discovering a part of the house that he assumed must have that dated from Roman times, he then discovered another stone slab, which led down more steps to a cave where he found two human skulls:

> It was plain to me that the house represented a kind of image of the psyche—that is to say, of my then state of consciousness, with hitherto unconscious additions. Consciousness was represented by the salon. It had an inhabited atmosphere, in spite of its antiquated style.
> The ground floor stood for the first level of the unconscious. The deeper I went, the more alien and the darker the scene became. In the cave, I discovered remains of a primitive culture, that is, the world of the primitive man within myself—a world which can scarcely be illuminated by consciousness.[2]

It is for this reason that houses are such powerful symbols, but they also provide ample opportunities for emotional encounters, shadowy secrets and unexpected revelations. The house is the most profound metaphor of our sense of identity, security and, consequently, of all our anxieties. Houses both comfort and unnerve. Magritte's famous surrealist 1954 painting *L'Empire des Lumières* (*The Empire of Lights*) exploits the schizophrenic nature of the home by presenting an impossible state of affairs: darkness at noon. A blue sky above the house in Magritte's painting fails to tally with the darkness of the view below, which is lit by a streetlamp. Two windows on the first floor are illuminated from within, suggesting inhabitants, and yet the scene is otherwise devoid of people. This is a house, presumably a place of security, but the dreamlike sense of contradiction makes us feel uncomfortable. The house is white and yet full of shadows. (It also has a tower, like Oakley Court, which Freudians might like to interpret as a phallic symbol, but which is certainly a place of vantage from which we may look out at the world, as we ourselves look out from our consciousness at what is going on around us.) In this picture, Magritte shows us both aspects of the house and its inherent contradictions. Our homes are havens against the outside world, but at the same time most accidents, some of them fatal, are domestic in nature, and we often die in our own beds. Home is where the heart is, but most of our family disputes take place behind closed doors. The house can shelter us but it can also trap us. Teenagers feel smothered by their parents' domestic certainties. Avaricious nephews covet the property of their wealthy aunts. Mortgages can crush us. Accumulated possessions can overwhelm us. Ghosts of the past can haunt us (even if only in our memories). Home is not always sweet, despite the song that tells us so.

Freud even regarded the appearance of a house in dreams as a possible metaphor of the separate portions of the body; thus, "in a dream caused by a headache, the head may be represented by the ceiling of a room covered with disgusting, toad-like spiders."[3] "On the other hand ... a very long street of houses may represent a stimulus from the intestines."[4] Houses, therefore, are our most potent symbol of the self, and as such are vital elements in psychological thrillers in which the self (represented by the hero or heroine under duress) is in various ways under duress.

In *The Man in Black*, Oakley Court stands in for the fictional Oakfield Towers. Searle explained in an interview with Mike Murphy that the building actually inspired the film:

> A gothic turreted monster, wonderfully scenic with grounds down to the Thames River. It was owned by a yacht millionaire and it was an extraordinary place, really quite beautiful inside. It had an enormous mechanical organ in the hall. I thought, "I've got to use that sometime" and I did in *Someone at the Door*.
>
> While we were at Oakley Court, I wrote a story for *The Man in Black*, because the surroundings were so right....
>
> The main problems were with the lighting, and where to put the second boom. Obviously, it was also very cramped and, whereas in a studio you can float anything, you can't float brick and mortar. But, really, this was half the fun because there was much more need for creative talents, unlike today where so much is mechanized.[5]

After the main titles, which play out before the shadowy features of the largely redundant Man in Black, we are introduced to the main characters. The first is Henry Clavering, played by Sid James, whose serious performance as a wealthy practitioner of Yoga is light years away from the kind of comedy roles for which he later became famous in the "Carry On" films. Here he is a man "obsessed with a fear of impending death." We are then shown Clavering's second wife Bertha (played by Bette Ann Davis), whom the Man in Black describes as "merciless, vindictive, evil." Janice, her equally unpleasant daughter (Sheila Burrell), follows, along with Victor Harrington, (Anthony Forwood, who later gave up acting to become Dirk Bogarde's partner and manager). The final member of the cast is Hazel Penwarden, who plays Joan Clavering. "Danger sought her in this house of terror," the Man in Black intones. We should note the emphasis on the word "house" here, rather than the people who actually attempt to commit the crime of driving poor Joan mad to claim her inheritance for themselves.

After this roll call we are shown an establishing shot of the most important member of the cast: Oakley Court itself. Searle makes sure we see the tower and the dolphin fountain clearly, surrounded by dark monkey puzzle trees on either side; the branches reach out as if to clutch viewers and draw them into the building. We then cut to a shot of the main entrance. The doors swing back as the Man in Black explains his interest in the philosophy of yoga. As he does so, the staircase in the hall is revealed, and Searle will exploit this on many occasions later. The camera pans to the left to take in a carving of a medieval man in armor playing with a dog, before traveling down the hall to observe the state of disarray in which the house now languishes. It appears that the house and its contents are up for sale. A tea chest at the foot of the stairs suggests this to be the case, as do the ticketed *objets d'art*. Eventually, having learned that Henry Clavering is dead, the Man in Black (whose point of view we are sharing) discovers a statue of the Indian deity Siva, which interests him. The aura of Oriental mystery is thus offered to tantalize us, but this is not a mystery dealing with some unspeakable Hindu thuggery; Hammer audiences had to wait until Terence Fisher's *The Stranglers of Bombay* (1960) for that. Nevertheless, the statue of Siva evokes the conflation of "East meets West," which informed so many Victorian and Edwardian mystery tales, thanks to the repressed guilt of Empire, and in order for that sort of story to work, it was vitally important that the Orient was placed in a domestic Western setting. From Wilkie Collins' *The Moonstone* (1868) onwards, the Oriental threat was perceived to undermine the security of domesticity at home in England. The House, therefore, harbors the "enemy within."

Having said that, the Orientalism in *The Man in Black* is a very diluted affair, and is basically a pretext for events later in the story. Even so, it does serve a psychological function. The Man in Black then encounters Joan Clavering, who tells him the story we are about to enjoy. It took place two years earlier and basically concerns the plot of Bertha Clavering to drive Joan insane so that she will be able to claim Oakfield Towers for herself. However, Henry Clavering is fully aware of his wife's avariciousness. He therefore decides to fake his own death and then impersonate the gardener to find out what has been going on. This he does and Joan is saved from her enemies. Clavering removes his disguise and Bertha is similarly unmasked.

We are given our first view of the entrance to Oakley Court, with its heraldic griffins on each side of the door, when Joan returns to the family home. Searle, so obviously fond of this location, uses it far more evocatively than Terence Fisher did in *The Brides of Dracula* (1960), where we catch only the briefest of glimpses of it as Peter Cushing's Van Helsing runs out of Chateau Meinster. While Fisher never used the interior of Oakley Court, Searle atmospherically dwells on the claustrophobic atmosphere of the hall with its fringed drapes parted over the double doors. Henry Clavering's will is then read in the dining room with its heavy Victorian furniture, Tudor arched fireplace and wood paneling. It is all rather grand in its *haute bourgeoisie* manner, but as Jung explained with regard to his own dream, such psychological landscapes are not necessarily related to our actual properties and acquisitions. He recognized the rococo style and antique paintings as "my house." Similarly, this is Joan's house, though it is in the process of being stolen from her. The brooding atmosphere of the place also reflects not only the machinations of her stepmother and stepsister, but also Jane's anxiety, which both women play upon in their bid to make her believe she is insane. Such anxieties are given eloquent expression by Searle's use of shadows in Joan's bedroom.

Into this nest of vipers comes Victor Harrington, who parks his automobile under the *porte cochère*, giving Searle another opportunity to dwell on the griffins flanking the door, thereby emphasizing the connection his film makes between Gothic romance and psychological thriller. Oakley Court's Thames-side location also comes in useful for the boating scenes during which Sid James displays his considerable skills as a master of disguise. He plays both the old gardener, Hodson, and Henry Clavering, even before Clavering starts to impersonate the old man. The results are therefore even more convincing. Hodson-Clavering significantly refers to Mrs. Clavering as "an old vampire…. You can always tell a vampire when you see one," thus anticipating Hammer's later association of such creatures with this particular location. Appropriately, given the vampire's traditional association with staircases, Searle has the old vampire herself glide up and down it, dressed in suitably threatening black, just as Christopher Lee's Count Dracula would ascend and descend the specially built staircase in Hammer's first Dracula film in 1958. The library is also shown to good effect during the scene between Mrs. Clavering and the family lawyer, Mr. Sandford (Lawrence Baskcombe). We see the somewhat oppressive monkey puzzle trees through the heavily draped window casements as Mrs. Clavering lights a cigarette and tells Mr. Sandford that Joan is losing her mind.

Searle regularly alternates interiors with exteriors. We are shown the elaborate wrought-iron gates of the estate through which Joan walks, alarmed by the sound of an apparent pursuer (this is all Mrs. Clavering's doing, needless to say). We then cut to another darkly lit shot of Mrs. Clavering on the stairs once more, with a grandfather clock at its foot and the elaborately carved newel post decorated with a figurine (which has not survived in the Oakley Court hotel as it is today).

Scenes in the conservatory between Victor and Joan also give a false sense of security: light is let in, but of course Victor is a cad and only pretends to love Joan. He jokes that Mrs. Clavering would "cut your throat for sixpence. As for me, I wouldn't do it for under half a crown," but, of course, this is not so far from the truth.

After Hodson-Clavering warns Victor to stay away from Joan, Victor encounters the real Hodson, who issues a similar warning. Victor hits him, unintentionally killing him, thus giving the plot a further twist when Hodson-Clavering appears later. This eventuality also introduces another important element that is to feature in Hammer's more mature psychological thrillers when apparent revenants and doppelgängers add to the tension: Joan later says she has been talking to Hodson, much to the surprise of Mrs.

Clavering and Janice, who know that Hodson has been murdered. Indeed, this scene anticipates the much more famous and critically praised moment in *Les Diaboliques* when the schoolboy insists he has seen the apparently dead headmaster: Hammer got there first.

The stone griffins of the main entrance to the Court were too atmospheric not to be used again for the scene in the family vault where Mr. Clavering is supposed to have been interred; his coffin is, of course, empty. Victor decides to drag the body of the real Hodson here, and when he finds, to his surprise, that the coffin is empty, he deposits the body there before running out. All Searle had to do was attach a crucifix to the door of the main entrance, light the griffins somewhat more moodily, and the feeling of a family vault is nicely created in a shot that passes too quickly for a casual audience to realize the cinematic subterfuge.

Mrs. Clavering also stages a fake séance, with Janice rapping out the "replies" of Mr. Clavering's spirit from behind a curtain. This foreshadowing of the séance scenes in Hammer's *Hands of the Ripper* (dir. Peter Sasdy, 1971) brings us to the dénouement, when Hodson-Clavering appears. Understandably, Mrs. Clavering and Janice think that the ghost of Hodson has come to haunt them, but Clavering removes his disguise and all is revealed. The disguise is a very convincing one, for it is certainly not immediately obvious that Sid James has been playing both roles. Disguises also help to propel the plots of *Nightmare*, *Paranoiac* and Hitchcock's *Psycho*, of course. In *Nightmare* we are asked to believe that a latex mask can give the convincing impression of the actress Clytie Jessop, while the mask used in *Paranoiac* is merely grotesque. Anthony Perkins' Norman Bates was not attempting verisimilitude in his various maternal posturings, but he is so possessed by the spirit of his mother that a wig and the merest of other accessories are all he needs to help him submerge his own personality beneath that of his alter ego. All these cases, however, discuss the conflict explored in other Hammer thrillers between appearance and reality, and this is most obviously the case in our next film.

4
Misogyny in *Stolen Face*
(dir. Terence Fisher, 1952)

Stolen Face anticipates the main theme of Hitchcock's *Vertigo*. It concerns the successful attempt of a plastic surgeon (Paul Henreid) to graft the face of his dead lover onto that of a disfigured female convict. Such an erotic obsession certainly foreshadows the attempt of James Stewart's Scottie to recreate the image of his own object of desire in *Vertigo;* but while both films obviously manipulate the ancient Pygmalion and Galatea story, *Vertigo* is without doubt the more poetic of the two treatments. *Stolen Face*, however, adds its own element of the grotesque, along with some gentle comedy, to a psychologically disturbing love story.

Stolen Face also explores the literally skin-deep superficiality of appearance, and in many respects the film is a grotesque paraphrase of Bernard Shaw's play *Pygmalion*. Instead of merely coaching a working-class woman in the speech inflections of the upper classes, as Shaw's Professor Higgins does with Eliza Doolittle, Henreid's plastic surgeon, Dr. Ritter, transforms the face of a scarred ex-convict into the features of a glamorous concert pianist with whom he has fallen in love, but who is engaged to someone else. Georges Franju would direct a rather more horrific variation on this theme in 1960's *Les Yeux sans Visage* (*Eyes Without a Face*), in which a much more deranged plastic surgeon attempts to craft successive new faces onto the shattered features of his daughter, who has been badly disfigured in a car accident. These attempts are not a success, unlike Dr. Ritter's operation, and the unfortunate daughter is forced to a wear a mask, which unnervingly reveals only her highly expressive eyes. The film is both horrific and surrealistic in its imagery, its ultimate message apparently being that who we are is far more significant than what we look like, though life is surely never quite as simple as that. In the final scenes, the daughter (played with astonishing eloquence, considering the restriction of her mask, by Edith Scob) releases the dogs and doves her father keeps for his experiments, stabs the nurse who assists him and walks away from the horror of her father's obsession with her face. The father is attacked by the dogs, thus executing a kind of grimly poetic justice. One could, of course, interpret Franju's film and *Stolen Face* along feminist lines, as indictments, in their respective ways, of male domination and oppression—the kind of misogyny, indeed, that found eloquent expression in Villiers de l'Isle Adam's 1886 novel *L'Ève Future*. In that work, another mad scientist creates the perfect female android that combines beauty and obedience with more soulfulness and intelligence than was possessed by the real woman on whom the android's face has been fashioned. The scientist of this tale, based on the real-life example of Thomas Alva Edison, informs his "client," "At first, I will reincarnate all this exterior, which is so exquisitely vital to you.... I will illuminate from your idealized melancholy the imaginary soul of this new woman who will be capable of astounding even the angels."[1] Hammer returned to this theme in *Frankenstein Created Woman* (dir. Terence Fisher, 1967) but instead had Peter Cushing's baron transplant a male soul into a female body.

All these films play with the central misogynistic idea that the purpose of women is to fulfill and serve male fantasies. That message is already suggested in the opening scenes of *Stolen Face* in which a vain and selfish middle-aged woman, Lady Harringay, visits Dr. Ritter to ask for a facelift. Ritter informs her that she is already too old for that. He wouldn't want to risk it, but he does risk a great deal more later on when he becomes emotionally involved with another woman, and this implies that he is not quite the knight in shining armor his name suggests. (Henreid's full real name was, coincidentally, Paul Georg Julius Henreid Ritter von Wassel-Waldingau.) "Learn to live with yourself as you are," Ritter hypocritically advises Lady Harringay. Lady Harringay is not amused and storms out.

The noble side of Dr. Ritter's character is immeasurably aided by Henreid's screen charisma. Henreid had been associated with romantic leading roles in Warner Brothers melodramas in the '40s, most notably in *Now Voyager* (dir. Irving Rapper, 1942), *Casablanca* (dir. Michael Curtiz, 1942), and *Deception* (dir. Irving Rapper, 1946), and such a background lent all the more authority to his apparently benevolent role in *Stolen Face*, where Ritter demonstrates his commitment to helping prisoners who have been disfigured. "Of all prisoners who have received your plastic surgery treatment," the prison governor remarks, "only one has been rearrested since leaving here." However, like his underlying approach to women, Ritter's approach to these people is paternalistic. As we see later in the film, he wants nothing to do socially with the people he helps in prison, and the film consistently equates the lower orders with crime and vulgarity. The rule here appears to be that nice people come from and belong to a higher social order, and as if to emphasize this prejudice, Ritter makes the "mistake" of thinking he can turn an untrustworthy, feckless working-class person into an respectable, reliable middle class person simply by fixing her face, dressing her appropriately and taking her to the right parties.

Lily, the woman he attempts to convert, has been horribly disfigured in the Blitz. Ritter thinks, like Frankenstein, that noble features will make a noble character. Though this is semantically the opposite of what Peter Cushing's baron says in *The Curse of Frankenstein*, it amounts to the same thing: "I admit he isn't a particularly good-looking specimen at present," Frankenstein tells his tutor, Krempe (Robert Urquhart), "but don't forget, one's facial character is built up of what lies behind it in the brain. A benevolent

Poster for *Stolen Face* (dir. Terence Fisher, 1952), with portraits of Paul Henreid and Lizabeth Scott.

mind, and the face assumes the patterns of benevolence; an evil mind, then an evil face. For this, the brain of a genius will be used, and when that brain starts to function within the frame, then the face and features will assume wisdom and understanding." Unfortunately, both Frankenstein and Ritter are proved disastrously wrong, even though Frankenstein's theory remains just about intact, due to the brain in question having been damaged in a tomb-side struggle with Krempe. Ritter, however, soon finds out that a pretty face can't change Lily's inherent morally degenerate, lower-class personality.

But before all that happens, he has to meet the original on which his copy is based. In need of a holiday, he leaves Harley Street and travels up to the north of England. Like Marion Crane in *Psycho*, he is caught in a rainstorm, turns on the windshield wipers and is forced to take refuge in a hostelry. However, Malcolm Arnold's score is nowhere near as foreboding as Bernard Herrmann's for Hitchcock. His job in the scenes set in the Dog and Duck pub is, by contrast, to create a mood of gentle romantic comedy. Nothing remotely sinister happens for a while. There is some charming interplay between Ritter and Alice Brent (Lizabeth Scott), who occupy opposite bedrooms in the pub. (Sangster recalled being shocked by Scott: "A very sexy Hollywood actress who astounded me on the first day of shooting by telling me that she wouldn't be available Wednesday or Thursday because she was due for a period. I remember asking her 'A period what?' I was very naïve in those days."²) Alice has a cold, blows her nose and sneezes. Ritter gets out of bed, slips a prescription under the door and eventually encounters his lover-to-be. Greatly aiding the scene, Arnold's music charmingly punctuates this farcical mime in the manner of cartoon music. It seems that we are a long way from a psychological thriller. Indeed, these and later scenes charting their blossoming holiday romance have much in common with Henreid's *Now Voyager*, another holiday romance. The only major difference here is that setting is in the United Kingdom. The montage which demonstrates time passing is also indebted to Hollywood: a hunting scene, a picnic, a fishing trip, a pony trap ride—all accompanied by appropriate music.

Alice plays some music herself on the pub piano (Beethoven's *Pathétique* sonata, which soon segues into a Liberace routine including a boogie-woogie, followed by a rendition of "Rolling Home" to which everyone in the pub sings along). But this idyll cannot last. Alice is engaged to her agent, David, played by Hammer stalwart André Morell, and so Ritter turns his attention to Lily, resolving to give her Alice's face. Ritter is a fine sculptor, and makes a pre-operative bust before getting to work on the flesh and bones. Here he resembles Dr. Georges Bonner (Anton Diffring) in Hammer's *The Man Who Could Cheat Death* (dir. Terence Fisher, 1959). Bonner, another doctor who dabbles in the plastic arts, unveils his new bust at the beginning of the film, but in the case of *The Man Who Could Cheat Death*, it is the doctor's face which changes: Denied the pituitary glands he needs for his elixir of life, he ages hideously at the end of the film.

Meanwhile, Alice's virtuoso career continues. Another montage follows, similar to the ones we see in *The Seventh Veil* (dir. Compton Bennett, 1945) and *Love Story* (dir. Leslie Arliss, 1944). Superimposition of piano keyboards, posters, applause, airports and the Paris Opera House all combine to give Arnold another opportunity to play out his big Romantic piano concerto theme, first heard during the main titles. A similar thing happens in *The Seventh Veil*, which, along with *Stolen Face*, looked forward to Hammer's *Crescendo*, all three films being in their different ways psychological dramas about professional musicians.

David now realizes that Alice's heart belongs to someone else. He releases her from their forthcoming marriage, but this comes too late to leave the field open for Ritter, because Ritter has by this time married Lily. Again like Berlioz and Harriet Smithson, Ritter has married a fantasy—to all intents and purposes an animated, evil-minded waxwork of Alice—and he has already begun to regret it. Indeed, his situation more accurately resembles that of Scottie in *Vertigo*, who similarly *creates* his fantasy ideal. Scottie buys Judy the right clothes, and he arranges her hair to make her resemble Madeleine (whom Judy had anyway been pretending to be in the first place). The fantasy cannot be sustained and ends in tragedy, as does *Stolen Face*.

"Stop trying to make me something I'm not," Lily shouts, happy to wear the expensive clothes Ritter buys for her but not so happy to behave like the well-bred young lady he wants her to be. This fake Alice isn't at all interested in classical music like the real one. The opera bores her. She much prefers jazz, and here the story becomes Shaw's *Pygmalion* in reverse, for instead of Professor Higgins taking Eliza to high society gatherings, Lily now takes her "creator" to a noisy night club, where he obviously feels uncomfortable. There, she introduces him to her low-life friends and her kleptomania returns, much to Ritter's acute embarrassment and disappointment.

This state of affairs is reminiscent of the tradition of the evil doppelgänger that was so close to the heart of German Romanticism. It formed the basis of several of Hoffmann's tales, particularly "The Doubles" but also "Die Elixiere des Teufels" ("The Devil's Elixir," 1815), and I will be returning to these stories in more detail when considering Hammer's *Crescendo* later. In Hoffmann's and other stories about doubles, the double is presented as a harbinger of death, and this is of particular resonance here. Freud explains this by pointing out that the double was originally "an insurance against the destruction of the ego, 'an energetic denial of the power of death,' as Rank says; and probably the 'immortal' soul was the first 'double' of the body."[3] He continues:

> The same desire led the Ancient Egyptians to develop the art of making images of the dead in lasting materials. Such ideas, however, have sprung from the soil of unbounded self-love, from the primary narcissism which dominates the mind of the child and of primitive man. But when this stage has been surmounted, the "double" reverses its aspect. From having been an assurance of immortality, it becomes the uncanny harbinger of death.... [The] extraordinarily strong feeling of something uncanny that pervades the conception ... can only come from the fact of the "double" being a creation dating back to a very early mental stage, long since surmounted—a stage, incidentally, at which it wore a more friendly aspect. The "double" has become a thing of terror, just as, after the collapse of their religion, the gods turned into demons."[4]

John Lash adds:

> To be "taken over" (motif of transference) or united with the double is fatal but, to complicate matters even more, total separation from it is equally fatal.[5]

Deodatus, the hero of Hoffmann's "The Doubles," says "it is only too certain that I have a Second Self, a double who persecutes me, who wants to swindle me out of life and rob me of Nathalie," his beloved.[6] We will be reminded of this line again when exploring *Crescendo*, but it also has considerable relevance to *Stolen Face*. Lily does indeed "take over" Alice, and threatens to rob her of happiness with Dr. Ritter. She also smashes Ritter's portrait bust of Alice, like Pygmalion smashing her own statue. Lizabeth Scott of course plays both roles, but the resulting duality also suggests a subtextual element of schizophrenia at work here, prompting us to ask, "Who is the real Alice?" The narrative has no doubt about that, but some of the characters within the narrative are nonetheless confused, and so too might be a more inquiring member of the audience. Could it be that there is an aspect of Alice that is more like Lily than Ritter would like to believe? Has he merely created a physical copy or, much more worryingly, unleashed something from within Alice's psyche, Jekyll and Hyde–style? This is certainly one way of looking at the situation. If Ritter *has* unleashed something, he desperately needs to exorcise it, which he eventually does, and this suggests a psychiatric process as much as the exercise in social snobbery, which the surface narrative of the film seems most concerned with.

Poe's story "William Wilson" (1839) notably shares the snobbish agenda of *Stolen Face*. The narrator describes himself as of "noble descent," but when he goes to a school in England, he meets a boy who, like him, is also called William Wilson. The other Wilson embarrasses the narrator because he is "plebeian," but gradually this alter-ego dresses and even starts to walk like the noble William Wilson. Eventually he comes to resemble him completely. Horrified, the noble Wilson leaves the school and goes to university, by which time he has become increasingly decadent and debauched. The other Wilson follows him and imitates the noble Wilson's various peccadilloes. In the end, the noble Wilson drags his doppelgänger into the antechamber of a ballroom in Rome and stabs him. The doppelgänger dies but the noble Wilson sees the apparently dead double reflected in the mirror and feels himself to be saying, "In me didst thou exist—and in my death, see ... how utterly thou hast murdered thyself."[7]

The parallels with *Stolen Face* here are intriguing. Like Lily, the second Wilson doesn't resemble the first at the beginning. He *grows* to resemble him. Like the noble Wilson's doppelgänger, Lily is also plebeian; and just as the noble Wilson grows degenerate, so too does Lily grow increasingly criminal in her activities. She steals a brooch (a scene which is played out, incidentally, on a staircase with rich black shadows, highly reminiscent of the staircase scene in *Deception*, in which Bette Davis shoots the character played by Claude Rains—and this might be yet another way in which Paul Henreid's career at Warners is being referenced here). Lily then steals a fur coat, which gives actor Richard Wattis a good opportunity to play a diplomatic but very knowing store manager. Then, Lily starts going out with Pete the criminal (Terence O'Regan), and before the end of the film Lily will be destroyed, just as the plebeian Wilson is murdered.

Lily throws a party in Ritter's flat, a scene which might be said to have anticipated the unruly gathering that opens Hammer's *Dracula A.D. 1972* (dir. Alan Gibson, 1972) in which a rock group and their groupies take over an elegant upper-class drawing room in Chelsea. The party scene is where *Stolen Face*'s inherent class conflict is played out to the full. The plebeian partygoers are presented as highly undesirable, and the upper-class Ritter throws them out, punching Pete on the jaw for good measure. The partygoers in *Dracula A.D. 1972* are similarly ejected, but not before Dracula's disciple Johnny Alucard (Christopher Neame) smashes one of the Chinese ornaments so dear to the heart of the upper-class hostess. Fashions may have moved on by 1972, but Hammer still retained its primarily middle class orientation and class prejudice.

Ritter now contemplates suicide, and we are also led to believe that he has begun to consider murdering Lily himself. The dénouement, like that of the occult thriller *Night of the Demon* (dir. Jacques Tourneur, 1957), takes place on a train. Alice discovers Ritter and Lily's carriage, and in a way in which everyone is allowed to be blameless in the eyes of the law, Lily is indeed killed, but the implication is that it is Alice who is basically responsible, just as William Wilson killed *his* alter-ego. She bursts into the carriage where Ritter and Lily are having a drunken argument, and Lily accidentally falls out of the door onto the tracks below. The film closes with the unavoidable moral lesson that nasty people are expendable so that the nice may live, but how much have Alice and Ritter killed in themselves by this stage? Ritter's idealism has suffered a severe blow, and his misogyny and snobbery have been exposed. Alice's bust has also been smashed, her beauty and Ritter's appreciation of it contaminated by Lily's appropriation of it, and perhaps aspects of her personality, which might otherwise have been hidden from view, have been revealed.

This situation is, in fact, a curious mirror image of an influential doppelgänger story by Hanns Heinz Ewers (1871–1943). His 1913 novel *Der Student von Prag* (*The Student of Prague*) was first adapted for the cinema in 1913 (directed by Paul Wegener and Stellan Rye). A remake followed in 1926, directed by Henrik Galeen, and a third version, directed by Arthur Robinson, came out in 1935. As Freud points out, the hero of Ewers' novel "has promised his beloved not to kill his antagonist in a duel. But on the way to the duelling-ground he meets his 'double,' who has already killed his rival."[8] The double here represents the subconscious intention of the student. The student *wanted* to kill his adversary and so the doppelgänger does it for him. Such an interpretation suggests a similar way of interpreting *Stolen Face*. Could it be that Lily does indeed represent aspects of Alice's subconscious? In the event, Lily, the evil doppelgänger, doesn't actually kill anyone, no matter how much she might want her rival out of the way. Because a happy ending was required, the situation was merely reversed: If anyone is responsible for Lily's death, it is ultimately Alice herself.

5

Narcissism in *The Snorkel*
(dir. Guy Green, 1958)

Hammer was always keen to import American stars into its thrillers. Bette Davis, Robert Webber, Kerwin Mathews, Tallulah Bankhead, Joan Fontaine, Stefanie Powers and Richard Widmark all appeared amid British talent such as Oliver Reed and Rita Tushingham. Of these American stars, only Joan Fontaine and Tallulah Bankhead had ever worked for Hitchcock, and they were outranked by Bette Davis, surely the biggest American star Hammer ever employed. (The attempt of Hitchcock regular and Hammer fan Cary Grant to play the Phantom of the Opera was rapidly squashed by the studio to whom he was contracted at the time.)

Made only thirteen years after the defeat of the Nazis in the Second World War, *The Snorkel* chose a different kind of star: a German, whose real name was Götz von Eick, but who called himself Peter van Eyck. Van Eyck was far more appropriate than any American star to resonate the echoes of Nazi atrocities with which the subtext of this film is concerned. War films of this period emphasized courage and adventure over the psychological trauma of the experience, a trauma that seems to have been much more successfully dealt with by post-war psychological thrillers like this than by conventional war dramas. Van Eyck plays a ruthlessly charming murderer, who dispatches his victims in distinctly Nazi style by poisoning them with gas. Van Eyck was familiar with such roles, having been cast as Nazi officers in previous films. He was also no stranger to the psychological thriller, having starred in Clouzot's *Le Salaire de la Peur*, and during his time in Hollywood he appeared in the "Safe Conduct" episode of the TV series *Alfred Hitchcock Presents* in 1956. Screenwriter Jimmy Sangster regards *The Snorkel* as a straightforward murder story, but as the psychological element is paramount here it simultaneously qualifies as a psychological thriller. The Nazi connection also raises the influence of the Marquis de Sade, whose writings certainly foreshadowed if not inspired later Nazi atrocities and which also inform elements of Hammer thrillers.

Another theme that runs through *The Snorkel* and many of Hammer's other thrillers is the aesthetic pride taken by the criminal in the artistry of his crimes. Such criminals are also fatally compulsive and in the end, like the narrator of Poe's famous psychological crime story "The Black Cat," they are betrayed both by their compulsion and the over-inflated self-confidence that goes with it. The first writer really to come to grips with this tendency was E.T.A. Hoffmann, in his 1819 story "Mademoiselle de Scudéry," wherein a jeweler, René Cardillac, murders his clients to regain the jewels he sold to them. He does this not because he needs the money but because he cannot bear to be parted from his creations, which he feels are an almost physical—certainly psychological—part of him. The condition is well known medically, and has since been called "Cardillac syndrome" by German psychologists.

Poster for *The Snorkel* (dir. Guy Green, 1958), with a portrait of Peter van Eyck wearing the eponymous snorkel and a rather fanciful depiction of his character's attempted murder of Candy, played by Mandy Miller, who looks nothing like this representation of her.

The Snorkel begins with music as we are shown a gramophone playing a waltz. This draws to a close after which the needle follows the lead-out groove of the record until a hand lifts the gramophone arm and the disc stops spinning. This in itself suggests something sinister—a termination—especially as the shot lingers on the still gramophone and all we hear is silence. By beginning the film with an object, the director, Guy Green, indicates the preoccupation of the film in general. It is all about objects. Van Eyck's protagonist, Paul Decker, views everything, including all the people and animals in the cast, as objects. He rearranges everything around him, as in a game of chess, to suit his own agenda. The only difference is that this is a deadly game. He kills one person, attempts to kill another, has already killed a third before the film begins and he lies to everyone he meets. Objects are his goal, money and materialism his only motivation. He is the ultimate aesthete, for whom ethics do not exist—the perfect Nazi, in fact. As Frederic Spotts perceptively observed, "Crime itself was forgivable in Hitler's eyes if committed by an artist"[1]—though one should qualify this by adding that it would only have applied to the right (non–Jewish) kind of artist. Decker is yet another example of the ruthlessness inherent in the aesthete, which had been exhaustively explored so long before by Kierkegaarde in *Either/Or*. Indeed, Kierkegaarde's description of Johannes in the "Seducer's Diary" section of that work could well be applied to Decker in *The Snorkel*:

> In the first case he savored the aesthetic element personally; in the second he savored his own person aesthetically. In the first case the point was that he egoistically, personally, savored what in part reality gave him and what in part he had himself impregnated reality with; in the second case his personality was volatilized and he savored, then, the situation and himself in the situation. In the first case, he was in constant need of reality as the occasion, as an element; in the second case reality was drowned in the poetic.[2]

Decker does indeed savor his ingenious, "aesthetically" elegant method of murder. He also savors his own person aesthetically. He too impregnates reality with his own aesthetic genda: Other people and animals that get in his way are removed without hesitation. The reality of others is of no interest to him until they start to impinge upon his own world. Again, he resembles Johannes in "The Seducer's Diary." As Kierkegaarde puts it, "to talk of his conscience awakening is to apply too ethical an expression to him. For him conscience takes the form simply of a higher level of consciousness which expresses itself in a disquietude that still fails to accuse him in a deeper sense, but which keeps him awake with no support beneath him in his barren restlessness. Nor is he mad; for in their diversity his finite thoughts are not petrified in the eternity of madness."[3]

The next shot shows us, in close-up, latex-gloved hands taping up a window. The next cut pulls back a little to show van Eyck's figure surrounded by an array of baroque objects which fill the room: a large cupboard on the right, which will prove to be his ultimate downfall, and, on the left, a statuette of a priest wearing a mitre. The religious iconography of the room is of course ironic, emphasizing, by contrast, the unethical behavior that is being perpetrated in its midst. The room is full of distinctly ornate objects: vases, pedestals supporting figurines, silk-upholstered antique furniture, paintings in elaborate frames, etc. It would appear that we are somewhere in Catholic Europe as the furnishings are rather more baroque than one would expect to find in England. We are, in fact, in Italy.

Decker, dressed in dark tee-shirt and close-fitting slacks, removes two glasses of milk from a table and flushes what remains of their contents down a basin in the adjoining bathroom. After checking the seal of the door one more time, he removes a coil of rubber tubing from the cupboard. Lifting the rug in front of the cupboard, he then accesses a trap door, and stepping down into it takes the tubing with him. As he makes his way beneath the scantlings, a small rat scurries over the rafters, providing an appropriate metaphor for the kind of man he is. He then crawls along in the dark, like the rat, and attaches the end of the rubber tubing to an outlet pipe. The attention to detail, as we watch him screw the tube to the pipe and pull them to make sure they are secure, again emphasizes the film's and Decker's obsession with objects and technique. There is also something vaguely but appropriately effete about van Eyck's performance. His movements are very precise and delicate, and on emerging from the trapdoor he carefully brushes the dust from his clothing. This indicates the inherent narcissism of the character he plays, which will eventually cause his demise. (Significantly, Harold Nicolson recorded Carl Burckhardt's observations that Hitler "is the most profoundly feminine man that he has ever met, and that there are moments when he becomes almost effeminate."[4])

Trapdoors and secret compartments are well-established devices, but it is significant, I think, that Hoffmann includes them in "Mademoiselle de Scudéry," which anticipates so many of the themes explored by Hammer's psychological thrillers. In Hoffmann's tale, Cardillac presses an iron knob in a wall, and a section of the wall "swung round, so that a man could easily slip through the opening and out into the street.... It is a piece of wood, plastered and whitewashed on the outside only. Set in it, on the street side, is a statue, also of wood, but colored exactly to resemble stone, and the whole affair, statue and all, moves on concealed hinges."[5] This device allows Cardillac to fool the police with regard to his murderous activities. Admittedly, the trapdoor in *The Snorkel* is rather less elaborate, but its lineage back to Hoffmann is clear.

Decker extinguishes the gas lights, plunging the room into darkness, and we then cut to a shot of a woman lying drugged, breathing heavily on a couch. Decker looks at her and then turns the gas back on without lighting it. He has created his very own domestic Auschwitz. The main title then fills the screen over a shot of him sitting down wearing his protective snorkel, now attached to the rubber tubing he had prepared earlier. The murderer waits patiently for the gas to take effect.

The horror of Auschwitz is almost a cliché today but this was not the case in 1958, even though its memory was still fresh in the minds of many people in the audience when *The Snorkel* was first shown. War films, favoring action, heroism and adventure, avoided the subject. Indeed, Auschwitz wasn't really discussed in a graphic cinematic manner until Steven Spielberg's *Schindler's List* in 1993. There had been romantic dramas which echoed the grimier aspects of the war, such as *Portrait from Life* directed, interestingly, by Terence Fisher in 1948. This stars Mai Zetterling, Guy Rolfe and Herbert Lom, and is partly set in a displaced person's camp in which ex–Nazis (one of whom is played by Lom) also find themselves interned. The echo of Auschwitz here is muted and oblique but it resonates nonetheless. Less muted, but transposed into the setting of Gothic fantasy were the echoes of Nazi atrocities to be found in Universal's horror films during the Second World War, which featured a variety of mad scientists, and one should not forget that Hammer's very own *The Curse of Frankenstein* had been critically received at the time of its release with the kind of moral indignation we would nowadays deem more appropriate for a film showing Auschwitz in action. The crimes of Dr. Mengele had even been anticipated by Charles Laughton's terrifying performance in *Island of Lost Souls* (dir. Erle C. Kenton, 1932), but generally speaking, there was a reluctance to deal explicitly with Nazi genocide in popular films from the immediate post-war period. Dirk Bogarde, one of the biggest British stars of the post-war period, had personally helped to liberate Belsen but even as late as 1995, he wrote with typically terse discretion about his traumatic experience of death-camp survivors in his memoirs:

> [H]aggard, hysterical, shaven-headed, weeping creatures crying out to us in a babel of tongues. Begging for food, clutching our hands, kissing the Jeep bonnet, sobbing in gratitude, urinating down their legs as they stood, from sheer joy.... We had a map, but strangely enough the Germans had never feared an invasion as we in England had. We'd removed all our signposts. They had left their intact. We gratefully followed the black and yellow signs to Bergen-Belsen.
> Where we lost our boyish laughter for ever.[6]

It was perhaps easier to deal with this difficult subject, even in 1958, by means of the psychological thriller. By choosing the blonde-haired, Aryan good looks of van Eyck as the face of their fiendish murderer, Hammer was able to suggest the Nazi subtext of *The Snorkel* in a subliminal manner.

The idea of a crime perpetrated in a sealed room is also a well-established mystery device. Edgar Allan Poe, again, had been instrumental in the development of this motif in his story "The Murders in the Rue Morgue" (1841) in which a corpse is discovered in a room that has been locked from inside, just as in *The Snorkel*. The major difference is two-fold in Poe's story: The corpse is discovered stuffed up a fireplace flume, and the perpetrator is discovered to be an escaped ourang-outang, which gained access to the room by climbing up a lightning rod. Similarly, Gaston Leroux, in his *The Mystery of the Yellow Room* (1907), set up an even more unlikely sealed-room scenario in which the victim actually inflicts her injuries upon herself. Having had a nightmare inspired by an earlier attack, she falls over a piece of furniture and fatally hits her head.

Decker has an even more ingenious plot, and would no doubt have succeeded in convincing the police of his innocence and his wife's apparent suicide had he not been the victim of his own hubris. His stepdaughter suspects that he has murdered his wife, but no one else believes her. If Decker had not allowed himself to be goaded by this rather annoying young woman (played by Mandy Miller), he would have gotten away with his crime, but he decides to murder her using the same method, and the plan backfires. His elaborate, "artistic" plot, so carefully thought out, is foiled when the heavy cupboard we saw right at the beginning is dragged over his hiding place, trapping him beneath the floorboards. (The way in which the cupboard is photographed—monumentalized and thus invested with symbolic significance—is indebted to Hitchcock, Clouzot and also Riefenstahl, as we have seen.)

As with the concept of the sealed room, the idea of the "artist of crime" also has several literary precedents. The most obvious one is Sir Arthur Conan Doyle's Professor Moriarty, whom Sherlock Holmes refers to as "the Napoleon of Crime"—a man who prides himself on his own ingenuity and even manages to pass off fakes of Leonardo da Vinci's "Mona Lisa" to gullible American millionaires in "The Final Problem" (1895). A rather more apposite precedent for Paul Decker's narcissistic approach to crime, and also a somewhat earlier example than Moriarty, is, as mentioned at the outset of this chapter, E.T.A. Hoffmann's René Cardillac, who is very much a prototype of the kind of villain we encounter in Hammer's psychological thrillers, and there are many issues pertinent to them which this remarkable story explores.

The artist Edvard Munch (1863–1944) to some extent suffered from Cardillac Syndrome, hating to part with his canvases, which he referred to as his "children." He therefore made multiple copies to overcome his sense of loss. Cardillac is similarly motivated by his own ingenuity and skill rather than the money he can make by them, and despite Decker's apparent motivation of acquisition, the plot of *The Snorkel* reveals that on a deeper level he is actually more enamored of his elegantly ingenious method of killing the opposition than by what he can gain by his crimes. In other words, he too suffers the Cardillac Syndrome.

Cardillac describes his delight in creation early on in Hoffmann's story:

> He accepted all commissions with eagerness and enthusiasm, and would name fees so moderate that they seemed to bear no proportion whatever to the work to be done. And once a commission was taken in hand it gave him no rest. Night and day he would be heard hammering in his workshop, and often when his task was almost finished he would suddenly conceive a dislike for the design, or begin to question the elegance of the setting of some of the jewels, or the form of even a little link. This was sufficient reason for him to throw all his work into the crucible, and begin it entirely over again. Thus every piece of jewelry that he created was a perfect and matchless masterpiece which excited the wonder of his patrons.
>
> ... It made little difference whether his customer was a rich townsman or an important nobleman of the court, Cardillac would throw his arms impetuously round his neck, and hug and kiss him, saying that now he was quite happy again, and that in eight days the work would be finished. Then he would run home, breathless, rush into his workshop and begin to hammer away, and at the end of eight days a masterpiece would be completed.
>
> But the moment the customer came to call for it, more than ready to pay the insignificant fee demanded, and anxious to take the finished ornament away with him, Cardillac would become testy, rude, and obstinate.[7]

We will encounter this psychology of perfection in other Hammer films, particularly as manifested in the elaborate penthouse suite in *Hysteria*. The villain in that film delights in the elaborate nature of the plan itself, and the expense and organization it involves, which is surely comparable to the ecstasy of creation experienced by Cardillac. The same thing could be said of the twin accomplices of *Nightmare*, who are similarly defeated by their own smug self-satisfaction with their elaborate hoax. In *Crescendo*, a woman equally obsessed by the artistic legacy of her dead husband, organizes another complex "jewel" of a plan to encourage her deranged son to finish his father's piano concerto. The motivation of the plot is really another MacGuffin from the point of view of the audience—and perhaps the aim in view has also been lost by the widow, who is so absorbed by the complexity of her plan that it becomes an end in itself.

"Mademoiselle de Scudéry" also discusses the ingenuity of poisoners, and this pre-echoes the post–Holocaust crime of *The Snorkel*, particularly in the following example, in which the poisoner uses a mask to prevent the inhalation of deadly fumes:

> The poisons which Sainte-Croix compounded were of such a potent nature that if the mixer exposed his face during the preparation of the powder (called by the Parisians

Poudre de Succession) a single inhalation might cause instantaneous death. Sainte-Croix therefore, when engaged in its manufacture, always wore a mask made of fine glass. One day, just as he was pouring a completed formula into a phial, his mask fell off; the fine particles of the poison reached his nostrils, and he instantly fell down dead.[8]

Though ostensibly motivated by the perverted ideal of ethnic cleansing, the Nazis revealed a similar fascination with their own criminal "artistry," which was manifested in the supreme organization, efficiency and secrecy of the operation. These qualities are shared by van Eyck's charmingly duplicitous performance of the equally methodical Paul Decker. Just as Nazi propaganda films cynically presented images of happy, well looked-after inmates of Buchenwald and Treblinka, so Decker smiles and professes to love the people he is about to kill. Indeed, the final scenes in which he attempts to deal with his troublesome stepdaughter, are an object-lesson in Nazi methodology, as we shall see.

The racial ideology and narcissism of the Nazis did not blind them to the economic advantages to be gained by mass extermination. Like all poisoners, this was an important consideration, but it was not the main motivation. In "Mademoiselle de Scudéry" the poisoner, Sainte-Croix, murders ostensibly for money but there is a more compelling psychological drive behind his crimes:

> Often, without any further purpose than the mere depraved pleasure of the thing, poisoners, like chemists who perform experiments for their own enjoyment, have destroyed persons whose life or death must have been a matter of perfect indifference to them.[9]

Cardillac is also an early manifestation in literature of psychological duality, which is reflected not only in *The Snorkel* but also in many other Hammer thrillers. He is described as "frank, generous, without guile" but he also has deep-set green eyes, which might lead one "to suspect him of hidden malice and viciousness."[10] He is, in other words, not what he might at first appear to be, and van Eyck portrays such duplicity with particularly suave ruthlessness. Also, like Decker, Hoffmann's anti-hero is quite calm after committing his murders: "Once it was over I experienced a peace, a satisfaction in my soul, which I had never before known. The specter had vanished, the voice of the fiend was still. Now I knew what my evil destiny required of me. I had the choice of yielding to it or perishing."[11]

When Decker is discovered by his stepdaughter's carer, Jean (Betta St John), he has his head in his hands and appears genuinely devastated by his wife's "suicide." "I can't understand it," he exclaims. "It just isn't possible. If there was anything worrying her, why didn't she tell me?" Who but the audience (and Candy, his suspecting stepdaughter) would realize he was lying? Van Eyck's mellifluous timbre and strangely unexpressive face contribute to the illusion he creates throughout the film of a man who might even manage to convince himself that he is innocent, or at least that his crime is so perfect that he deserves to get away with it. ("Crime itself was forgivable in Hitler's eyes if committed by an artist.") Hoffmann suggests the same frame of mind in "Mademoiselle de Scudéry," where he is able to elicit sympathy and even support for Cardillac from his readers. There is, of course, far more to Cardillac that a mere murderer. Again, we admire the *artist* in him, which greatly mitigates the censorious response we might expect ourselves to feel when faced with his crimes. Similarly, audiences of *The Snorkel* are to some extent on Decker's side. We admire his ingenuity, if not his brittle charm. Early in the film, just after the body of his murdered wife has been discovered, there is a moment of danger: Decker is still hiding under the floorboards when Candy's dog, Toto (a soulful eyed spaniel), picks up his scent and starts to scratch at the rug that conceals the trapdoor. A classic moment of tension ensues but, as with the comparable moment in Hitchcock's *Rope*, in which two students serve dinner to the parents of the man they have just murdered on a chest in which the dead body has been deposited, we do not want the crime to be discovered just yet. We are momentarily on Decker's side, intrigued and even delighted by his Mephistophelean daring. The sweat of van Eyck's face and his expression of anxiety are ours as well. There would be no tension here if we were not to some extent in sympathy with him.

Hoffmann explains our attraction to crime stories (and "Mademoiselle de Scudéry" is, like Hammer's thrillers, essentially a crime story approached from a psychological point of view) by drawing our attention to "the most secret blood lust and murder ... which may be hidden in the best of us."[12] It is not quite as simple as blood lust, however, which is a more erotic drive. The identification we feel in the case of *The Snorkel* is intellectual and concerned with the Nietzschean Will to Power, which we have already discussed. Like many of the villains in such stories, Decker is an obsessive. Such criminals are also victims of their own compulsions and, as such, worthy of a certain amount of sympathy. Cardillac is obsessed by his own jewels. "I would brood and dream of sparkling diamonds and ornaments of gold,"[13] he confesses, an obsession that has a great deal in common with Paul Mallen, the jewel-obsessed anti-hero of *Gaslight*, as played by Anton Walbrook in Thorold Dickinson's classic 1940 British cinema adaptation of Patrick Hamilton's 1938 play. Indeed, *Gaslight* [*Angel Street* in the U.S.] also prefigures Hammer's much-used theme of trying to turn the victim mad. (This theme also surfaces in *The Snorkel*, as we shall see.) "Rubies!" shouts Mallen's wife Bella (played by Diana Wynyard). "You killed a woman for them. And me! You tried to kill my mind! You made me mad! 'Witless as an animal,' you said! And now you're helpless and I'm mad!" Mallen's crucifying obsession also encourages us to pity the monster he has become. In the end, Mallen scoops up his precious rubies at the moment he is handcuffed. "Better let him hold them," says the arresting policeman, who feels a similar pity and speaks for the audience.

However, any sympathy we might have for Decker disintegrates for all but the most hard-hearted when he steps into the realm not merely of crime but also of animal cruelty. To explain how this happens requires the story being brought up to date. Like Bella Mallen in *Gaslight*, not to mention the unfortunate Joan Clavering in *The Man in Black*, the heroine, Candy, is accused of madness. "You think I'm mad, don't you?" she shouts, having correctly (though without any hard evidence) accused Decker of having killed her mother. "They all thought I was mad when I said he'd killed my daddy," she complains. The difference here is that at first no one attempts to make Candy mad. Indeed, at one stage Jean says to her, "We mustn't start imagining things that didn't happen"—quite the opposite of the situation in *Nightmare* and *Hysteria*. "Do you think I'm mad, Jean?" Candy asks. "Of course not," Jean replies, but similarly no one believes that Paul Decker could be a murderer. As there *is* no evidence for that, it appears to the other characters that Candy has become unbalanced due to jealousy and grief.

Having accused Decker to his face, Candy's future is now under threat. At first, Decker plays on the idea of Candy's deranged mind, subtly suggesting that this is indeed the case. His duplicity is quite hypnotic in its suavity: "Now listen to me, Candy," he pleads after her initial outburst. "I love you. You are all I have left. We must help one another. Won't you try? We could have such fun you and I. We did have fun a long time ago, didn't we?"

"That was before you killed my daddy," Candy scowls back.

Decker has indeed killed her father. He drowned him and Candy witnessed it. Decker also murdered her mother, but the evidence arranged by Decker suggests that this is quite impossible. Not only did the death take place in a room locked from inside, but a letter to his wife arrives soon after the discovery of her body. It is from Decker:

> I miss you very much, but it is almost worth it. The book is coming along marvelously. I hope to finish it by tonight but whether I do or not, I can't stand being away from you, so I'm going to start back first thing in the morning. In fact, I may reach you before this letter does. Longing to see you, darling,
> Your own Paul

Of course, Decker has not been away at all; he has arranged the delivery of the letter as carefully as every other aspect of his plan. His apparently innocent charm is so convincing that the only explanation of Candy's accusations seems to be an unbalanced mind. The whole tension of the plot, of course, is whether Decker will be found out or not. If we are partly rooting for him at the beginning, it is also hard to warm to Mandy Miller's goody-two-shoes performance as Candy. It takes a dog to turn the tables and strip Decker of any humanity he might still have left.

Toto, Candy's doe-eyed but intelligent spaniel, discovers Decker's snorkel in the wardrobe of his hotel room. At first, Candy doesn't make the connection. She is more interested in trying to find Decker's passport to prove that he was not in France as he said he was when his wife apparently committed suicide. Decker has anticipated this, and arranged things accordingly, but he did not anticipate the dog finding his snorkel. After the dog has stared up at him accusingly, having dropped the snorkel at his feet, he callously poisons the animal, even making it beg for the drug that will kill it. This consolidates the film's Nazi allegory (despite the fact that Hitler was in fact a great dog lover). The corollary here is the way in which the unfortunate new arrivals at Auschwitz were soothed by telling them they were merely going to take a shower. Toto's death is so touchingly performed by Flush the dog, that Candy's role almost becomes superfluous.

Candy carries the dog's corpse back to Decker's room, where he continues his perfectly convincing duplicity, but Candy knows the truth. "You're going to have to kill me too," she shouts, "because if you don't, I'm going to kill you."

"These were her exact words," Decker explains, repeating them to Jean later that day, using them to imply that Candy is indeed going mad. "I can't forget the way she looked at me. It was so abnormal," he adds.

Decker then moves in on Jean, and implies that he would like to marry her. He plays with her emotions as if he is arranging a vase of flowers. The "romantic" love scene between them, played out ironically against moonlight on an exotic sea-front, reveals in one shot the cynical smile of Decker as he marvels at the effect of his own manipulative charm. One might compare that smile with the fleeting expression of half-surprised self-congratulation on Hitler's face in Riefenstahl's *Triumph of the Will*, after a particularly enthusiastic response to part of the speech he was making at the time.

While all this is going on, Candy creeps up to the villa to search for clues. An element of traditional Gothic creeps in here, with the silent house, the shuttered windows, the cicadas on the soundtrack, shadows on the stairs and Francis Chagrin's gently threatening ostinato for harp and celesta accompanying the whole. *The Snorkel* was made just after Hammer's *The Curse of Frankenstein* and around the same time as the company's even more famous Gothic masterpiece *Dracula*, so it is tempting to think of such a scene as having been influenced by both. The fact that *The Snorkel* was made in black-and-white also supports my contention that monochrome was regarded by Hammer as more realistic and contemporary than their Gothic fantasies in full color. The religious iconography of *Dracula* also seems to have been anticipated in *The Snorkel* as we now get to see a sculpture of a Madonna and Child in the same room in which Decker had gassed his wife. This might be suggesting that the forces of good are on Candy's side—though, having said that, they failed to help Decker's wife. Such iconography is intriguing, though, as it plays no other role in the action. Suddenly, Decker appears, having realized that Candy might be here. "I don't like naughty girls," he says, staring at her and now planning to do to her what he did to Toto.

During a day on the beach, Candy observes a man with a snorkel and begins to ask awkward questions concerning how snorkels are used. Having made Decker distinctly uncomfortable, she feels much happier. "It was as though she saw you clearly for the first time," says Jean, unaware of the irony here, and merely happy to see Candy happy again. But Decker takes the opportunity of attempting to drown Candy when she swims out too far in the sea, and during this compelling sequence, Chagrin brings back the film's opening waltz, weaving it into his dramatic underscore for the scene. Fortunately for Candy, Jean swims to the rescue as well, and Decker's murder attempt is foiled. When Candy accuses Decker of trying to kill her, Jean slaps her and seriously begins to think that Candy is deranged. "I know you lost your mother," she shouts, "but did you ever stop to think about Paul? He lost his wife." Finally, she admits, "It's not good making excuses for her any more. There's something wrong."

"I suppose you're right," Paul agrees, with apparent reluctance, but Candy is adamant.

"You can't see that I'm telling the truth," she complains to Jean, "because he's fooling you, the same as everyone else!"

Having failed to drown Candy, Decker now decides to repeat the plan that worked so well with his wife. Again, he sets up an alibi and lures Candy back to the villa. There he explains he has discovered a letter from her mother. A more consummate performance of callous duplicity than van Eyck's here would be hard to find. He offers his stepdaughter drugged milk and reads:

> Let's read it quietly before anyone else gets here: "My two darlings, Paul and Candy. You must forgive me for the terrible thing I have to do. You see, I went to the doctor the other day and he said that in a very little while I was going to die. He said I would undergo terrible pain. I could not face that—not because of myself but for the looks on your two faces if I were to suffer, so it is better to end it quickly like this.... I know that you will take care of each other, and that gives me great comfort. You will have such fun together. Bless you both—and Candy, I send you a kiss from your mummy.

Such cynicism expresses, as far as a popular entertainment of the time could express, the appalling cynicism of the Nazi slogan "Arbeit macht frei" ("Work will set you free") on the gates of the Auschwitz concentration camp. Decker's line, "I send you a kiss from your mummy," delivered so softly and tenderly by van Eyck, is profoundly shocking. Candy bursts into sobs but then notices that the letter is blank. Decker has made it all up. She collapses, Decker applies his latex gloves (in the sinister style that has been much lampooned in comedy sketches since) and repeats the opening scene. But a car pulls up with Jean and her ambassadorial friend, Wilson (played by William Franklin), and Candy is saved. They threaten her with a mental home, however, when she tells her story. As Decker has crawled back under the floorboards, they assume she has tried to kill herself. Humoring her, they agree to search for Decker, whom Candy insists must be hiding somewhere. They pull out the large cupboard and this now covers the trap door. Having convinced her that she has made up the whole story, they take her away—the threat of a lunatic asylum having been diminished as she promises not to persist in her "delusions." But Candy, unable to resist looking one more time, rushes back when Jean and Wilson are in the car. Decker shouts for help, but Candy ambivalently replies, "It's just my imagination. I must keep my promise."

Originally, the film was to have ended there, with the cupboard burying Decker alive, but as Sangster explains,

> Somebody, I'm not sure who ... maybe it was the censor, maybe the American distributor Columbia or maybe even Jim Carreras ... got cold feet about this one. Anyway I had to write a final scene where the girl walks into the local police station to tell them that Paul is trapped, thus saving his life. It was something I really didn't want to do at the time and I still think the movie would have been better if I'd kept to my original version. At least it would have given the audience something to discuss/argue about when they left the cinema. Always a good thing.[14]

(Hitchcock called such discussion "ice-box talk," which Donald Spoto explains as being what people chatted about "when they returned home from a movie and were rummaging through the refrigerator for a snack."[15])

The Snorkel also set a precedent for Hammer's later thrillers by placing the action in attractive, affluent European locations (in this case the Italian Riviera). Sangster confesses that the main reason for this was that it was a perk of the job, which he exploited to the hilt, but it also reflects the growing aspiration of the British cinema audience to visit such places themselves. As the late 1950s moved into the 1960s, package tours became more popular, air travel more affordable and the exotic locations once only available to the minority became increasingly accessible. The plot motivation of such films, invariably the desire to steal an inheritance, also reflects the then-current change in British society towards greater affluence, social mobility and materialism. The so-called lower orders were indeed beginning to get their hands on much more cash, and were probably disconcerting their former superiors in the process. As prime minister Harold MacMillan put it in a speech made only one year before the release of this film: "Indeed let us be frank about it—most of our people have never had it so good." Dirk Bogarde, by then already an established British star, wasn't so happy about the situation. In 1967 he wrote of then prime minister "Mr. [Harold] Wilson and his incompetent government. There is not one of them I trust. Nationalizing everything from Coal to Railways and nothing nationalized works. I'm all for the working man having fair shares, but not without incentive of some kind. With this government handing out free medicine, social aid, and all the other bits and pieces, no one need work at all. And the Unions are growing stronger and stronger and asking for more and more. There is no question that Britain is bent on a slow, determined, bloodless revolution … but where in God's name will it lead?"[16]

Bogarde, who assured his readers that his political opinions had mellowed considerably by the time that letter was published in 1989, never made a Hammer film, even though his partner, Anthony Forward, had appeared in one, Christopher Lee had appeared alongside him in *A Tale of Two Cities* (dir. Ralph Thomas, 1958), and he himself had been directed by Terence Fisher. He was enjoying a different kind of popularity as one of the cinema's most lovable medics in the Doctor films. But Hammer also specialized in doctors of a more worrying kind, and none were more disturbed and disturbing than the psychiatrist of their next psychological thriller.

6

Psychiatry in *The Full Treatment*
(dir. Val Guest, 1961)

With the exception of *The Two Faces of Dr. Jekyll* (dir. Terence Fisher, 1960), Hammer did not return to the psychological thriller genre until 1961 with *The Full Treatment*. Fisher's way with the Jekyll and Hyde story was typically "novel" in that it transformed Jekyll into a bearded old bore and made Hyde dashing, handsome and debauched. The psychological elements at work here are fairly obvious, principally being a dramatization of the Freudian concept of sexual repression and release, which Stevenson's original story had disguised, emphasizing a more theological conflict between good versus evil instead. Rouben Mamoullian's much more engaging 1931 adaptation, starring Fredric March, was the first film version to elaborate the sexual ramifications of the story. It highlighted the characters of Ivy Pearson, the music hall singer (Miriam Hopkins), and Muriel Carew (Rose Hobart), Jekyll's upper-class flame, both of whom had been grafted onto the story by Thomas Russell Sullivan in his 1887 stage adaptation. Fisher's film went on to make the sexual element paramount, featuring nightclub scenes with a snake-fondling belly dancer, which echoed Franz von Stuck's celebrated symbolist painting "Die Sünde" (1893). In fact, the composer for the film, Monty Norman (the creator of the James Bond theme the following year), was charged with the commission to hire the dancer in question.[1] Fisher's melodramatic approach to the lurid goings-on makes this film far more of a psychological fantasy than a psychological thriller, indicated once again by its use of poster-paint color as opposed to the more sober black-and-white imagery of *The Full Treatment*.

Hammer's involvement with this adaptation of Ronald Scott Thorn's novel *The Full Treatment* was disguised not only by Val Guest's rather different way of handling things but also by the fact that Hammer's subsidiary company, Falcon Films, joined forces with Guest's own company, Hilary, and Hammer's name did not appear on the titles. These are accompanied by Stanley Black's energetic jazz (standing in for radio music from the crashed car), which further distances the film from any connection with Hammer's Gothic style. The crew was also a rather different mix than usual. The result was nonetheless one of Hammer's very best but most underrated achievements in this field. Guest's style is much faster paced than Fisher's more sober, solid approach, and yet the film actually has a much longer running time than most Hammer films. The overall style is also rather slicker than even the best of Hammer's other thrillers.

At first, *The Full Treatment* appears primarily to be concerned about the psychosis of Alan Colby, a racing driver (played by Ronald Lewis, who would go on to play the chauffeur in *Taste of Fear*). After a serious car accident while on his honeymoon, he develops a mysterious compulsion to murder his wife. "The man is emotionally unstable," insists one of the doctors who has been treating him; and Colby is certainly fueled by a high level of testosterone, with mood swings that change as fast as the cars he drives for a living. He takes his wife on a second honeymoon, and Guest then transports us to another exotic location, this time a luxurious hotel in the South of France. (Ironically, Hammer's Gothic horrors set in Mitteleuropa rarely ventured further than Black Park in Berkshire.) "Is this as expensive as it looks?" Colby laughs, as he parks his sports car in front of the hotel's entrance with its elegant flight of steps; but already, Colby has given us signs that he is disturbed in some way. On the journey he put his hands around the throat of his wife, Denise (Diane Cilento), and when he discovers that Denise has booked a room with two single beds he demands to know if the doc-

American poster for *The Full Treatment* (dir. Val Guest, 1960), retitled *Stop Me Before I Kill,* with somewhat unrealistic portraits of Ronald Lewis, Diane Cilento and Claude Dauphin. The cat, which gives the greatest clue as to the true nature of Dauphin's mad psychiatrist, also plays its part here.

tors have told her he is too dangerous to risk having sex with. There is obviously something wrong; but the real motivation of the plot only gradually emerges with the appearance on the scene of a French psychiatrist, Dr. David Prade (played with astonishing brio by Claude Dauphin).

Prade first encounters Denise while Colby is on a cable car that leads to and from the beach below. "It's a mechanical device," he explains. "You know, they all break down sooner or later when the stresses and strains reach a sufficient pitch of tension.... Well, I suppose human beings follow the same laws more or less." Having guessed that something is wrong with Colby, Prade invites the couple to his nearby villa, just as Dr. Ravna invites the hapless Harcourts to his chateau in *The Kiss of the Vampire*. Indeed, Prade later watches Denise through a pair of binoculars, much as Ravna spies on the Harcourts in their motorcar through his impressive telescope.

Once seated at Prade's elegantly spread table, one of the guests is startled by a spider, and this gives Prade another opportunity to comment on Colby's psychological condition: He points out that female spiders eat the males of the species, with the implication that that is why men want to kill women. Again, Colby is outraged and storms out.

It would therefore appear that this film is about Colby's sex drive and its possible homicidal consequences. "I daren't make love to my wife," he complains. "I daren't sleep with her because sometimes when I hold her, I feel a kind of emotional compulsion"— a compulsion that seems to be focused on her neck. Surely we are not talking about vampires here? No, we are not. Colby is boisterous, possessive, hectoring, unpredictable, always smacking his wife's bottom. Similarly, Guest's trademark style of direction is appropriately frenetic and upbeat, and the dialogue of all the actors is delivered in the upper register of their voices. The neurotic mood is greatly enhanced by the way in which Guest paces the action.

Colby now begins to suspect that Prade is having an affair with Denise. This is not the case, but certain details lead us to suspect that Prade is not to be trusted. For a start, there is his vampire-like villa and the episode with the binoculars. The unmarried Prade also lives with his mother and, as we have already discussed, popular prejudice decrees that this is always a sign of abnormality. We then see him answering the telephone while stroking a Siamese cat in the manner of Dr. No, by which Guest is obviously signaling Prade's repressed sexuality. At one stage the cat is juxtaposed with a close-up of Denise's hair, consolidating the connection. Prade has indeed fallen in love with Mrs. Colby, and we begin to suspect there is more to his apparently disinterested desire to help her relations with her husband when Guest shows us the cat squirming erotically at Prade's feet. We might also ask why the good doctor never charges Denise and Colby for his presumably expensive Harley Street services.

As we eventually learn, Prade has conceived an elaborate plot to make Colby look as though he is insane, but it is the psychiatrist who is the truly unbalanced character, and this state of affairs is reminiscent of the situation in Hitchcock's *Spellbound*. Indeed, the analysis scenes in *The Full Treatment*, in which a forgotten memory is gradually revealed, are comparable to those in Hitchcock's earlier psychiatric thriller. Stylistically, however, they are very different. Hitchcock's surrealistic dream sequences contrast starkly with Guest's much more restrained, naturalistic approach. To suggest our joint plunge into Colby's subconscious, the lighting remains subdued and sometimes the faces of the two men emerge from entirely black backgrounds. A previous shot of Prade's bookshelves reveals a copy of Freud's *Interpretation of Dreams*, but Guest has no need of Dali's visual gimmicks. Instead, he shows us Colby's point of view as he looks up at the ceiling with its elaborate plaster rose. The camera then moves to a cabinet surmounted by a Chinese ginger jar, and, after that, to the fireplace. These ordinary objects are monumentalized to reflect Colby's concentration and anxiety, and Guest makes excellent, somewhat ambivalent use of close-ups of the two protagonists' faces during pauses in their dialogue. Prade glances down at Colby's fingers, which twist the upholstery braid of his chair and tap the end of his cigarette before stubbing it out. The chiaroscuro of Dauphin's dimly lit face, with its sinister, ambivalent expression photographed against a black background, are portrait studies worthy of Karsh in their texture and lighting. As such, they are unrivaled by any other Hammer film.

During these sessions, we learn that Colby's compulsion to kill his wife is due to guilt arising from the opening car accident. While adjusting the chain of Denise's crucifix, he swerved the car and crashed into the oncoming vehicle. He then thought he had killed his wife and, as the psychiatrist explains, "You felt like killing her ever since. In the moment of terror you have just re-lived on that couch, you thought you had killed Denise, the object of your love; you felt so guilty you wanted to punish yourself. The only way of diminishing your guilt was by suffering what you should have suffered if she had been killed.... See how even your method of killing her was conditioned by the accident: your hand on the gold chain around her neck, the association of strangling at a time of maximum shock."

Prade's approach is very much the kind of thing Richard Webster criticized Freud for in his study *Why Freud Was Wrong*, to which Richard Noll refers in *his* controversial book on Jung:

> In placing what was, in effect, a confessional ritual at the very heart of the psychoanalytic movement, it seems clear that Freud was not, as he himself believed, engaging in a form of scientific innovation. Rather, he was unconsciously institutionalizing his own profound religious traditionalism at the same time that he was creating for himself a ritual stage on which he could pay out his own "God complex" in relation to patients he regarded as inferior and in need of redemption.[2]

Prade certainly exhibits a strong God complex, believing he can manipulate his patient into believing he is a psychopath. At this stage, however, whatever vague doubts the audience might have about Prade's motivation, we are still under the impression that he is genuine. His approach seems to be following the therapeutic aims outlined in his copy of Freud's *Interpretation of Dreams*:

> I have been engaged for many years (with a therapeutic aim in view) in unravelling certain psychopathological structures—hysterical phobias, obsessional ideas, and so on. I have been doing so, in fact, ever since I learned from an important communication by Josef

Breuer that as regards these structures (which are looked on as pathological symptoms) unravelling them coincides with removing them.... If a pathological idea of this sort can be traced back to the elements in the patient's mental life from which it originated, it simultaneously crumbles away and the patient is freed from it.[3]

Prade also extracts Colby's imagined method of disposing of his wife's body: Colby confesses that he would dismember it and eject it through the waste disposal chute. (Later, Prade enacts this imaginary scenario, sacrificing one of his own beloved cats to smear surgical instruments which had once belonged to Colby's father with the necessary blood and hair.) Having been thus set up, Colby thinks he really has gone mad. He runs away, and Prade now assumes the field is clear for his own advances on Denise. But Colby finds out what has been going on, and the psychiatrist, unmasked, is accidentally killed in a culminating chase scene involving the cable car with which the whole affair started.

The idea of duality is central to the presentation of Prade's character. He is, after all, a figure of trust who is untrustworthy. No one expects a doctor to be criminally insane, just as we do not immediately associate an artist with murder. Indeed, Prade's literary ancestor is, once again, René Cardillac. A less compelling version of an untrustworthy doctor appears in Hammer's later *Hysteria*; but the idea of a mad psychiatrist derives from Poe's famous 1845 story "The System of Doctor Tarr and Professor Fether," in which a lunatic asylum is eventually revealed to be run by its inmates. Prade suggests the connection with this story when he replies to Colby's confession that he distrusts psychiatrists: "I know. Crazy, the lot of them. Inhuman monsters with tangled minds and perverted sense of humor. We know all that."

The narrator of Poe's tale visits a *Maison de Santé* in "the extreme southern provinces of France"[4] (a location also shared by *The Full Treatment*). Introduced to the director, Monsieur Maillard, the narrator eventually finds himself having dinner with a group of eccentric guests who discuss the peculiarities of previous inmates.

> "We had a fellow here once," said a fat little gentleman, who sat at my right,—"a fellow that fancied himself a tea-pot; and by the way, is it not especially singular how often this particular crotchet has entered the brain of the lunatic? There is scarcely an insane asylum in France which cannot supply a human tea-pot. *Our* gentleman was a Britannia-ware tea-pot, and was careful to polish himself every morning with buckskin and whiting."[5]

Gradually, the narrator realizes that he's dining with madmen:

> "And then," said some other one of the party,—"then there was Bouffon Le Grand—another extraordinary personage in his way. He grew deranged through love, and fancied himself possessed of two heads. One of these he maintained to be the head of Cicero; the other he imagined a composite one, being Demosthenes' from the top of the forehead to the mouth, and Lord Brougham's from the mouth to the chin."[6]

A lady then begins to crow like a cock, while another starts screaming, and eventually the truth is revealed: The patients have overthrown the directors of the establishment.

> Monsieur Maillard, it appeared,... had, indeed, some two or three years before, been the superintendent of the establishment; but grew crazy himself, and so became a patient. This

fact was unknown to the travelling companion who introduced me. The keepers, ten in number, having been suddenly overpowered, were first well tarred, then carefully feathered, and then shut up in underground cells. They had been so imprisoned for more than a month, during which period Monsieur Maillard had generously allowed them not only the tar and feather (which constituted his "system"), but some bread and abundance of water. The latter was pumped on them daily. At length, one escaping through a sewer, gave freedom to all the rest.[7]

The Full Treatment is not as melodramatically grotesque as Poe's tale, but it shares the same premise, exploring the implication of a deranged psychiatrist along psychological lines with far more tension and insight than films such as the somewhat obscure *The Keeper* (dir. Tom Y. Drake, 1976), in which Christopher Lee plays the director of the Underwood Asylum. He hypnotizes his patients to swindle them of their money before persuading them to commit suicide. Some arty shots of his hypnosis machine reference the spirals and eyes of *Vertigo*'s main title, but the film has little else to compare usefully with Hitchcock's masterpiece or Guest's underrated thriller. *The Full Treatment* is also a much more mature exploration of the possibilities of such a situation than the nonetheless enjoyable Amicus portmanteau film, *Asylum* (dir. Roy Ward Baker, 1972).

7

The Gothic in *Taste of Fear*
(dir. Seth Holt, 1961)

Hammer's thrillers are studies in terror, and as such have certain things in common with the Gothic romances of Ann Radcliffe at the turn of the eighteenth-century. Hammer's approach to Gothic horror, on the other hand, owed much more to the style of Radcliffe's most celebrated imitator, Matthew Lewis, whose novel *The Monk* (1796) was so successful that he became known as Matthew "Monk" Lewis on the strength of it. The distinction largely conforms to Todorov's tripartite categorization of fantasy mentioned in the introduction, with Lewis' approach belonging to the "marvelous" and Radcliffe's being "uncanny." Radcliffe was truly horrified by Lewis' novel, but not in the way he might have hoped. *The Monk* was not at all the kind of tribute to her art that she approved of, feeling, quite rightly, that the adolescent Lewis had entirely missed her aesthetic point. His eighteenth-century equivalent of date rape, his rebellious blasphemy, his much cruder, poster-paint literary style (which prefigures Hammer's more lurid manner) and, most of all, his manifestation of the supernatural in the novel's sensational dénouement were not to Radcliffe's taste at all. A child of the age of enlightenment, she always explained her supernatural suggestions away, and that was all they remained: *suggestions*. The Devil certainly never made an appearance in her eagerly awaited romances, which, for all Jane Austen's satire in *Northanger Abbey* (aimed, it should be emphasized, at Radcliffe's besotted, immature readers, rather than the novels themselves), were models of moral rectitude and decorum. With the possible exception of *The Italian* (1797), the evocation of terror, rather than horror, was always her overriding aim. Mystery, reversal, anticipation, fear, the anxiety of environments, of interiors and objects, exotic European locations, the melancholy of solitude, plots revolving around the inheritance of money or property—these were her chosen subjects. Sex may have been threatened but was never actually described, and the moral proprieties were never overlooked. What she lent to Hammer's Gothic horrors were the castles and sublime scenery, but the rest of her effects had much more in common with Hammer's psychological thrillers, which in their various ways tick the boxes of all the abovementioned categories.

Taste of Fear was released in 1961, a year after the phenomenal appearance of *Psycho*.

American poster for *Taste of Fear* renamed *Scream of Fear* (dir. Seth Holt, 1961) with Susan Strasberg's famous scream and *Vertigo*-inspired spirals.

However, with its plot to drive a disabled young woman insane in a luxuriously appointed villa in the South of France, it has more in common with *Les Diaboliques*, not to mention those echoes of Radcliffe's romances. Needless to say, the plot is eventually foiled. Seth Holt's direction has certain things in common with Guy Green's for *The Snorkel*, particularly in the way in which he isolates and monumentalizes everyday objects: the sinister pool in which the corpse is submerged, the garage doors and the car itself, the wheelchair of the heroine, the photograph of her father, the disorientating camera angles from which the piano is shot—the piano that the heroine thinks she hears being played before discovering that the room in which it stands is empty. By isolating these ordinary objects and imbuing them with significance, Holt was able to create many terror effects out of the most trivial of things.

Whereas *The Snorkel* is set on the Italian Riviera, *Taste of Fear* takes place on the French Riviera. Such sophisticated European locations have more resonance than merely their similarity to the locations of Ann Radcliffe's Gothic Grand Tours, which similarly took her readers to France and Italy, where, by implication, anything could happen. Hammer's choice of location not only echoes the French setting of *Les Diaboliques* but also reflected a change in British tourism. On May 1, 1960, BOAC introduced lower fares on their propeller aircraft, and at the end of the month started flights using the new Boeing 707 aircraft, which had been introduced in 1958. Although still expensive, fares were gradually dropping in price. In 1962, BOAC introduced the lowest ever (under £100) transatlantic fare—still a large amount of money but a taste of things to come and one which *Taste of Fear* capitalized upon. Combined with Harold MacMillan's legacy of never having had it so good, the growth of the package tour and the increasing wealth of younger people, the continent was now closer to England than before, and Hammer's locations were tapping into that aspiration in their audiences at home.

Because he was producing as well as writing the film, Jimmy Sangster found himself in charge of finding suitable locations. The Villa de la Garoupe, overlooking Cap d'Antibes, served as the exterior of the Appleby residence, and he also arranged to film at Nice Airport ("a much smaller and friendlier place in those days").[1] All the interiors were filmed at Borehamwood Studios which had the facilities to construct the required swimming pool along with the rest of Bernard Robinson's complex set:

> It was a huge composite set, taking in the entrance hall, living room, the girl's bedroom, leading out onto the patio with garage, chauffeur's quarters, swimming pool and pool house, then some rocks climbing to a small promontory which was supposed to overlook the sea. If we'd done the movie at Bray [Hammer's usual headquarters] it would have involved at least five sets.[2]

Robert Murphy eloquently describes *Taste of Fear* as "a suspense film worthy of Hitchcock, where plot implausibilities only surface long after the film has ended. Douglas Slocombe's glistening black and white photography and Bernard Robinson's simple but convincing sets give an almost formal perfection to the film. But in contrast to *Psycho* or *Vertigo*, where the characters carry an unbearably sad weight of experience on their shoulders, Susan Strasberg, Ronald Lewis, Ann Todd and Christopher Lee, good though their performances are, exist only as part of the mechanics of a complex plot."[3]

Taste of Fear begins (without music) with a prologue set in Switzerland. Hammer had begun *X—The Unknown* without music over the main titles (apart from an introductory flourish from composer James Bernard), but the company's usual practice was to use attention-grabbing symphonic signaling. The lack of music indicates that this film is a very different event from a typical Hammer horror. Instead we hear only the naturalistic ambience of the lakeside setting as we are informed that this is a Hammer Production and are shown the names of the three main stars. The silence signals ambivalence and mystery and complements the film's publicity strategy, which released only one still of Susan Strasberg screaming. (In this, Hammer imitated Hitchcock's publicity gimmick for *Psycho*, which insisted that no one was allowed to enter the theater after the film had started.)

An impressive matte shot of alpine scenery turns the actual lake-side location of Black Park in Buckinghamshire into a very different place. Swiss-German dialogue without subtitles also indicates not only the film's "difference" but also its "sophistication." A policeman is dredging the lake and eventually finds a corpse, which is dragged into the rowboat. A shot of this provides the background to the full main titles sequence, with Clifton Parker's score. Christopher Lee's name appears in large capitals, even though he has only a supporting role. Sangster commented on this casting choice:

> "Why Chris Lee?" people asked me when they heard. "He's Dracula and the Mummy, the ultimate villain."
> For me he wasn't the ultimate villain, he was the ultimate red-herring.[4]

Lee's appearance provides an interesting tension between Todorov's "marvelous," "uncanny" and "fantastic" categories, prompting the audience to ask what kind of film this is. Lee was almost wholly associated with the "marvelous" at the time *Taste of Fear* was first released, and his presence in an "uncanny" film suggests that he *has* to be the villain, which, of course, he was not—quite the opposite, in fact. The other stars also brought appropriate connotations with them. Ann Todd had notably starred in *The Seventh Veil*, a psychological thriller that was neither "uncanny" nor "fantastic" but with its brooding Svengali character (played by James Mason) and its psychiatric context (the psychiatrist was played by Herbert Lom, a later Phantom of the Opera for Hammer), it has similarities with *The Full Treatment*. The parallels between classical music and psychosis in *The Seventh Veil* also connect *Taste of Fear* with *Crescendo*. Ronald Lewis had starred in *The Full Treatment* and Susan Strasberg provided the "required" Hollywood glamour.

The action proper begins with a shot of a plane landing at Nice airport, an instant signifier of affluence, which is consolidated by the arrival of a Rolls-Royce, driven by Robert, the chauffeur (Ronald Lewis). Strasberg's Penny Appleby is wheelchair-bound, hence vulnerable. She wears dark glasses, as though attempting to hide herself from the world—and yet all is not as it appears, as we ultimately discover that she is not Peggy Appleby at all but in fact Peggy's friend Maggie. This revelation, saved until the very end of the film, does not, as Robert Murphy points out, stand up to much scrutiny when watching the film for a second time, as this character simply would not have behaved in the way she does once we know this. But, as with Sangster's model, *Les Diaboliques*, the effect of the revelation is dramatically effective.

Whereas the dialogue in the prologue was in Swiss German, the opening scenes of the action proper are in French, again without subtitles, once more lending an air of sophistication to the proceedings as well as echoing the Gallic ambience of *Les Diaboliques*. Robert informs Peggy that her father is away on business after a period of illness. Peggy apparently has no idea that her father has been ill. In fact, he is already dead.

To emphasize the locale, Holt cuts to an impressive shot of the Rolls driving up a winding mountain road, with the sea in the distance. This leads us to the Villa, on the steps of which Jane (Ann Todd) appears, wearing a Chinese-style silk trouser suit, which conveys a slightly alien, certainly uptight quality. The costume also taps into the cultural stereotyping and racial prejudices of writers such as Sax Rohmer, subtly suggesting movie memories of Myrna Loy in *The Mask of Fu Manchu* (dir. Charles Brabin, 1932) and Anna May Wong in her various Oriental *femme fatale* roles. Jane's wardrobe consists of variants of these trouser suits, which reinforce her ambivalence. The conspiracy between her and Robert to drive Peggy insane and claim her inheritance is, with hindsight, nicely suggested by Jane's cold manner towards him and her frequently averted eyes, though Robert gives very little away.

Jane shows Peggy a photograph of her father, played by Fred Johnson, who had played Father Stepnik in Terence Fisher's *The Brides of Dracula* the previous year. His lantern jaw, beetling eyebrows and a posture that leans towards the camera does not present a reassuring image. Even more unnerving is the sound of the crickets outside, which chirrup incessantly throughout these and other scenes. This effect is a crucial element in the creation of the tense atmosphere, and far more evocative and unnerving than any music could be. Indeed, music is rationed in a highly disciplined manner throughout the film, and reserved mainly for the principal shock scenes. Naturalistic sound effects also create a much more realistic mood and help to create the counterbalance required for the creation of Todorov's "uncanny" quality.

Next, Holt introduces us to the black waters of the swimming pool, one of the film's most obvious references to *Les Diaboliques*, but nothing more is made of this image at this stage, Holt being quite content for the time being to let it resonate in the audience's collective imagination. Candles flicker during a conversation between Peggy and Jane over dinner, lending, through association, a vague sense of the Gothic to this scene. Jane herself ironically enhances this mood with her line: "Did you expect me to be like the wicked stepmother in the fairy stories?"—which, of course, she is.

We now advance towards the shock scene in which Peggy confronts the dead body of her father. He has been murdered by Jane and Robert, though we don't know this yet, and neither does Peggy (though all the time the Maggie who is pretending to be Peggy does). As part of the build-up, she is awoken by the sound of a window shutter banging in the wind. Again, the uncanny effect is created solely by the sound of an ordinary object. Nothing supernatural occurs and yet the sound implies the supernatural. Significantly, Hammer's *Dracula with Christopher Lee* LP issued in the 1974 contains the line, spoken with sepulchral sonority by Bill Mitchell, "You did lock the doors—latch the windows? Didn't you?" Peggy has done neither. The camera hovers over her lying on her bed in restless sleep. She wakes and turns on the bedside light, which illuminates that foreboding portrait of her father. Maneuvering herself out of bed, she hauls herself into the wheelchair and wheels herself over to close the shutter. Here is one of the moments that do not make much sense once we know she is only pretending to be Peggy. Why does she maintain the charade of paralysis in the privacy of her own room? But perhaps she is aware that something might happen which would expose her subterfuge if she did not act out her pretense at all times. Alternatively, it might be better to ask such questions at all.

When she notices a light flickering in the pool house, Clifton Parker's underscore resumes, and is unnervingly combined with the squeaking of the wheelchair and the persistent crickets. As Peggy opens the door, Parker employs a musical device similar to one of James Bernard's gestures in both his music for Hammer science fiction and vampire films, and which also appears in *The Devil Rides Out* (dir. Terence Fisher, 1968). It is basically a string glissando that rises and falls, creating a graphic musical equivalent of the effect of spine-tingling nervous excitement. Inside the pool house, amid a chaotic array of *bric-à-brac*, we see a stuffed eagle. If the pool reminds us of *Les Diaboliques*, the stuffed eagle surely reminds us of *Psycho*. This is a bird not so much of ill omen as of prey, which is more appropriate to an "uncanny" story about a woman who is being persecuted. We also see a Victorian flower arrangement under a glass dome, itself suggestive of entrapment, suffocation and death. Then, up-lit by a candle at its feet and slumped threateningly in a chair, the corpse of her father stares sightlessly out at her, the large eyebrows eloquently emoting the demonic. Fred Johnson's pose here curiously resembles that of Daniel Chester French's famous statue of Abraham Lincoln at the Lincoln Memorial in Washington, D.C., Johnson's hands resting somewhat more awkwardly on the arms of the chair than Lincoln's do. In fact, the angular arrangement of Johnson's arms is more in the manner of the right arm of Lucifer in Franz von Stuck's 1890 painting of that name, and Lucifer is certainly an appropriate figure to echo here, as are the patriarchal connotations of Lincoln. Of course, neither of these references may have been consciously intended, but the image, like French's statue of the president, does seem to be referencing the accounts of Phideas' statue of Zeus in the Parthenon. Seth Holt certainly intends to create a statue-like quality here, and the way in which Johnson's Mr. Appleby is lit transforms any paternal benevolence he may have had when alive into pure malevolence now that he is dead. This is an image of fatherhood inverted, suitably monumentalized by means of close-up.

Here, given that we are in the midst of a psychological thriller, Freud's comments on dream-images of "the father" might prove useful. We must remember that Peggy has lived apart from her father nearly all her life. Indeed, they are virtual strangers to each other. Peggy felt abandoned by her father, especially after her mother's death. Added to this, Peggy is not, of course, Peggy at all, but Peggy's friend Maggie, pretending to be Peggy. Such a complicated state of affairs might suggest that any serious analysis of what is going on here is misplaced, but I think what Freud has to say about dream images of the father helps us to understand the deeper resonance of this scene, which is so powerful because it taps into common dream imagery of our own parents and the ambivalence we all feel with regard to them:

> [A] man who had nursed his father during his last illness and had been deeply grieved by his death, had the following senseless dream some time afterwards. *His father was alive once more and was talking to him in his usual way, but* (the remarkable thing was that), *he had really died, only he did not know it....* While he was nursing his father he had repeatedly wished his father were dead; that is to say, he had had what was actually a merciful thought that death might put an end to his sufferings. During his mourning, after his father's death, even this sympathetic wish became a subject of unconscious self-reproach, as though by means of it he had really helped to shorten the sick man's life. A stirring up of the dreamer's earliest infantile impulses against his father made it possible for this self-reproach to find expression as a dream; the fact that the instigator of the dream and the daytime thoughts were such worlds apart was precisely what necessitated the dream's absurdity....
>
> It very commonly happens that in dreams of this kind the dead person is treated to begin with as though he were alive, that he then suddenly turns out to be dead and that

in a subsequent part of the dream he is alive once more. This has a confusing effect. It eventually occurred to me that this alternation between death and life is intended to represent *indifference* on the part of the dreamer. ("It's all the same to me whether he's alive or dead.") This indifference is, of course, not real but merely desired; it is intended to help the dreamer to repudiate his very intense and often contradictory emotional attitudes and it thus becomes a dream-representation of his *ambivalence*.[5]

The particular scariness of the dead father in *Taste of Fear* is not, therefore, just the result of simple, though superbly executed shock tactics. It is frightening—and "uncanny" (in Freud's rather than Todorov's use of the term)—because it releases an emotion from the subconscious that "ought to have remained ... secret and hidden but has come to light." The imagery of the dead father can also be interpreted as a representation of what Jung referred to as the animus—the male archetype in the unconscious of the female psyche:

The father endows his daughter's animus with the special coloring of unarguable, incontestably "true" convictions—convictions that never include the personal reality of the woman herself as she actually is.

This is why the animus is sometimes, like the anima, a demon of death ... that lures women away from all human relationships and especially from all contacts with real men....

A strange passivity and paralysis of all feeling, or a deep insecurity that can lead almost to a sense of nullity, may sometimes be the result of an unconscious animus opinion. In the depths of the woman's being, the animus whispers: "You are hopeless. What's the use of trying? There is no point in doing anything. Life will never change for the better."[6]

Peggy is similarly passive and insecure. Her physical paralysis suggests the paralysis of her emotional world. She has had little experience of "real men" and feels so hopeless that, as we learn at the very end of the film, she actually committed suicide before the film began! Peggy is ruled by a negative animus, and the vision of her dead father which haunts her is therefore suitably terrifying.

Douglas Slocombe photographs Mr. Appleby as a thing of shadows rather than of light—"darkness visible," indeed, to quote Milton's *Paradise Lost*. When we cut to an even more monumentalized close-up of the dead, staring eyes, surrounded by the deep shadows of the lines and wrinkles around them, the image is far more graphically ghoulish than anything one might find in Hitchcock. Just as Val Guest and his photographer Gilbert Taylor created Karsh-like portraits of Claude Dauphin in *The Full Treatment*, Holt and Slocombe create a cinematic Carvaggio here—the cinematic equivalent of Carvaggio's head of Goliath, held aloft by David (c. 1607), or that artist's other horror painting of Judith beheading Holofernes (1598–1599).

We may now temporarily put aside psychological interpretation and concentrate instead upon the Gothic tradition to which such a scene belongs. As I mentioned at the beginning of this chapter, *Taste of Fear* owes much to the example of Ann Radcliffe, and various shock scenes in *The Mysteries of Udolpho* (1794) form illuminating literary parallels with this film. The successive sightings of Mr. Appleby correspond, indeed, to the horrible secret that Emily, the heroine of Radcliffe's novel, glimpses behind a veiled picture. Radcliffe refrains from revealing what the horror is until the very end of the novel, and this delay caused intense speculation among the novel's fanatical readers. In *Northanger Abbey*, Jane Austen has a delightfully gossipy conversation between her heroine, Catherine Morland, and her friend Isabella:

> "Have you gone on with *Udolpho*?"
> "Yes, I have been reading it ever since I woke; and I am got to the black veil."
> "Are you, indeed? How delightful! Oh! I would not tell you what is behind the black veil for the world! Are you not wild to know?"
> "Oh! yes, quite; but what can it be?—But do not tell me—I would not be told upon any account. I know it must be a skeleton, I am sure it is Laurentina's skeleton."[7]

Radcliffe describes the moment referred to by Austen in the sixth chapter of the second volume of her Gothic masterpiece, and in her build-up to the revelation we can see how much Peggy's approach to the pool house and what she sees inside it owes to Radcliffe's example.

> This brought to her recollection the veiled picture, which had attracted her curiosity, on the preceding night, and she resolved to examine it. As she passed through the chambers, that led to this, she found herself somewhat agitated; its connection with the late lady of the castle, and the conversation of Annette, together with the circumstance of the veil, throwing a mystery over the subject, that excited a faint degree of terror. But a terror of this nature, as it occupies and expands the mind, and elevates it to high expectation, is purely sublime, and leads us, by a kind of fascination, to seek even the object, from which we appear to shrink.
> Emily passed on with faltering steps, and having paused a moment at the door, before she attempted to open it, she then hastily entered the chamber, and went towards the picture, which appeared to be enclosed in a frame of uncommon size, that hung in a dark part of the room. She paused again, and then, with a timid hand, lifted the veil; but instantly let it fall—perceiving that what it had concealed was no picture, and, before she could leave the chamber, she dropped senseless on the floor.
> When she recovered her recollection, the remembrance of what she had seen had nearly deprived her of it a second time. She had scarcely strength to remove from the room, and regain her own; and, when arrived there, wanted courage to remain alone. Horror occupied her mind, and excluded, for a time, all sense of past, and dread of future misfortune.[8]

Radcliffe saves an explanation of what Emily actually saw until the end of volume three:

> It may be remembered that, in a chamber of Udolpho, hung a black veil, whose singular situation had excited Emily's curiosity, and which afterwards disclosed an object, that had overwhelmed her with horror; for, on lifting it, there appeared, instead of the picture she had expected, within a recess of the wall, a human figure of ghastly paleness, stretched at its length, and dressed in the habiliments of the grave. What added to the horror of the spectacle was that the face appeared partly decayed and disfigured by worms, which were visible on the features and hands.... The history of it is somewhat extraordinary.... A member of the house of Udolpho, having committed some offense against the prerogative of the church, had been condemned to the penance of contemplating, during certain hours of the day, a waxen image, made to resemble a human body in the state to which it is reduced after death. This penance, serving as a memento of the condition at which he must himself arrive, had been designed to reprove the pride of the Marquis of Udolpho.[9]

As we have seen, however, what Peggy sees in *Taste of Fear*, though related to the Gothic tradition of Radcliffe, actually has far more psychological resonance than the ghastly waxwork of Udolpho. There are other similarities. Imprisoned in Signor Montoni's gloomy castle in the Apennine mountains, Radcliffe's heroine wanders around its echoing chambers, much as Peggy wheels herself around her father's admittedly more modest but luxuriously appointed villa; and Emily also resembles Peggy in that she is orphaned and is being cared for by her aunt. Emily's aunt is merely foolish rather than malevolent like Peggy's, but the parallel remains.

Back in the pool house, Peggy's screams punctuate Holt's various close-ups of her dead father's staring eyes. She wheels herself away, Holt notching up the tension by showing us the wheels of the wheelchair spinning dangerously close to the edge of the pool, and, as we expect, she falls in. Robert the chauffeur comes running to the rescue.

We then fade into the first shot of Christopher Lee as Dr. Gerrard, his face, solemn, serious and sinister, half in shadow. He stares down at Peggy while taking her pulse, but the implication is that he might be about to lunge upon his victim as he did in *Dracula*. This was the first time Lee had spoken with a foreign accent in a Hammer film, and the effect must have been slightly disorienting to the film's first audiences, adding to the confusion. Unlike Dr. Prade in *The Full Treatment* and Dr. Keller in *Hysteria*, Lee's Dr. Gerrard is entirely trustworthy, even though we are strenuously encouraged to believe that this is not the case. Holt positions his camera at a low angle during these scenes to give us Peggy's eye-line, and also to make Lee seem more threatening. It is a technique that Holt uses throughout the film.

No one believes Peggy when she insists she has seen her father's corpse. "Don't treat me as though I were a mental defective," she insists, which is exactly what Jane has in mind. They check out the pool house and Jane gives the interior one last look before departing, like the good housekeeper she obviously is, having removed all evidence of a wet corpse in record time. Lee is shown watching her, suggesting collusion, but actually expressing suspicion.

The following day the crickets are silent and instead the air is filled with the calm sound of birdsong and waves on the beach. These ambient sounds are a highly effective way of creating a completely different mood, but Jane is intent on gently planting doubt and fear into Peggy's mind:

"Your father told me how you were when you were a little girl," she explains, "imaginative, fanciful, slightly…"

"Neurotic?" Peggy suggests.

"No, I didn't men that." (But she did.)

"I was, though," Peggy agrees. "I was afraid of everything. Dark, wind, thunder, lightning."

"Most children are."

"They grow out it."

We then cut to a seaside scene. The wheelchair is parked at the edge of the cliff—an image that will recur at the end of the film. Robert, as usual, is giving a very convincing impression of being sympathetic and trustworthy, but he plants doubt in Peggy's mind nonetheless. He recalls that Peggy's father drove away in the small car and "he doesn't like the small car."

Holt then monumentalizes a telephone. Objects, to an even greater extent than in *The Snorkel*, are invested with a sinister quality throughout this film. By showing us such mundane objects in close-up they almost become characters in their own right; consequently, we respond to the imagery with a greater sense of curiosity and attention. Peggy is summoned to the phone to talk to her father—a hoax that is never explained, but the implication must be that Jane has arranged for someone to impersonate him. The voice used on the soundtrack is actually that of Fred Johnson, however.

When the conversation is over, Jane looks back at Peggy from halfway up the stairs, and this expression confirms the doubts both we and Peggy have about her. Robert then tells Peggy that he has to pick up Dr. Gerrard, but Peggy asks why he didn't pick him up the previous night. Robert agrees that it seems odd that Gerrard just "seemed to be here." Robert also brings her some shavings of candle wax that he "discovered" in the pool house, proving that she at least did not imagine the candle at the feet of her dead father.

Gerrard is present again at lunchtime, and Peggy accuses him of insinuating that if she doesn't control her imagination, she will become insane and have to be locked up. Later that night, alone in the house (or so she thinks), Peggy hears a car drive into the garage, and this sets up the second big shock scene. Wheeling herself out to the terrace to investigate, she calls for Robert. The garage door is half-raised but it suddenly slams down with a shocking clatter—a classic, highly effective way of making everyone in the audience jump out of their skins. She advances to the garage where she discovers the small car, suggesting that her father has indeed returned. Again, Holt and Slocombe manage to invest an ordinary everyday object with intense malevolence here. Lit from above, the white bonnet contrasts starkly with the jet black shadow of the windshield, echoing the dark glasses Peggy likes to wear. We wonder if there is anyone inside the car, and Holt lingers upon the image of the still, sinister vehicle to increase its unnerving effect, while the crickets in the background also do their work. Like the telephone, the car is filmed in such a way as to suggest it is a living presence, and this uncanny quality is of course related to the way in which Hoffmann often imbues inanimate objects with a life of their own in his stories.

The third shock follows quickly. Having returned inside, Peggy hears Chopin's E-minor piano prelude, with its hypnotically repetitive chords that gradually change their harmonies under a melancholy monotonous melody. As she wheels herself into the corridor to investigate, we see light under the threshold from the room beyond. We cut to the interior of the room, where we find that the lid of the piano is closed and there is no sign of a pianist. From a low angle, the camera observes Peggy throw wide the double doors of the room—an action that helps create a greater sense of space and vacuity. We then cut to a shot of the piano from Peggy's point of view, the camera angle distorted to create an unnerving sense of disorientation in one of Holt's greatest monumentalizations. The piano, like the car and the telephone before it, appears predatory even though inanimate, just like Mr. Appleby's corpse. Only Mr. Appleby played the piano, so with the return of the small car, the piano music seems to confirm his return. The influence of *Les Diaboliques* is very apparent here, though the sheen of Slocombe's photography and the formal sophistication of Holt's direction are actually superior to Clouzot's technique.

Mysterious music is also a classic Gothic convention, first made famous by Radcliffe in *The Mysteries of Udolpho*. Towards the end of volume two, Emily hears lute music, actually played by her lover who is imprisoned in another part of the castle, which also reminds her of her father:

> A superstitious dread stole over her; she stood listening, for some moments, in trembling expectation, and then endeavored to re-collect her thoughts, and to reason herself into composure; but human reason cannot establish her laws on subjects, lost in the obscurity of imagination, any more than the eye can ascertain the form of objects, that only glimmer through the dimness of night.
>
> Her surprise, on hearing such soothing and delicious sounds, was, at least, justifiable; for it was long—very long since she had listened to any thing like melody....
>
> When her mind was somewhat more composed, she tried to ascertain from what quarter the sounds proceeded, and thought they came from below; but whether from a room of the castle or from the terrace, she could not with certainty judge. Fear and surprise now yielded to the enchantment of a strain, that floated on the silent night, with the most soft and melancholy sweetness. Suddenly, it seemed removed to a distance, trembled faintly, and then entirely ceased.
>
> She continued to listen, sunk in that pleasing repose, which soft music leaves on the mind—but it came no more. Upon this strange circumstance her thoughts were long engaged, for strange it certainly was to hear music at midnight, when every inhabitant of the castle had long since returned to rest, and in a place, where nothing like harmony had been heard before, probably, for many years. Long-suffering had made her spirits peculiarly sensible to terror, and liable to be affected by the illusions of superstition. It now seemed to her, as if her dead father had spoken to her in that strain, to inspire her with comfort and confidence, on the subject, which had then occupied her mind.[10]

Taste of Fear merely updates the action of this passage to 1961 and replaces the lute with a grand piano.

The third shock, after Peggy observes that the small car has disappeared, takes us back to the pool house once more. The same sequence of events and music is reprised but this time the climax is bathetic as there is no corpse, only a candle flickering in front of the empty chair. The flame goes out as soon as Holt presents it in close-up. Peggy wheels herself out and Holt arranges a stunning shot of her entering the screen from the left to initiate a new scene, with the swimming pool glittering in all its blackness behind her. The shot is very simple but it has an unnerving effect due to the way in which she enters the frame and our sense of sudden proximity to her. (Peter Sasdy repeated the effect in 1970's *Taste the Blood of Dracula* when Christopher Lee's vampire enters a shot unexpectedly from the right of the screen.) As Peggy circles the pool, the lights from the main house are turned off, darkening the terrace. Holt also concentrates on the sound of the wheelchair, in much the same way that Thorold Dickinson had used the sinister ostinato of the countess' rustling robes and her wooden stick in *The Queen of Spades* (1949) to create a leitmotif out of simple sound effects. Holt further increases the tension by dwelling on the wraith-like effect of the play of light from the pool on the wall behind Peggy. As she enters her room, we see it from her point of view. The camera advances towards a table lamp, Holt again investing another object with a sinister resonance by means of another close-up. Peggy reaches out to switch on the lamp but it doesn't work. Another shot from her point of view takes us to the shadow-laden sideboard against the wall behind her—and emerging from the darkness, we again see her father's corpse. Its head drops down and Peggy screams before wheeling herself off to Robert, who runs into the room to investigate. Here again, Holt demonstrates his directorial mastery. Robert looks around the room, accompanied by a pause chord in Parker's underscore. The camera follows his eye-line to reveal Jane silhouetted in the doorway. Holt holds this shot for a few moments before she turns on the light, and by this means her sinister role is confirmed.

A different use of shadows occurs a short while later when Holt decorates the set of Peggy's bedroom with the shadows thrown from Venetian blinds. The same effect had been used to considerably more disorientating effect by Mark Robson in *Isle of the Dead* (1945). Here, it is less overt but certainly aids the mood of uncertainty.

Robert next discovers that the chair in which Peggy saw her father's corpse is still wet. He then points out to Peggy that Jane and Gerrard will inherit all her money if she is found to be "incapable" so, putting two and two together, they determine to find where Jane is keeping Mr. Appleby's body. At dinner that night, Gerrard suggests that Peggy's problem might be hysterical paralysis. As he knows who "Peggy" really is, he also knows that Peggy isn't paralyzed at all, so this conversation is presumably for Jane's benefit. The audience, however, is still unaware of the subterfuge at this point. Hysterical paralysis was well known to Freud, and it adds another subtle layer of psychological resonance to the plot. Peggy counters Gerrard's proposition with one of the film's best lines: "You say my mind is affecting my legs. You're wrong. It's my legs that are affecting my mind." Jane looks on, wearing another figure-hugging Chinese-style outfit, and the awkward dinner party is nicely framed by a fringed lampshade in the foreground.

The fourth shock concerns the opening of the deep freeze where Robert thinks Appleby's corpse might be being stored. Holt treats the deep freeze as he treated the small car: A simple chest freezer is made to attain the macabre significance of a coffin. It stands against a wall in an unnaturally immaculate and deserted kitchen. The emptiness and order of the place, with its adversarial checkerboard floor, creates the same kind of ominous anticipation we encounter in the paintings of Georgio de Chirico (1888–1978) or the rather different deserted spaces of Edward Hopper (1882–1967). As nature abhors a vacuum, dramatic space anticipates action, and an empty space even more so. But Holt increases the anticipation by concentrating on the most mundane of activities (unscrewing the metal plate to which the freezer's padlock is secured). Parker's restrained string tremolo and timpani accompaniment further raises the tension. But nothing is found inside.

Again, this scene has its precedents in Gothic literature. The bathetic effect of a sinister cabinet that is revealed to have nothing of interest inside it formed part of Jane Austen's satire of the genre in *Northanger Abbey*. Catherine Morland finds herself intrigued by a cabinet in the eponymous Gothic pile to which she has been invited to stay. Like Holt, Austen makes sure that we first have a "close-up" of the cabinet by means of detailed description, followed by effective delaying tactics to increase the tension felt by the reader:

> She took her candle and looked closely at the cabinet. It was not absolutely ebony and gold; but it was Japan, black and yellow Japan of the handsomest kind; and as she held her candle, the yellow had very much the effect of gold. The key was in the door, and she had a strange fancy to look into it not however with the smallest expectation of finding anything, but it was so very odd, after what Henry had said. In short, she could not sleep till she had examined it. So, placing the candle with great caution on a chair, she seized the key with a very tremulous hand and tried to turn it; but it resisted her utmost strength. Alarmed, but not discouraged, she tried it another way; a bolt flew, and she believed herself successful; but how strangely mysterious!—the door was still immoveable.... Again therefore she applied herself to the key, and after moving it in every way possible for some instants with the determined celerity of hope's last effort, the door suddenly yielded to her hand: her heart leaped with exultation at such a victory.... It was entirely empty.[11]

Peggy's wheelchair is again seen on the cliff top the next morning, and Robert and Peggy are back at the seaside engaged in a heart-to-heart conversation; but when Robert ends his ministrations with a kiss, the camera pans to the left of the perilously perched wheelchair to where Jane has been watching developments with a very worried expression. Back at the villa, she warns Peggy not to grow too friendly with the chauffeur, and suggests that they might have the pool cleaned: "Then you could swim, perhaps?" Again, we are reminded of the pool-cleaning sequence in *Les Diaboliques*, and Jane's comment now suggests to Peggy where the body is hiding. Holt skillfully implies her thought processes by means of juxtaposition between the pool and Peggy's face, a close-up of and pan across her features indicating that the penny has dropped.

The problem with the pool is that it is quite tiny and nowhere near as big as the underwater scenes to which we are soon treated suggest. Nonetheless, Robert obliges and dives in. Amid the weeds he indeed discovers the corpse floating like one of Francis Bacon's screaming pope pictures, its eyes staring wildly in a manner that also calls to mind the hideously degenerating painting in Albert Lewin's *The Picture of Dorian Gray* (1945).

The discovery made, we are ready for the dénouement. Having failed to drive Peggy insane, Robert and Jane opt for out-and-out murder. Though viewers aren't meant to know this yet, they put the corpse in the Rolls, and Robert drives Peggy to the police. Jane flags them down, Robert makes sure the hand-break is off and the car rolls over the cliff. The story will be that Mr. Appleby took his daughter for a spin and had a terrible accident. Peggy apparently screams her last and Robert and Jane are finally revealed to be the conspirators in the very Clouzot-esque reversal that follows.

We now cut sharply to the interior of the villa. The same Chopin prelude is playing again. Jane listens and enters the music room. The camera pans to reveal a tape recorder.

Robert turns this off and kisses Jane, who regrets having been forced to murder. He, however, enthusiastically reveals how he drowned Mr. Appleby. "I dragged him under and I held him there," he explains, reminding us, perhaps, of Paul Decker in *The Snorkel*. After a scene at the police station, Dr. Gerrard appears from behind a door after Jane and Robert have been interrogated, indicating, in the second reversal, that he is actually on the side of law and order. Robert must next identify the car. On the cliffs, Holt uses a close-up of Robert's expression to convey his anxiety when the policeman tells him that Peggy's body has not been found. Then, back at the villa, Leonard Sachs appears as the family solicitor, and reveals to Jane that Peggy committed suicide three weeks earlier in Switzerland, so we now know the identity of the body that was being recovered from the lake in the film's prologue.

The woman whom Jane assumed to be Peggy is waiting on the cliffs in her wheelchair and she finally reveals herself to be Peggy's friend, Maggie. She is not paralyzed and she knows everything about Jane and Robert's plot. She told Mr. Appleby of Peggy's suicide, but three weeks later she received a letter supposedly from Mr. Appleby asking for Peggy to visit. Obviously something was wrong. Together with Dr. Gerrard, they decided what to do.

Crushed by this revelation, Jane sits down in the wheelchair, which allows Holt to indulge in the film's final twist, for when Robert sees who he assumes to be Peggy, he pushes the wheelchair into the sea, only realizing the truth when its too late to save her.

Sangster explained that he first saw *Les Diaboliques* and *Psycho* within a few days of each other "and, like the guy in *A Chorus Line*, I figured 'I can do that.' So I set to work and four weeks later out came the first draft of *Taste of Fear*." Quite rightly, he claims that the film "holds up well. It is exciting, suspenseful, scary, and it has more twists than most other movies of its type. If that sounds like I'm blowing my own trumpet, I am. And why not?"[12] Why not, indeed?

8

Love and Landscape in *Maniac*
(dir. Michael Carreras, 1963)

Some psychological thrillers use landscape as a way of articulating the unconscious and expressing mood. Hitchcock's *North by Northwest* is a prime contender for this category; so, also, is *Vertigo*, with its dream-like evocations of locations around San Francisco. One British thriller using landscape in a particularly integral way is *And Soon the Darkness* (dir. Robert Fuest, 1970), in which two girls on a cycling holiday in France are terrorized as much by the deserted vistas and lonely roads as by the serial killer who is stalking them.

Hammer never used landscape quite so effectively in its own thrillers, though it did manipulate that favorite location of Black Park to suggest a comparable psychological landscape of fear in *The Kiss of the Vampire*. Perhaps of all Hammer's psychological thrillers, *Maniac* is the most concerned with landscape. It is also a love story. Instead of a woman in distress, the victim is a man, and the nature of the deception practiced upon him undermines the atmosphere of romance which the film so carefully sets up. Love here is ultimately shown to be a deception. The hero rejects the woman who truly loves him and falls for the one who merely uses him to further her plans to be with another man. That man is a maniac, and love is therefore revealed to be not necessarily a force for good in the world. Many people genuinely loved Adolf Hitler, after all.

Carreras chose a widescreen format for this film, appropriate for the landscape element, which screenwriter Jimmy Sangster originally intended to be much more in evidence. "Michael didn't take as much advantage of the locations as he could have," he said. "The sheer, stark emptiness of the area, which made me choose it in the first place, didn't come across. But I guess nobody went to the movie to watch the scenery. [For] a film with such a potentially vast, visually exciting background, the whole thing turned out, for me, to be slightly claustrophobic."[1] This is rather too critical, as the film does contain some very impressive uses of landscape, adding considerable atmosphere to a plot, which, as Sangster also admitted "could have been located anywhere."[2] The claustrophobia to which he refers is certainly present, but it is intensified by the positive agoraphobia of its punctuating vistas. The contrast between the two creates considerable emotional tension.

The landscapes of the film are presented as sublime in many of the ways Edmund Burke defined that term in his *Philosophical Enquiry* of 1757. For Burke, the sublime is anything that excites "the ideas of pain, and danger, that is to say, whatever is in any sort terrible, or is conversant about terrible objects."[3] Solitude is sublime because "absolute and entire *solitude*, that is, the total and perpetual exclusion from all society, is as great a positive pain as can almost be conceived."[4] Vastness is sublime; so too is Infinity, which "has a tendency to fill the mind with that sort of delightful horror, which is the most genuine effect and truest test of the sublime."[5] Even horses are sublime for Burke, and they are certainly presented in *Maniac* along the lines he describes them in the *Philosophical Enquiry*: "The horse in the light of an useful beast, fit for the plough, the road, the draft, in every social useful light ... has nothing of the sublime; but is it thus that we are affected with him, *whose neck is cloathed with thunder, the glory of whose nostrils is terrible, who swalloweth the ground with fierceness and rage, neither believeth that it is the sound of the trumpet?*" In this description the useful character of the horse entirely disappears, and the terrible and sublime blaze out together."[6] Carreras doesn't dwell on the horses in his film, but they are certainly presented in a heroic, sublime manner, as, for example, when Eve (Nadia Gray) and Geoff (Kerwin Mathews) gallop two fiery steeds along a deserted beach, with the sea rolling in orgasmically beside them.

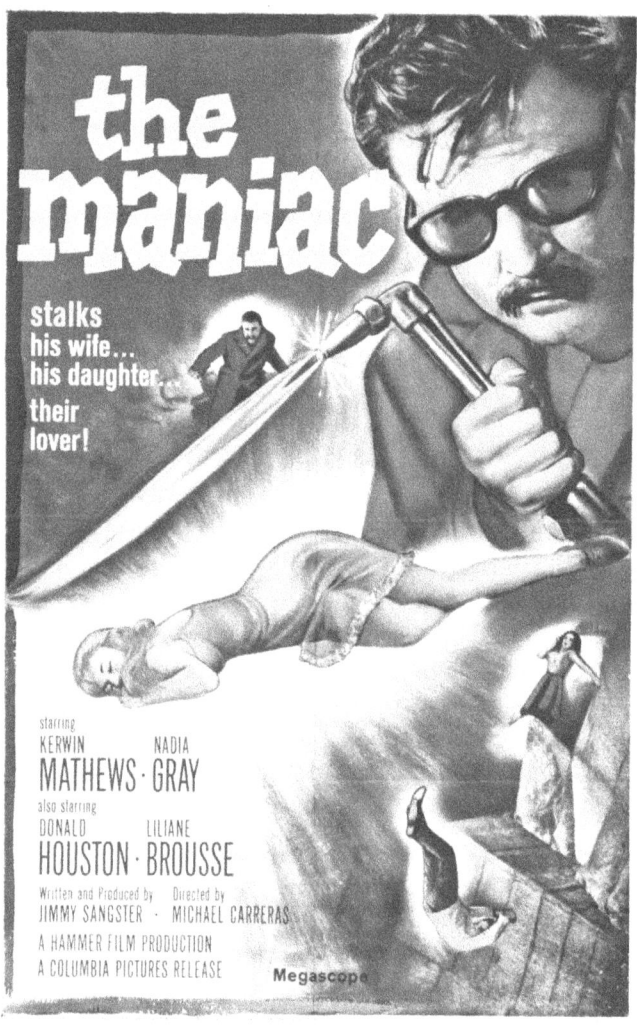

Poster for *Maniac* (dir. Michael Carreras, 1963), incorrectly advertised with a definite article, with a rather unreliable portrait of Donald Houston as the acetylene killer. Below, a representation of his eventual demise.

Maniac contrasts the inherently sublime terrors of the landscape with the claustrophobic terrors of the characters' actions within it: a rape in a field, an attempt to dispose of a corpse in open countryside, two women alone inside a deserted Roman amphitheater ("To the sublime in building, greatness of dimensions seems requisite," says Burke[7]). The finale similarly juxtaposes weird grandeur (the caves of Les Baux) with an attempt to murder the heroine (Liliane Brousse), thus increasing the terror of the girl's predicament. Only the acetylene murders themselves are set in a truly claustrophobic space, Georges' old garage, but the confined space is made all the more claustrophobic due to the contrast it makes with "outdoors." It is in this very important respect that *Maniac* becomes a rather different film from Hammer's other psychological thrillers, which are much more claustrophobic and largely set-bound.

We open with a wide vista of plain, populated only by cattle, over which a card explains, "The Camargue ... a remote area in Southern France where wild horses roam, fighting bulls are bred, and violence is never far away." The shot has about it something of the American photographer Ansel Adams (1902–1984), who specialized in similarly unpopulated vistas (seascapes, lakes, deserts, mountain ranges) all characterized by sharp focus and dramatic contrasts between light and shadow. One might categorize their sublime manner as "sophisticated primitivism." Adams' photographs epitomize one of the main consequences of photography as identified by Susan Sontag: "So successful has been the camera's role in beautifying the world that photographs, rather than the world, have become the standard of the beautiful."[8] Sontag also observed the following in publicity copy for a book of photographs by Ansel Adams: "The creations of man or nature never have more grandeur than in an Ansel Adams photograph, and his image can seize the viewer with more force than the natural object from which it was made."[9] Such a quality perhaps applies less to *Maniac* than to a film such as *The Kiss of the Vampire* which manipulates what is in fact the very ordinary—indeed municipal—British woodland to suggest a sublime middle–European environment. The landscapes in *Maniac* are much more "genuine" but they are nonetheless photographed in a self-consciously "aesthetic" manner, which distances them from Hammer's Gothic fare. Their careful composition and sophisticated lighting encourage us to interpret them in a particular way, and such a style reflects the ambitions Michael Carreras had for Hammer Films at the time. Prior to directing *Maniac*, he had temporarily moved away from Hammer:

> The reason I broke away was that I wanted—like I think everyone does at some point—just to have a fresh scene.... There was a very rigid pattern at Hammer at the time—a successful pattern but nevertheless a rigid one. By the same token, I wanted to gather a wider experience so that when I rejoined Hammer, which I always expected to do, it being a family concern, I would be able to bring this experience with me.[10]

Sangster's opinion of Carreras as a director: "He wasn't as good as Terry Fisher, but he was better than half a dozen others who worked for Hammer, whom I won't name. Technically, he knew it all; artistically, maybe he could have been a little better."[11] Even though Sangster felt that the landscape could have been more successfully integrated into the action, what landscape there is (and it is quite sufficient for the needs of the drama), was beautifully photographed by Wilkie Cooper, and it gave Hammer its most impressive location work to that date. When it came to *She* (dir. Robert Day), which Carreras produced in 1965, the landscapes of desert vistas photographed by Harry Waxman were far less aesthetically independent, their purpose being merely to furnish the action; but Cooper's shots of the Camargue in *Maniac* could quite easily stand alone, away from the rest of the film, as photographs in their own right.

It is also significant that the leading man, Kerwin Mathews, plays a landscape artist. Having separated from his girlfriend Grace (a small part for Justine Lord), he decides to stay on in the Camargue to paint the scenery. We see one of his attempts in the film, by which time we have been led to think he has been killed. (The painting is given away to the policeman played by Norman Bird.) It shows some standing stones, executed with considerably less panache than Cooper's photography, but the important thing here is that the character's profession helps to consolidate the film's awareness of its own environment; and the long, empty vistas evoked in the film undeniably add to the mood of anxiety—particularly at a time in the early 1960s when "abroad" was much more exotic and alienating than it is today.

After the opening establishing shot of the Camargue plain, we cut to a close-up of a watching eye, and this echoes the staring eye that appears in Saul Bass' opening titles for *Vertigo*. The imagery therefore not only serves the plot ("Who is this who is watching?") but also identifies the genre ("Ah! This film will be like an Alfred Hitchcock movie!"). We are then shown both eyes of the peeping Tom. They stare out at the audience, which, of course is similarly watching, reminding us of Spoto's observations about the voyeuristic connotation of mirrors and staring eyes in *Psycho*: The audience of *Maniac* is just as much complicit in voyeurism as the man who is watching Annette Beynat, the girl played by Liliane Brousse. Sangster wanted the rape scene to be much more explicit, and blamed the censor for preventing this,[12] but his intention does beg the question about the audience's moral position. The staring eye is very much our own.

Next we see the face that belongs to the staring eyes. It is a man's face, and he licks his lips as he observes Annette step off the school bus to walk home. We see her first in long shot, but when it comes to a close-up Carreras makes sure we see her legs first. Only then does the camera move up to her face. The rapist, whom Annette knows as Janiello (Arnold Diamond), drives his truck up to her and offers her a lift. Again significantly, the dialogue is in French through out this scene, not only consolidating the location but also providing the intended sense of sophistication that Carreras was keen to exploit in his aim to move away from Hammer's Gothic horror image.

The rape itself takes place under a tree to the left in another flat landscape shot. The image is desolate, but the score by Stanley Black is up-tempo (in fact a somewhat watered-down version of John Barry's James Bond idiom). The mood is, in fact, one of excitement rather than of tragedy or horror. We are meant to be titillated rather than censorious, though we also look forward to watching the rapist being punished. In other words, we are eating our cake and having it too, much as the popular press screams moral indignation over pedophiles in its headlines while simultaneously devoting its inside pages to soft pornography.

A boy from the school bus has followed Janiello and Annette on his bicycle but rather than take on Janiello himself, he cycles off to fetch Annette's father, Georges. When they arrive back at the scene, Annette staggers from her ordeal and collapses in front of them. Georges grabs a heavy spanner and advances towards the rapist. He takes him back to his garage, where the camera moves slowly over its close-up of two gas canisters. The rhythmic activity of the music now lessens to emphasize the ominous significance of the canisters, which are a grotesque equivalent of Annette's violated legs. The punishment would appear to fit the crime, for these canisters are connected to an acetylene torch. Georges ignites this, and as we cut to a shot of Annette watching the proceedings from her bedroom, Janiello's screams indicate the manner of Georges' vengeance.

The action that immediately follows this up-tempo prologue is very slow-burning, seemingly belonging more to a romantic drama than a psychological thriller. The timeline has moved ahead four years and we are shown the exterior of a café-bar owned by Georges' second wife, Eve. Geoff has some words with Giles, the ferryman (Jerold Wells). Giles has no lines but will play a vital part in the plot. Inside the bar, Norman Bird's policeman, Salon, is enjoying a drink served by Annette. When Geoff's girlfriend Grace arrives, they argue. She drives away never to return, and this leaves Geoff with nothing to do but paint the scenery and become involved in the plot.

Then Eve appears on her horse and agrees to rent Geoff a room. He offers to mend her jukebox and the following scene gives Annette and Geoff an opportunity to dance together. Sangster remembered this as being "sexy as hell" when they shot it but added, "Now it looks just plain stupid."[13] Perhaps both opinions are too extreme. The charming Brousse and the sensitive Mathews both appear to have genuinely enjoyed filming this elegant flirtation, but when Annette and Geoff attempt to dance in each other's arms they are prevented by Eve, who asks Annette to help her behind the bar.

Geoff cannot sleep due to the heat. Sangster's script specified that the weather throughout the film "is very hot, like the story."[14] Night noises (animals, birds, insects, etc.) provide an ambience similar to the incessant crickets of *Taste of Fear*. Geoff jumps out of bed, looks out of the window and sees someone on a horse watched by another figure in the undergrowth. Though these people are later revealed to be harmless gypsies and have no more to do with the plot, they are sufficiently intriguing to make Paul pull on his trousers to investigate. Once outside, he bumps into Annette who is also unable to sleep. They have another drink together and play a game of dice. Annette starts to call him "Geoff" rather than "monsieur." They kiss and it appears they are falling in love with each other. But this is not to be, as Eve appears and makes more successful advances on Geoff herself.

We cut to a particularly impressive rocky landscape, in fact the heights of Les Baux de Provence in the Alpille mountains with its magnificent ruined chateau-fortress—another Gothic element that makes a discreet contribution to the mood here. Geoff is attempting to paint, but he should really have been taking lessons in photography from

Wilkie Cooper, who chose a spectacular vantage point that captures both the incredible rock formations and the distant sea, 15 miles away. Eve arrives with a picnic lunch, which they eat by the ruins. Eve now explains what happened to Annette, and how Georges is incarcerated in a lunatic asylum; but this is only the beginning of her plan, which will take time to mature, as her dialogue suggests:

"How are you getting on with your painting?" she asks.

"Oh, I'm still waiting for inspiration."

"Well, like most things, if you wait long enough, it will happen eventually."

Indeed it does, but not quite as Eve expects.

Back at the café, Annette serves Geoff his dinner. Geoff asks her if he will allow her to paint her portrait, as she is such a beautiful young woman, but by this time he is emotionally more interested in Eve. Annette is understandably put out and increasingly upset. Eve invites Geoff to go riding with her, and the next scene takes us to the beach at Saintes Maries de la Mer, the same location that Van Gogh famously painted and drew during a week's visit there in 1888. The view inspired Cooper to achieve his most Adams-like imagery: a long shot of the couple against the vast horizon. (This shot also looks forward to the shot of Tadzio pointing out to sea at the end of Visconti's *Death in Venice* eight years later.) Eve gives Geoff an opportunity to dry her off, removing her shirt and revealing her breasts to him (though not to the audience).

Annette watches Eve and Geoff return to the café, where they kiss. She slams the door and bursts into tears on her bed. Eve, by contrast, confesses, "I feel I've come alive again, thanks to you," and Geoff, who shares her feelings, agrees to accompany her on her next visit to her husband. Eventually, Eve persuades Geoff to help her husband to escape. She doesn't believe Georges is insane, and explains that he has agreed to release her from her marriage vows, consequently making her free to marry Geoff, if they will do this last good deed for him. Geoff agrees (though at this stage in the proceedings it seems unclear why he is needed, as Eve could surely do alone all that is required, which is no more than to provide a car and drive Georges away).

As they wait for the rendezvous to take place, a parrot squawks in its cage on the town square, suggesting the bird imagery of *Psycho*, but only very briefly. The detail is significant, however, especially considering Hitchcock's use of birds as symbols of disorder and misrule. Georges appears to have been delayed, so they return to the car, where Georges suddenly appears from the back seat, exploiting a classic shock tactic of raising his hand before revealing his body. A couple of awkward glances suggest Eve's deception: She knows that Georges is not the real Georges at all, but rather his nurse, with whom she has fallen in love. But this, along with Geoff's real role in the plot, has yet to be revealed. Together, they drive "Georges" to the docks where he apparently plans to sail away to a new life.

Now George Pastell appears as the policeman who has been assigned to investigate the disappearance of Georges and his nurse. Pastell's last two appearances for Hammer had been in Terence Fisher's *The Mummy* (1959) and *The Stranglers of Bombay* (1960), but here he is strictly non-malevolent, his function purely to further the narrative. He does, however, provide a sense of continuity, which helps identify this as a Hammer product. So too, for that matter, does Kerwin Mathews, who had appeared in Hammer's *The Pirates of Blood River* the previous year.

At a market in Arles, Eve asks Geoff to put their groceries in the back of the Citroën, and it is there that he discovers a corpse. Eve allows Geoff to assume that this is the body of the nurse who helped Georges to escape, and Geoff now understandably revises his opinion of Georges' sanity. They attempt to dispose of the corpse in a river, but the appearance of two Camargue horsemen prevents this. According to Sangster's original script, the horsemen were originally to have been two traffic cops, in a scene reminiscent of the one in *Psycho* when Janet Leigh's character is pulled over by a policeman, but the traffic cops were cut due to financial considerations.

Temporarily foiled, Eve and Geoff return home with the corpse, pending another attempt to dispose of it. Meanwhile, a couple of acetylene gas canisters are delivered to the garage, "ordered by phone this morning," according to the delivery man. It can only have been Georges who did this, implying that he never caught the boat in the first place. Carreras again invests the canisters with malevolent significance by means of a threatening close-up, and Geoff now presumes that Georges is plotting revenge on both Eve and himself for having fallen in love with each other. They eventually succeed in dumping the unidentified body, which, as Geoff correctly points out, now makes them as guilty as Georges.

Back at the café it seems that Georges has returned to his old habit of playing with the acetylene torch. Annette watches it flash and flare through the windows and cracks in walls of the dilapidated garage, which splendidly aids the impression of there being, as Sangster himself put it, "something nasty in the woodshed."[15] Annette bravely goes out to investigate like a good Gothic novel heroine, but there is no one inside, only the torch, attached in a vise and burning against a sheet of metal.

There follows a particularly atmospheric scene reminiscent of Alain Resnais' *Last Year at Marienbad* (1961) in its uncanny calm, and the balletic movement of the camera as it encircles the two silent women. Eve and Annette have gone to the amphitheater at Arles to meet Georges and find out what is happening—or, at least, that is Eve's story. In fact, Georges is not there. He is back at the garage where he plans to murder Geoff. Sangster was unhappy with the way the Arles amphitheater was filmed, but it is a particularly effective scene, despite being relatively short. Carreras manages to evoke the terror of place even though nothing happens. The eerie de Chirico mood is palpable, aided by the fluid camerawork, and the elegant, statuesque poses of the two women in the midst of the vast enclosed space is highly reminiscent of Resnais' silent, statuesque guests in the formal gardens in *Marienbad*. Hammer would never again achieve such continental elegance in the visual style of its films.

Now it is Geoff's turn to notice flashing lights in the garage. He runs in to discover "Georges," who knocks him out. When Geoff comes round, he has been tied to the acetylene canisters. "Georges" explains that he intends to burn Geoff's body and then blow up the garage. The police will therefore assume that Georges has repeated his crime and been killed by an accidental explosion. The charred bodies will be taken for those of Georges and his nurse. Then "Georges" will be officially dead and able to escape from the law forever. It is a perfect plan, which would no doubt have worked if the conversation hadn't been overhead by Giles, the ferryman.

After the explosion, which takes place off-screen, Pastell's policeman arrives at the scene and repeats "George's" dialogue almost word for word. It would appear that Giles was listening closely and has informed the police all about the plot—but too late. When Eve and Annette arrive back from Arles, the policeman explains:

> We found two bodies in the debris. Your husband, I'm afraid, was one of them. The other, the male nurse that helped him escape. It seems your husband was attempting to recreate the crimes he committed four years ago. A typical pathological pattern. Then suddenly the equipment must have blown up in his face.

He adds that "one of them is alive. Burnt but still alive," and Eve immediately assumes that this is Geoff. She visits him in hospital, and the bandaged patient who awaits her foreshadows the bandaged "mummy" at the end of *Blood from the Mummy's Tomb* (1970). That film was completed by Michael Carreras after its original director, Seth Holt, died of a heart attack during the shoot, and it is tempting to assume that Carreras had this shot from *Maniac* in mind when filming the ambivalent epilogue to that later adaptation of Bram Stoker's Egyptian romance *The Jewel of Seven Stars*. In it, we are not sure if the bandaged victim is Margaret Fuchs, the daughter of the Egyptologist who discovered the tomb of the evil Queen Tera, or Queen Tera herself, whose perfectly preserved body was kept in the Egyptologist's cellar. The cellar in which the dramatic dénouement of that film takes place collapses, crushing everyone present, much as the acetylene gas blows up the garage in *Maniac*.

Eve looks down at the man on the hospital bed and confesses her plot: "Georges" is not Georges. The real Georges is the corpse she and Geoff tried to dump in the river. While visiting her husband in the lunatic asylum, Eve fell in love with Georges's nurse. Geoff's real role in all of this was to provide the required body to make the police assume that both the nurse and Georges had perished. Eve then ruthlessly removes Geoff's drip-feed and thinks she is finishing him off for good.

But now Annette is troubled by what Eve has (rather unnecessarily) told her. Eve did not give away the whole plot to her, but for some reason she does confess her conviction that the other man in the explosion was Geoff. The only reason for so doing is to move the plot forward, as the film needs to end with a climax in which Annette's life is threatened. Annette insists that Eve should tell the truth (as much of it as Annette knows, anyway) to the police, and this is the cue for Eve to set the final scene in action. She persuades Annette to go shopping with her, but Giles watches them leave and telephones the police to let them know the turn of events.

We cut to the police station where Geoff is discovered alive and well, having acted out the hospital scene to extract the truth from Eve and exonerate himself from his complicity in the plot by assisting the police with their inquiries. Giles, we are now told, alerted the police before "Georges" could implement the explosion. This was later staged by the police for Eve's benefit.

Eve takes Annette to the caves outside Les Baux de Provence, which provide a suitably surreal location for the final chase sequence in which Georges reveals his true identity to Annette. He falls to his death, and the police arrive to escort Eve into the arms of justice and the corpse of "Henri" to the cemetery.

Maniac is Hammer's least known psychological thriller, but also one of its most rewarding. Combining ravishing landscape, a love story that inverts the love story genre, and a typically complex plot of reversals, it is Sangster's most aesthetic response to *Les Diaboliques*, with some of the most accomplished photography in any of Hammer's oeuvre.

9

Sex and the Dead in *Paranoiac*
(dir. Freddie Francis, 1963)

Paranoiac was Hammer's adaptation of Josephine Tey's 1949 novel *Brat Farrar* in which the eponymous Farrar colludes with a disaffected actor, Alex Loding, to impersonate Patrick Ashby ("Tony" in the film), who was believed to have committed suicide some years before. Loding's plan is to pass Farrar off as Ashby, to whom he bears a close resemblance. Once re-established as the long-lost elder son returned, Farrar will inherit the family fortunes, from which Loding will take a cut. There is, however, the suspicion and jealousy of his younger brother, Simon, to contend with.

Jimmy Sangster changed various aspects of Tey's novel in his screenplay, particularly by delaying the exposure of the impostor. In the novel, Farrar is introduced and exposed as an impostor right from the start. By delaying the revelation of character's true identity, Sangster creates the possibility of a supernatural explanation, and thus conforms to Todorov's definition of the "fantastic" category, when it is "impossible to determine whether the bizarre events which occur are figments of a fevered imagination of manifestations of the supernatural." Tey toys with this by referring to a newspaper headline inspired by the return of "Patrick," which screams "Back from the Dead." Patrick's sister Eleanor also comments that Brat-Patrick "looked so tired that he looked like a *dead* man,"[1] but the structure of the novel reduces these references to dramatic irony, rather than elevating them to ambivalence and mystery.

Sangster also entirely removed the horse-racing background of the novel (presumably on grounds of expense). All that remained of the equestrian element is one brief mention of a pony called Clinker, a birthday present given to "Tony" from the family solicitor Mr. Kosset. In the novel, Simon attempts to dispose of his fake brother by letting him ride on a particularly unruly horse—"a nice piece of vicarious manslaughter"[2] which fails to have the desired effect. Sangster has Simon tamper with the engine of a car instead. He also injected a degree of grotesque terror that is quite absent in Tey's story. In the film, Simon (played by Oliver Reed) is a psychopath who has been protected by his devoted Aunt Harriet (Sheila Burrell). She dresses up in a grotesque mask to deter anyone from discovering Simon in his more unbalanced moods. During these periods he plays the organ *à la* the Phantom of the Opera, overcome with remorse at having killed his brother, whose rotted away corpse he keeps in a secret compartment behind the organ. None of this features in Tey's much more sober novel where Simon is certainly the callous murderer of his hated elder brother, but not an organ-playing psychopath to boot. The fact remains, however, that though Simon knows Tony (Alexander Davion) is a fraud, he cannot expose him as that would mean exposing his own guilt; but Tey's Simon is nowhere near as paranoid as Sangster's. Tey also gives Farrar a considerable back history. He is an orphan with a colorful maritime past, but we know very little about the character called Tony in the film other than that he has colluded with one of the junior partners of the family's solicitor. Simon Ashby, who is a less well-defined character in the book, becomes, especially as played by Oliver Reed, the central figure.

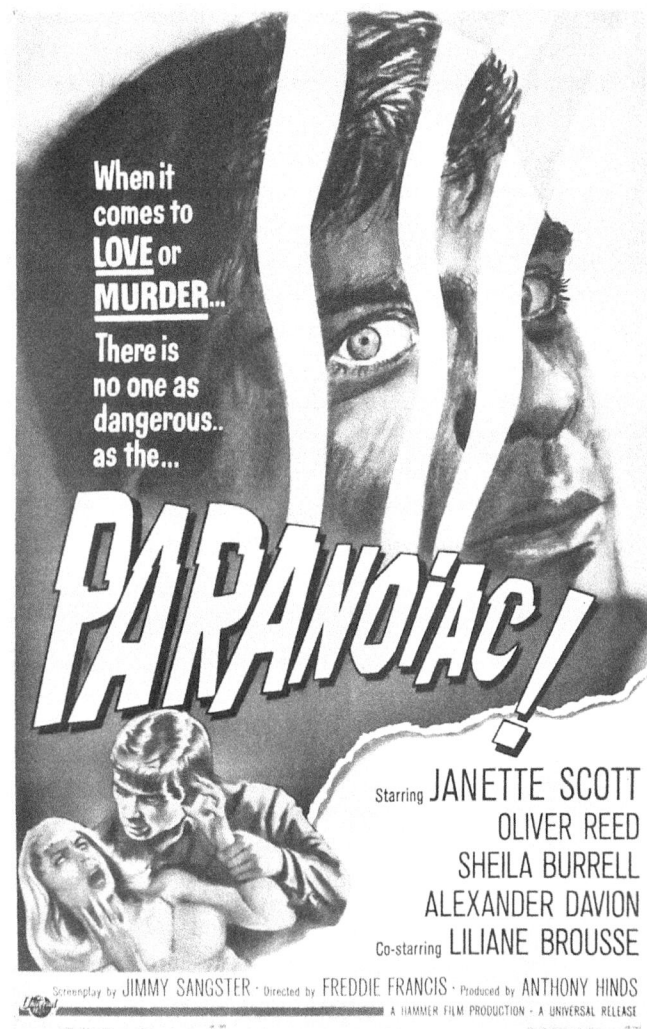

Poster for *Paranoiac* (dir. Freddie Francis, 1963). A portrait of Oliver Reed is slashed by schizophrenic symbolism.

Reed, who had already starred in Hammer's *The Curse of the Werewolf* (dir. Terence Fisher, 1960) and appeared in *The Pirates of Blood River* (dir. John Gilling, 1962), gives a performance as Simon that pulsates a psychotic brooding sensuality (demonstrating all three of the levels of passion he categorized as "Moody One, Moody Two or Moody Three" when working with Ken Russell[3]). Simon's behavior, fueled by drink on a scale that Reed no doubt personally identified with, is a cocktail of interesting Freudian complexes. Along with the paranoia and guilt, there is also an unhealthy dose of sibling rivalry, recalling the Biblical story of Cain and Abel. There are also some sexual anxieties. That was nothing new for a Hammer film. Indeed, the sexual tension of this one has much in common with *The Full Treatment*; but due to Reed's brooding charisma, especially in the scenes with Liliane Brousse, who plays Françoise, the nurse of Janette Scott's Eleanor, *Paranoiac* is certainly the one in which sexuality and psychosis are most notably to the fore. "You like me hurting you, don't you?" he smirks as Françoise yields to another of his brutal kisses. Later in the film, after another violent kiss, he strangles her and pushes her head under the waters of a lake on the grounds of the Ashby mansion. All these elements, combined with what we have already learned about the significance of houses, and certain perversities gleaned from the example of the Marquis de Sade, which are yet to come, reveal how Hammer brought increasing complexity to their psychological thrillers; but such a combination of sex, guilt and the idea of the revenant can be traced back to nineteenth-century Gothic tales such as "Wake Not the Dead," (1832), attributed to the German Romantic writer Johann Ludwig Tieck (1773–1853), in which a dead wife is summoned from the grave by her distraught husband. The wife in question turns into a vampire and preys on the husband's second wife and his children. Though *Paranoiac* draws the line at such "marvelous" developments, Eleanor Ashby's grief for her brother Tony, which has driven her almost insane, has much in common with the substance (if not the literary style) of Walter's grief for the dead Brunhilda in "Wake Not the Dead."

> "Wilt thou for ever sleep? Wilt thou never more awake, my beloved, but henceforth repose for ever from thy short pilgrimage on earth? O yet once again return! and bring back with thee the vivifying dawn of hope to one whose existence hath, since thy departure, been obscured by the dunnest shades. What! dumb? for ever dumb? Thy friend lamenteth, and thou heedest him not? He sheds bitter, scalding tears, and thou reposest unregarding his affliction? He is in despair, and thou no longer openest thy arms to him as an asylum from his grief? Say then, doth the paly shroud become thee better than the bridal veil? Is the chamber of the grave a warmer bed than the couch of love? Is the spectre death more welcome to thy arms than they enamoured consort? Oh! return, my beloved, return once again to this anxious disconsolate bosom." Such were the lamentations which Walter poured forth for his Brunhilda, the partner of his youthful passionate love.[4]

This is the atmosphere Sangster aimed to inject into his reworking of Tey's story, along with the horror of incest, which we will address is due course. Tieck's conflation of graveyard imagery with bridal beds was also exploited by Gottfried Bürger (1747–1794) in his once very famous poem "Lenore" (1773), in which a young woman prays for the return of her lover from the wars. He does return, but as a corpse, and they ride together to the bridal bed, which is now the tomb.

> But hark to the clatter and the pat pat patter!
>   Of a horse's heavy hoof!
> How the steel clanks and rings as the rider springs!
>   How the echo shouts aloof!
> While silently and lightly the gentle bell
> Tingles and jingles softly and well;
> And low and clear through the door plank thin
> Comes the voice without to the ear within:

> "Holla! holla! unlock the gate;
>   Art waking, my bride, or sleeping?
> Is thy heart still free and faithful to me?
>   Art laughing, my bride, or weeping?"
>
> "Oh! wearily, William, I've waited for you, -
> Woefully watching the long day thro,' -
> With a great sorrow sorrowing
> For the cruelty of your tarrying."
>
> "Till the dead midnight we saddled not, -
>   I have journeyed far and fast -
> And hither I come to carry thee back
>   Ere the darkness shall be past."
>
> "Ah! rest thee within till the night's more calm;
> Smooth shall thy couch be, and soft, and warm:
> Hark to winds, how they whistle and rush
> Thro' the twisted twine of the hawthorn-bush."[5]

Paranoiac also offers a parallel to Bürger's frightening ride of the wife and her dead lover, in the scene in which Tony takes Eleanor for a spin in a sports car. It very nearly ends in the death of them both thanks to Simon's tampering with the engine.

Even more relevant is E.T.A. Hoffmann's tale "Das Gelübde" ("The Vow," 1817), in which a woman is convinced that her lover has returned to her, but the man is in fact only someone who resembles the lover. Like Tony with Eleanor in *Paranoiac*, this man then falls in love with the woman, but goes even further than Tony by making her pregnant. These stories have relevance to *Paranoiac*, because although Simon doesn't believe in the impostor, his sister desperately wants to believe her brother has returned to her. Like Eleanor, the heroine of Hoffmann's tale "in sorry confusion found herself incapable of separating the emotion from the image and the image from the resemblance." Later, Hoffmann's unfortunate heroine, Hermengilda, realizes her mistake, when the impostor, like Tony in the film, confesses his deceit:

> The officer, flushed and trembling, utterly disconcerted, drew back a step and gently extricated himself from Hermengilda's passionate embrace. "This is one of the happiest moments of my life," he stammered out, "but I cannot permit myself to—revel—in delights—that are only mine by mistake—in fact, I am not Stanislaus—ah, definitely not!"
>
> Now Hermengilda drew back, appalled, and when a calmer scrutiny of the officer convinced her that she had been misled by an utter stranger's remarkable resemblance to her lover, she fled to her room, moaning and sobbing to herself.[6]

Eventually, Hermengilda "for all her intense preoccupation with Stanislaus, was pleased, none the less, to permit Xavier to court her more and more overtly."[7] And the same process occurs in *Paranoiac* when Eleanor, aware that the impostor is not her brother, nonetheless saves him from the final conflagration and runs off with him.

Paranoiac opens with a widescreen shot of cliffs and the sea. The words "A Hammer Film Production" were by then a guarantee of a certain kind of entertainment and a set of expectations but, as with *Maniac*, the black and white "artiness" of these opening shots, with their widescreen format and Elisabeth Lutyens' restrained scoring, indicate a more sophisticated, perhaps more cerebral event than the visceral full-color pleasures of the company's previous Gothic horrors. Indeed, since 1961, Hammer's output had concentrated on this different approach. Only Fisher's *The Phantom of the Opera* had resembled their horror classics. Among a couple of comedies (*A Weekend with Lulu*, directed by John Paddy Carstairs in 1961, and Wolf Rilla's *Watch It Sailor!* the same year) there had been Michael Carreras' refugee drama *Visa to Canton* (1961) and four matinee adventures: *Captain Clegg* (dir. Peter Graham Scott, 1962); *Pirates of Blood River* (1962) and *The Scarlet Blade* (1963), both directed by John Gilling; and Anthony Bushell's curious *The Terror of the Tongs* in 1961, with Christopher Lee warming up for his later incarnation as Fu Manchu. Peter Cushing also turned up in Quentin Lawrence's bank robbery drama *Cash on Demand* in 1963, but all the other films released in this period were psychological thrillers, or what one might call psychological science fiction in the case of Joseph Losey's *The Damned* (1963). *Paranoiac* brought this experimental period to a close, and thereafter Hammer would alternate psychological thrillers with more traditional Gothic horror, while expanding into more lavish territory with epics such as *She*.

Though not as interested in landscape for its own sake as Michael Carreras was in *Maniac*, Freddie Francis nonetheless uses the coastal imagery in the opening shots of *Paranoiac* as a counterpoint to the claustrophobic interiors that dominate the action. They not only remind the audience of the location of Tony Ashby's supposed suicide but also signal deeper resonances about death and love. (Wagner's *Tristan und Isolde*, the ultimate meditation on that juxtaposition, similarly uses the sea as such a metaphor: "Öd und leer das Meer!" sings Tristan in Act III—"Bleak and bare the sea!") In particular, Francis' imagery here summons memories of Revelation, chapter 20, verse 13, "And the sea gave up the dead which were in it; and death and hell delivered up the dead which were in them: and they were judged every man according to their works." These words, of course, inform the service for "The Burial of the Dead" in the Book of Common Prayer: "and the sea shall give up their dead; and the corruptible bodies of those who sleep in him shall be changed." Thus, the very opening of the film suggests far more than merely establishing a location, particularly as Francis photographs the unusual rock formations in epic style. Indeed, Francis was chosen to direct the film due to his masterful camerawork on *The Innocents* (dir. Jack Clayton, 1961). As Sangster put it: "Camerawise, he was a master at creating suspense. He could light a set so you would be scared as soon as it appeared on screen."[8] Indeed, in *Paranoiac* Francis reprised his technique of obscuring the edges of the frame, which he had used to such effect in *The Innocents* and would adapt to vaguely psychedelic effect in *Dracula Has Risen from the Grave* in 1968. In that instance, the color distortion at the edges of the frame connoted Dracula's presence, whereas in Clayton's film, the fuzzy edges created a subtle sense of ambivalence and uncertainty. Francis was keen to inject this mood into *Paranoiac*, particularly in the scenes involving Eleanor.

Eleanor was played by Janette Scott, daughter of Thora Hird (who had appeared in Hammer's *The Quatermass Xperiment*) and she is given top billing, not only reflecting her status at that time (Oliver Reed is credited in smaller lettering) but also the importance of her role, which Sangster considerably expanded from Tey's original. It is Reed, however, who dominates the action.

As the seagulls cry, Lutyens' melancholy score accompanies the main title sequence's wide pan of the cliffs and the sea. After this, we fade to the exterior of a very British parish church. Francis realized how important it was to establish a distinctively British ambience, not only to anchor the film in a native tradition of Gothic romance but also to provide the social context that generates the plot. The Ashbys are respected members of the community, and it is to maintain this veneer that Aunt Harriet (Aunt Bee in the novel) goes to such trouble to maintain with regard to her tearaway nephew, Simon. Simon's behavior is an embarrassment to her as it would have been to 1960s British society; but it was also rather exciting to the young British audience to whom this film was principally marketed. England in 1963 was rapidly becoming the fashion hub of the swinging '60s, and Simon's conspicuous consumption, his fast cars and sharp suits, were very appealing to the aspirational young generation that was rejecting their parents' post-war austerities. In particular, we learn of Simon's holidays abroad. Though these are only briefly referred to by the morally disapproving solicitor Mr. Kosset (Maurice Denham), who is in charge of Simon's financial affairs, the mere mention of them is enough to reflect the fact that such holidays were now becoming possible for Hammer's target audiences in a way that had never been possible before. All this becomes a very heady mix when combined with Reed's sexually charged and dangerous performance. As Sangster remembered, "The critics went crazy for him."[9]

And so, Francis allows Arthur Grant's camera to rove through the graveyard past the tomb of John and Mary Ashby, the parents of Simon and Eleanor, and also to pause over the joint memorial to Anthony. The camera then moves towards the door of the church; inside, a vicar conveniently explains the family history. John and Mary died eleven years ago in a plane crash. Anthony, apparently "blinded by grief," was believed to have drowned himself shortly thereafter, leaving behind him Aunt Harriet, Eleanor and Simon, shots of whom accompany the vicar's respective introductions. Simon is waiting in the organ loft, nonchalant and cynical, smoking and stubbing out his cigarette on the organ itself—the very incarnation of what would emerge as teenage rebellion in October 1963 with the first appearance of Beatlemania and the more violent behavior of Mods and Rockers, which began to steal the headlines the following year. Simon may wear a suit and tie but that does not imply conformity to the status quo. Suits and ties were anyway ubiquitous in 1963, and Simon is, after all, a member of the upper middle classes, soon to be very rich.

But as Simon plays the organ, a figure appears at the entrance of the church. Eleanor looks at the man and faints, for she thinks she has seen Tony, and the audience also thinks the same, even though Tony is meant to be dead. Sangster extends the possibility of Tony being a revenant as long as he possibly can, making *Paranoiac* a much more compelling experience than Tey's novel (which, incidentally, receives no credit whatsoever on the main titles).

Eleanor is attended to by Françoise, and Simon speeds away in his sports car. We are then shown the Ashbys' very respectable mansion, which is typical of the kind of stockbroker-belt real estate to be found in the Home Counties. Dirk Bogarde lived in similar properties during the 1950s. After leaving Bendrose House, in Amersham, Buckinghamshire, he moved to Nore, in Hascombe, Surrey, in the early 1960s: "At Nore," he reminisced, "we sat around the fire, ran movies in the cinema at nights, read the papers, talked endlessly and walked miles across the fields with dogs and raincoats and a carried assortment of boots and stout sticks."[10] One can imagine Aunt Harriet doing the dog walking, and Simon running the movies with a decanter of brandy by his side. Both of them talk endlessly. The topiary that surrounds the Ashbys' house also lends a certain Continental formality to the proceedings, again reminding the attentive viewer of Resnais' *Last Year at Marienbad*. The impression is understated but adds a dash of sophistication to the film's overall ambience.

After Simon drives away from the church, Francis presents us with another ambivalent shot of "Tony" looking at his own grave. Such a situation had, in the past, been shared by Scrooge in Dickens' *A Christmas Carol* ("'Am *I* that man who lay upon the bed?' he cried, upon his knees."[11]), and also for comic purposes by Mapp and Lucia in E.F. Benson's 1934 novel *Mapp and Lucia*, which describes how the two socialites of Tilling are washed out to sea and later assumed to have perished. (The gravestone erected in their memory reads "IN DEATH THEY WERE NOT DIVIDED." "I've never heard of such a thing," cried Lucia. "I call it most premature of Georgie, assuming that I was dead like that. The inscription must be removed instantly."[12]) In *Paranoiac*, however, the situation provides an excellent example of Todorov's "fantastic" category.

Bernard Robinson's set for Eleanor's bedroom includes a room divider composed of turned wooden columns, which consciously or not echoes a similar feature in *Les Diaboliques*; and just as in that film, all is not as it at first appears. Françoise, the nurse, brushes Eleanor's hair (compare the hair-brushing in *Rebecca* and *The Nanny*) as Eleanor explains how close she was to Tony; and her dialogue here is in substance just what Walther gushes at the beginning of "Wake Not the Dead." Again suggesting the possibility that the man she saw is indeed Tony back from the dead, she sobs, "People who were as close as Tony and I were in life—we can't just be separated by death." She adds that she has "faith in the dead," and "I knew he would come for me." Françoise, disturbed by all this, insists, "You can't possibly have seen Tony. He's dead."

Simon's sports car now roars to a halt outside, and we can hear music by Chopin drifting from inside the house. Hammer was particularly fond of using Chopin as a macabre mood setter. We have already encountered it in *Taste of Fear*. In *Paranoiac* we hear the famous D-flat Major Nocturne, which will also be played by Carl Ravna in *The Kiss of the Vampire*. However, unlike Marianne in *Kiss*, Simon is not listening to a live performance. This Chopin is being played on a record in the sitting room where Aunt Harriet is awaiting Simon's return. Their conversation (Harriet's disapproval of Simon's behavior, Simon's indifference to it) is constructed in such a way that we have no idea about the secrets they share. Simon insists that Eleanor is "insane"—an opinion that seems to be justified when they subsequently see her walking about in the garden like a ghost. In fact, Eleanor is just about to see a ghost (or what seems like one) when she comes face to face with "Tony" in the garden. His expression is emotionless and he says nothing. When Eleanor turns in response to Harriet's voice, he vanishes in yet another example of Sangster's delaying tactic.

After dosing Eleanor with sleeping pills, Françoise goes to her room where Simon is found lying on her bed. Françoise seems to have been expecting him, and we soon learn they are having an affair. We also discover that Françoise is not a nurse, her function presumably being to report Eleanor's moods and behavior to Simon and be available when he is in an amorous mood. So far, Simon has demonstrated his violence and cynical streak. He reveals his psychotic nature when, in the next scene, he shouts at the butler, demanding more brandy; but as the butler points out, the brandy cannot be replenished because Simon has already spent his allowance. Reed's amazing performance of these terrifying rages recalls his transformations into a werewolf when playing Leon in *The Curse of the Werewolf*. In fact, they are even more disturbing here because they are all the more naturalistic. One expects a werewolf to be violent, but such a tantrum coming from a man in a dining room wearing a suit and tie is more of a shock.

"I suppose it had entered your mind that with Eleanor out of the way, you'd come into her share of the money as well as your own?" the stuffy lawyer, Kosset, suggests in the next scene. "Yes, it had entered my mind," Simon replies, and this, of course, has been his plan all along. Keith (John Bonney), the solicitor's son, is now introduced, and Simon, fully aware of how much Keith has been embezzling from the family fortunes, uses this knowledge to blackmail him into giving him a hundred pounds. What Simon does not know is that Keith is the one who has primed the impostor with sufficient information to make "Tony" so convincing. In Tey's novel, the role of Keith belongs to the actor called Alec Loding, but Sangster rightly decided that it would be much more economical and indeed logical to make him the son of the family solicitor. This information has yet to be released to the audience, but Sangster skillfully introduces Keith to the audience at this stage to prepare the later revelation.

As in *Taste of Fear* we are now shown the victimized heroine, Eleanor, gazing out to sea. Unknown to her, high above on the cliff top she is being watched by Tony. She is overcome with her own neuroses and grief, and life has become too much for her; she hurls herself into the sea. Tony rescues her and brings her back home. The butler is astonished at the impostor's resemblance to the real Tony, but still Sangster teases us with regard to how corporeal Tony really is by having him vanish once again, as soon as backs are turned. Simon is next in line to be shocked by the resemblance and he drives off in a panic after having nearly knocked Tony down in his sports car.

Harriet now interrogates the new comer. She doesn't believe he is who he says he is, but he answers her questions correctly. As Tony's body was never found, his story is plausible: he left a suicide note and then ran away "because I couldn't stand being with you for another minute, Aunt Harriet," as he politely informs her. We are beginning to understand that Harriet is very controlling. Tony accuses her of driving Eleanor insane, and as Keith's plot hasn't been revealed yet, we wonder if this is the reason behind

Tony's appearance. If he is not the real Tony, perhaps he is someone else who cares for Eleanor…

Now Tony is subjected to various tests by Harriet, Simon and Kosset. He passes all of them with flying colors. He even knows where his old room is situated. Keith has done his work well. Only now does Sangster reveal what Tey made no bones about from the very beginning—that "Tony" is an impostor. But we never get to know his real name, or indeed, anything else about him. Keith now introduces the next psychological element: "Watch it with Eleanor," he warns his protégé. "After all, she *is* meant to be your sister." This hint of implied incest will be developed later.

Next, the rattled Simon gets very drunk in a pub and in a truly frightening moment he threatens a man at the bar with the darts he pulls from a dartboard. Reed was, of course, accustomed to such behavior in real life. Sangster recalled, "Oliver Reed became a friend later, more of a drinking companion than a friend, but, as in most things, he overdid that too and rather scared me off."[13] Reed is truly scary here. "A bit barmy, isn't he?" one of the worried girls at the bar remarks. That is surely an understatement. Tony later drives him home. "I don't know who found you or where but you're Tony to a tee, I'll give you that," Simon admits. "Pompous, self-opinionated, holier-than-thou and dull."

Later that night, events take a fresh turn when Eleanor hears mysterious organ music accompanying a choirboy rendition of Mendelssohn's "Hear My Prayer." Tony hears it too and they both go their separate ways downstairs to an old chapel where we glimpse a cowled figure playing the organ. Tony is then attacked by a choirboy wearing a grotesque mask. This incident has nothing to do with Josephine Tey, but is typical of Hammer's approach. Having slashed Tony's wrist, the masked figure runs away and Eleanor comes to the rescue. She explains that she has heard the music before but seems to have been the only person to do so and consequently put it down to her imagination. Once more, therefore, we enjoy the Gothic convention of mysterious music drifting up to an imperiled heroine.

Now Freddie Francis arranges one of the key suspense scenes. We see Simon tampering with the MG sports car and soon discover what he is planning. He is determined to rid himself of this impostor even if it means killing his own sister in a car accident. A picnic on the cliffs with Tony and Eleanor follows, the only illogical element here being that they have obviously driven the car to this location earlier and have had no difficulty with the brakes, which is not the case when Eleanor reverses for the return journey and very nearly plummets over the edge of the cliff. Tony rescues her in the nick of time in a beautifully arranged widescreen shot of the cliff tops and the sea, which rounds off the scene and defuses the considerable tension in a very picturesque way. When Tony and Eleanor return home, Simon literally weeps with rage, and this alerts Françoise that all is not well with her boyfriend's state of mind.

The mysterious organ music recurs the following night, and this time we see that it is Simon at the organ accompanied by a mysterious choirboy. A gramophone is in fact responsible for the vocals, which Eleanor says sounds just like Tony when he was a boy. During the ensuing struggle, the mysterious figure is revealed to be Harriet. She has been protecting Simon, whom she believes to be insane and haunted by some kind of guilt over his brother's death. She has no idea that he actually killed the real Tony but she has tried to bring him peace by dressing up as his brother. She wears the mask to frighten people away; masks will return in Francis' *Nightmare*. Again, E.T.A. Hoffmann anticipates these facial deceptions in "The Vow," in which a nun wears a skin-tight mask to help atone for her past sins. The nun's mask is even more grotesque than Harriet's, and closely resembles Franju's skin-tight creation for Edith Scob in *Les Yeux sans visage*. All of these masks, however, share the unnerving quality of eyes staring out from an immobile face. Hoffmann describes the nun's mask as having "no distortion of feature, only a deathly pallor, a marble white face out of whose sunken eye-sockets a strange light blazed forth.... [T]he eyes blazed in their hollow sockets ... while lips fixed like a cipher, open and unmoving, sent forth cries of anguish."[14]

Tony agrees that Harriet is right about Simon: "The brakes in your car didn't just fail by themselves," he perceptively observes to Eleanor, just before finding himself in a passionate embrace with her. They kiss and suddenly the whole issue of incest explodes. Eleanor shrieks, "I'm insane. I'm dirty!" and tries to slash her wrists. Tony, running to the rescue, now explains that he is an impostor, just as Xavier does to Hermengilda in Hoffmann's "The Vow." And now, Tony's position as an impostor and embezzler is rather forgotten, as he races to the aid of a neurotic woman who has an insane brother. Françoise, however, cannot forget Simon's reaction to the sight of Tony and Eleanor returning from their picnic. "You've always known I wasn't exactly the blue-eyed boy," Simon retorts, before killing her. At this point, Francis indulges in an effective shot of Simon's face filmed underwater from the dead Françoise's point of view.

The final plot twist of *Paranoiac* again has much more to do with Hammer horror than Josephine Tey. It involves the revelation of the real Tony's corpse. The fake Tony discovers it bricked up behind the organ pipes, and in the dénouement, Simon explains how he forced his brother to sign a suicide note a year or two before he killed him. Harriet now bursts in shouting, "Simon belongs to me"—a curious echo of what Stoker's Count Dracula says to the vampire women who are about to enjoy Jonathan Harker ("This man belongs to me!")—before setting fire to the chapel. But Eleanor rescues the impostor and the final shots show us Simon in the arms of his brother's skeleton.

10

Loss and Deception in *The Kiss of the Vampire*

(dir. Don Sharp, 1964)

The Kiss of the Vampire has much in common not only with Hitchcock's themes and technique but also with a Gainsborough film co-directed by Terence Fisher and Anthony Darnborough in 1950. This featured Dirk Bogarde as English artist George Hathaway who helps the distraught Vicky Barton (Jean Simmons) discover what has been going on in a Parisian hotel at which Vicky's brother Johnny (David Tomlinson) has mysteriously disappeared. So too has the brother's bedroom and apparently all knowledge of his existence by everyone save Vicky herself and Hathaway, who remembers borrowing a 50 franc note from him the night before. What has actually happened is that Johnny has been taken ill in the night and, this being the time of the Great Exhibition in 1889, the hotel proprietors hush it up for fear of losing business. The film was *So Long at the Fair* (1950), based on Anthony Thorne's 1947 novel of the same name, and *The Kiss of the Vampire* borrows its basic idea, turning it into a vampire story structured on a Hitchcockian suspense model.

The Kiss of the Vampire might also be claimed as Hammer's unofficial remake of Edgar G. Ulmer's 1934 occult thriller, *The Black Cat*, with Noel Willman's Dr. Ravna as a version of Boris Karloff's villain, Hjalmar Poelzig; Clifford Evan's vampire hunter, Professor Zimmer, as Bela Lugosi's Vitus Werdegast; the honeymooners Mr. and Mrs. Harcourt (played by Edward de Souza and Jennifer Daniel) standing in for *The Black Cat's* David Manners and Julie Bishop as Mr. and Mrs. Alison, and Dr. Ravna's clutch of distinctly middle class vampires substituting Poelzig's coven of well-bred satanists. Poelzig's Bauhaus mansion is just as creepily clean and tidy as Dr. Ravna's more aesthetic but no less bourgeois, environment. Fort Marmorus and Chateau Ravna are both equally remote from civilization, and each offer their own dubious hospitality to the stranded couples.

Hammer's approach to Gothic horror was generally a very middle-class state of affairs, and *The Kiss of the Vampire* is no exception to that. In sharp contrast to the approach of Universal Studios, Hammer's production designer Bernard Robinson always made sure

Double-bill poster showing the bat finale of *The Kiss of the Vampire* (dir. Don Sharp, 1964) and a portrait of Oliver Reed reaching out for Lilian Brousse in *Paranoiac* (dir. Freddie Francis, 1963).

that the residences he created for his various vampires were always very well-swept and comfortable. Consequently, there are no cobwebs in Dr. Ravna's "ornate coffin" of a chateau, and Dr. Ravna himself (played with perfect suavity by Noel Willman) is, in fact, a much more interesting character than Christopher Lee's increasingly one-dimensional Count Dracula, whom Hammer relentlessly boiled down in successive pictures to a monosyllabic monster, much to Lee's often justifiable chagrin. Dr. Ravna is not an aristocrat. Presumably struck off for some medical misdeed, he is a decadent, middle class aesthete, a man of great sophistication judging by the artwork and grand piano of his home, but also, as one would expect, very dangerous when crossed. Dr. Ravna is indeed a kind of Dorian Gray figure with echoes of Baudelaire and J.K. Huysman's Des Esseintes about him.

The lack of cobwebs, so to speak, and the very bourgeois context of the action actually make *Kiss* rather more of a thriller and less of a Gothic horror than Roman Polanski's affectionate satire of it in *The Fearless Vampire Killers* (1967). In Polanski's film, people travel by horse and sleigh, but in *Kiss* Gerald and Marianne Harcourt enjoy their honeymoon travels on a De Dion Bouton motorcar. As usual in a Hammer horror film, they don't get much further than Black Park in Buckinghamshire, but Polanski's much bigger budget permitted a lavishness of production values and location work (in the Dolomites) to which Hammer could not hope to aspire at the time. Polanski has vast snowy vistas, and immense—very cobwebby—sets, dressed in faded baroque splendor, but he also indulges in many virtually direct references to *Kiss*: There is an inn which is terrorized by the local vampire, Count von Krolock (played by the excellent Ferdy Mayne, who is perhaps the most frightening vampire of all, despite—or perhaps because of—his ironic sense of humor). Von Krolock vampirizes the innkeeper's daughter and initiates her into his society of the undead back at the castle, just as Dr. Ravna has abducted Tanya (played by Isobel Black), the daughter of hotel owner Bruno (Peter Madden). Both von Krolock and Ravna are presented as cult leaders as well as Byronic outsiders, and Polanski models the presentation of the abducted girl at the end of his film in a very similar way to Sharp in *Kiss*. The heroes also infiltrate the castles and attempt to rescue the respective daughters. In both films, too, the son of the principal vampire plays the piano (or harpsichord in the case of Polanski's film, the vampires of which belong more to an earlier historical milieu).[1] Von Krolock even has a telescope with which to spy on the villagers just as Ravna does. Crucially, both films also feature elaborate ball scenes, though, with its demonic invocation and flying bat dénouement, the finale of *Kiss* is much more overtly occult than anything to be found in *The Fearless Vampire Killers*.

Kiss remains one of Hammer's best made and most inventive vampire films, which is no doubt why Polanski modeled his own film on it. Eschewing horror for suspense, Sharp created a tense thriller which has more in common with Hitchcock than the example of Terence Fisher, whose films Sharp nonetheless made a point of studying (he had never seen a horror film before directing *Kiss* for Hammer) but whose approach he did not wish merely to imitate; and, of course, Anthony Hinds' script, written under his pseudonym of John Elder, with its emphasis on terror and suspense rather than horror, revenge and chase, dictates a rather different approach anyway.

The suspense elements in *Kiss* revolve around the habitual Hitchcockian theme of appearance and reality. The vampires here appear to be a perfectly normal family. They are, of course, the complete opposite of a normal family, as is their "extended" family of disciples who hold regular meetings at Chateau Ravna. That ultimate bourgeois musical

10. Loss and Deception in The Kiss of the Vampire

instrument, the piano, ("the very altar of homes" as the late–Victorian artist Sir Edward Burne-Jones described it[2]), also has an important role to play in the scene that showcases James Bernard's celebrated "Vampire Rhapsody," and it bears comparison with the similar use of the piano in Hitchcock's *Rope*. In *Rope*, Philip (Farley Granger) plays Poulenc's "Mouvement Perpetuel," which, as Donald Spoto explains, is appropriate "not only because the camera is in perpetual motion throughout *Rope* [the film was shot in unprecedented ten-minute takes], but because, ironically, the inner state of the principal characters is an endless cycle of only apparent movement which is itself spiritual stasis."[3] When Carl Ravna (Barry Warren) plays the "Vampire Rhapsody" in *Kiss*, the apparently civilizing nature of music (as suggested by his previous playing of a Chopin Nocturne) is also inverted and corrupted.

The Van Helsing figure in *Kiss*, played by Clifford Evans, is Professor Zimmer, a scholar of the occult who is as gruff as Jack MacGowran's Professor Abronsius is cheerful in *The Fearless Vampire Killers*. Zimmer's daughter has also been corrupted by Ravna's cult (the subtext of syphilis is unmistakable with his description of her as having been "riddled with disease"), and he uses his knowledge of the occult to summon a force of evil that destroys itself, hence the bat finale already mentioned; but this exploits the imagery of *The Birds* in a merely vampiric manner, rather than Hitchcock's more complexly psychological one.

Barry Warren as Carl Ravna, working a musical vampire spell in *The Kiss of the Vampire* (dir. Don Sharp, 1964).

Polanski's original title for *The Fearless Vampire Killers* was *Dance of the Vampires* and this refers to the final scenes where a whole graveyard of von Krolocks emerge from their various tombs to attend a ball, much as Ravna's disciples have a lavish party in *Kiss*. In fact, the party in *Kiss* disguises a much more sinister motive: to kidnap the film's heroine, Marianne (Jennifer Daniel). The imagery of the illusory nature of a party is shared by Hitchcock's *Rope* where, as we have seen, guests are invited to dine on the chest in which the two male protagonists have deposited the corpse of the man they murdered at the beginning of the film. Hitchcock often uses party scenes to expose what lies behind the elaborate veneer of conventional social behavior. Paul Branch has explored in some detail Hitchcock's approach to party scenes, which is equally applicable to Sharp's in *Kiss*. Branch states that "the party denies reality and embraces pretense."

One dresses in one's nicest suit, makes the least offensive conversation, and enjoys hors d'oeuvres and rich desserts. Partygoers aim to forget difficult truths of the world as they strive to make positive impressions on the other guests. "Charm" becomes the by-law: to be charming, and be charmed in turn, is the agreement to render oneself pleasant, and by exchange recognize pleasantry in others. The ultimate effect is a form of mutual deception, in which all attendants quietly applaud the magnified virtues of their compatriots without attention to the mirrors and smoke which make up the illusion. The parties Hitchcock throws in his films are doomed to failure in this sense because of his insistence on sullying them with the darker features of life, populating his guest-list with spies, murderers, and blackmailers.[4]

James Bernard's music towards the end of the party scene in *Kiss* encapsulates this duality. While the dance music itself continues in the background, Bernard lays much more sinister music over it as Carl exchanges his own mask for an identical copy of the one he gave to Gerald, thus allowing him to make Marianne think he is actually her husband. Earlier, Sabina, Ravna's vampire daughter, played by Jacquie Wallis, offered Gerald a drugged glass of champagne ("a special glass of champagne" is how she puts it) to put him out of the picture until the following morning.

When Gerald wakes up, Carl insists that he has no idea who he (Gerald) is. "You came here alone," Carl insists—the very words used by the proprietor of the hotel in *So Long at the Fair* when Vicky insists she arrived there with her brother. Poor Gerald is thrown out of the chateau, and when he returns to the hotel he finds that all of Marianne's clothes are missing. An even more surreal situation awaits Vicky Barton in *So Long at the Fair*: Her brother's entire bedroom has vanished (or has, rather, been re-numbered as "20" instead of "19"). Again like Vicky, Gerald examines the hotel register, but the page in which he had signed his name has been ripped out. Vicky too finds that her brother's name is not in her hotel's register. In *Kiss*, hotel manager Bruno and his tight-lipped wife (Vera Cook) are both under orders by the Ravnas to deny that Gerald has ever checked in. Gerald's reaction is as understandably distraught as Vicky's but he is rescued by Professor Zimmer. (Vicky has Bogarde's Hathaway to help her.) The behavior of the Ravnas and the various hotel proprietors in both films has much in common with the duplicity of characters such as Dr. Murchison in *Spellbound* and Gavin Estler in *Vertigo*, while Dr. Ravna is even more drastically obsessive than Scottie in *Vertigo* in his attempts to transform Marianne into his own vampiric ideal.

The idea of losing the one you love at a party also has an intriguing literary antecedent in Arthur Schnitzler's 1926 novel *Traumnovelle* (*Dream Story*), which went on to inspire Stanley Kubrick's *Eyes Wide Shut*, (1999) starring Tom Cruise and Nicole Kidman. There is no evidence that Anthony Hinds' *Kiss of the Vampire* screenplay was in any way consciously influenced by Schnitzler's novel, but the similarities are striking. In the novel, Fridolin meets a pianist called Nachtigall who performs blindfolded at a secret gathering where the female guests are naked but everyone wears masks. Here we might think of Carl Ravna playing his own piano, along with the masked ball at the Chateau Ravna. Fridolin doesn't take his wife to the ball, as Gerald takes Marianne, but he does encounter a woman whose body he later tries to find in a morgue. Like an undead vampire, the fin-

10. Loss and Deception in The Kiss of the Vampire

Left to right: Jacquie Wallis (as Sabena), Barry Warren (as Carl), Isobel Black (as Tania), Noel Willman (as Ravna), Jennifer Daniel (as Marianne), Edward de Souza (as Gerald Harcourt) and Stan Simmons (as the Ravnas' servant) in *The Kiss of the Vampire* (dir. Don Sharp, 1963). Production designer Bernard Robinson's spectacular astrological window looms over all.

gers of this corpse "seemed to be attempting to move and take hold of his."[5] Much of Schnitzler's imagery is darkly Gothic. A closed coach is described as resembling a hearse,[6] and at the ball Fridolin encounters a woman wearing a black veil, "her blood-red mouth glistened beneath her lace mask."[7] There is also a torture scene which could be compared to the moment in *Kiss* when Gerald Harcourt is about to be initiated into Ravna's society, his hands tied behind his back, as Tanya advances upon him in one of Hammer's most disturbing examples of vampire imagery. In *Dream Story*, the torture scene is dreamed by Fridolin's wife:

> All became quiet and the princess made a sign, bidding you to come to her, and I knew that she had decided to pardon you. But you didn't notice her, or didn't want to notice. Suddenly, still with your hands tied but wrapped in a black cloak, you were standing opposite her, not in her chamber but somehow hovering in mid air. She was holding a sheet of parchment in her hand—your death sentence, in which your guilt and the reasons for your execution were recorded. She asked you—I could not hear her words and yet I knew— if you were prepared to become her paramour, in which case your death sentence could

be remitted. You shook your head as a sign that you refused,… whereupon you suddenly found yourself in an underground vault being chastised with whips, though I was unable to make out the people who were wielding them. The blood flowed from you in streams, and, seeing it flow, I was aware of my own horror without being surprised by it.[8]

And as if all that isn't enough, one of the characters to whom Fridolin is attracted is also called Marianne.

11

Dreams and Visions in *Nightmare*
(dir. Freddie Francis, 1964)

Nightmare recapitulates many of the themes already explored, including the use of Oakley Court in its early scenes. We also have characters who turn out not be who they pretend to be, and who attempt to drive the heroine (played by Jennie Linden) insane. The two villains are in fact lovers. One of them impersonates the other's wife by means of a very realistic disguise. By wandering around the house late at night, she so unnerves her victim that when the real wife appears, the girl stabs her to death. (The working title of the film was *Here's the Knife Dear—Now Use It*.) The death of the unwanted wife allows the lovers to marry and inherit the girl's estate now that she has been packed off to an asylum for the criminally insane. Eventually, however, justice is done.

All this is interesting enough, but with a film called *Nightmare* we need first to explore something of the imagery of dreams. In the nineteenth century, dream imagery and even insanity became fashionable because of the Romantic movement's preoccupation with instinct and irrationality. Some artists exploited their own very real mental illnesses—one thinks of Van Gogh, Munch, Strindberg and, in the musical world, Schumann and Scriabin, the latter probably saved from complete insanity by his unexpected early death. Though most classical composers were not insane, film companies have frequently reinforced the connection between music and madness, no doubt because of the powerful way in which music affects the emotions. *Hangover Square* (dir. John Brahm, 1945), the various versions of *The Phantom of the Opera*, *The Seventh Veil*, *Dangerous Moonlight* (dir. Brian Desmond Hurst, 1941), and not least the discordant lute improvisations of Roderick Usher in Roger Corman's *House of Usher*, all explored this apparent connection. Munch and Van Gogh expressed their inner turmoil in images, Strindberg charted his mental collapse in the pages of his *Inferno*, and Scriabin believed that it was only through irrational states of intoxication (musical or alcoholic) that one could attain the truth, whatever that is. Many other creative individuals flirted with madness while remaining quite sane, but the aim they all shared was to access the inner workings of the mind, the psychological drives of the unconscious and consequently the wellsprings of creativity. If the world is our own creation in the sense that we can only know it through the interpretation of the sense impressions we receive and interpret in our brains, the mind itself is the most important aspect of reality. And because the mind can distort sense impressions according to the emotional needs of the individual, "reality" is arguably a highly mutable affair—a mere symbol of the mind, unprovable and unknowable, entirely subject to interpretation. Indeed, it might not even exist at all, being merely our own creation.

Film offers more potential for realizing the unconscious mind than any other medium, as it is able to manipulate or distort reality surrealistically. Its many illusory techniques permit the seemingly impossible. Strindberg aimed for cinematic effects in his *A Dream Play*, written in 1900, the same year as Freud's *Interpretation of Dreams*. In the preface, he explained:

> In this dream play the author has, as in his former dream play, *To Damascus*, attempted to imitate the inconsequent yet transparently logical shape of a dream. Everything can happen, everything is possible and probable. Time and place do not exist; on an insignificant basis of reality the imagination spins, weaving new patterns; a mixture of memories, experiences, free fancies, incongruities and improvisations. The characters split, double, multiply, evaporate, condense, disperse, assemble. But one consciousness rules over them all, that of the dreamer; for him there are no secrets, no illogicalities, no scruples, no laws. He neither acquires nor condemns, but merely relates; and, just as a dream is more often painful than happy, so an undertone of melancholy and of pity for all mortal beings accompanies this flickering tale. Sleep, the liberator, often seems a tormentor, but when the agony is harshest comes the awakening and reconciles the sufferer with reality—which, however, is yet a mercy, compared with the agony of the dream.[1]

Nightmare is nowhere near as surreal as Strindberg's vision, but it is significant that it equates dream states with insanity. Freud, understandably, was also interested by this equation and discussed it in his *Interpretation of Dreams*. He pointed out that at the time he was writing, very little research had been carried out with regard to this subject but that, on the other hand "attention was long ago directed to the underlying kinship between dreams and mental disorders, exhibited in the wide measure of agreements between their manifestations."

> Kant writes somewhere, "The madman is a waking dreamer." Krauss (1859, 270) declares that "insanity is a dream dreamt while the senses are awake." Schopenhauer calls dreams a brief madness and madness a long dream. Hagen describes delirium as dream-life induced not by sleep but by illness. Wundt writes: "We ourselves, in fact, can experience in dreams almost the phenomena to be met with in insane asylums."[2]

Freud adds, "Radestock (1879, p. 228) sums up his views, and those of many others, by declaring that 'insanity, an abnormal pathological phenomenon, is to be regarded as an intensification of the periodically recurrent normal condition of dreaming.'"[3] But Freud takes issue with this, concluding:

> The indisputable analogy between dreams and insanity, extending as it does to their characteristic details, is one of the most powerful props of the medical theory of dream-life, which regards dreaming as a useless and disturbing process and as the expression of a reduced activity of the mind. Nevertheless it is not to be expected that we shall find

the ultimate explanation of dreams in the direction of mental disorders; for the unsatisfactory state of our knowledge of the origin of these latter conditions is generally recognized. It is quite likely, on the contrary, that a modification of our attitude towards dreams will at the same time affect our views upon the internal mechanism of mental disorders and that we shall be working towards an explanation of the psychoses while we are endeavoring to throw some light on the mystery of dreams.[4]

Freud is also in agreement with Strindberg that "pain and unpleasure are more common in dreams than pleasure.... And apart from these dreams, which carry over into sleep the various distressing emotions of life, there are anxiety-dreams, in which that most dreadful of all unpleasurable feelings holds us in its grasp till we awaken."[5]

Freud is quoted at length here to demonstrate that even over 60 years since the publication of *The Interpretation of Dreams*, and Freud's attempt to

Poster for *Nightmare* (dir. Freddie Francis, 1964), with portraits (from top to bottom) of Clytie Jessop, David Knight, Moira Redmond and Jennie Linden.

distinguish between dreams and insanity, popular culture was still quite happy to reinforce the connection. However, *Nightmare* also makes effective use of dream symbolism that Freud glossed in sexual terms in his famous book. *Nightmare* makes even more psychological use of the house in which the majority of its action takes place than a film like *The Man in Black*. For Freud, the appearance of house symbolism in dreams is a metaphor for the body itself: "[A] very long street of houses may represent a stimulus from the intestines. Again, separate portions of a house may stand for separate portions of the body; thus, in a dream caused by a headache, the head may be represented by the ceiling of a room covered with disgusting toad-like spiders."[6] "In 'dreams with a dental stimulus,' an entrance-hall with a high, vaulted roof corresponds to the oral cavity and a staircase to the descent from the throat to the oesophagus."[7]

> It is true that I know patients who have retained an architectural symbolism for the body and the genitals. (Sexual interest ranges far beyond the sphere of the external genitalia.) For these patients pillars and columns represent the legs (as they do in the *Song of Solomon*), every gateway stands for one of the bodily orifices (a "hole"), every water-pipe is a reminder of the urinary apparatus, and so on.... The ugliest as well as the most intimate details of sexual life may be thought and dreamt of in seemingly innocent allusions to activities in the kitchen; and the symptoms of hysteria could never be interpreted if we forget that sexual symbolism can find its best hiding-place behind what is commonplace and inconspicuous. There is a valid sexual meaning behind the neurotic child's intolerance of blood or raw meat, or his nausea at the sight of eggs or macaroni.[8]

In terms of *Nightmare*, the recurring image of the kitchen knife is photographed in such a way as to make it a phallic symbol *par excellence*. On a deeper level than its shared function as a prop that is vital to the narrative, it is also symbolic of the female heroine's various anxieties and neuroses. Freud also points out the sexual signification of "steps, ladders or staircases, or, as the case may be, walking up or down them."[9] The opening dream sequence of *Nightmare*, with its hospital corridors, could certainly be interpreted along Freudian lines: "[P]enetrating into narrow spaces and opening closed doors are among the commonest sexual symbols."[10]

Nightmare indeed begins with a complex of classic dream symbols. We are shown the facade of an imposing house behind wrought-iron gates. We also hear dogs barking, a particularly desolate sound at night. (Hammer used it to similar effect in the LP version of *The Legend of the Seven Golden Vampires*.) We then fade to a lamp in a darkened corridor. We move down the corridor towards a door. A shadow passes the door, and the camera passes down another corridor, following the shadow that is projected onto other doors. Though the plot of *Nightmare* has no *overt* sexual element, a strong sense of sexual anxiety is nonetheless present in its imagery. (Janet [Jennie Linden] is an adolescent girl; the part was originally intended to be played by Julie Christie, who was released from her contract with Hammer at the eleventh hour, enabling her to star in John Schlesinger's *Billy Liar*. Though Linden does a perfectly good job, Christie would no doubt have given the role an extra layer of sexual vulnerability and energy.) Such corridor and door imagery is perfectly natural for an adolescent to dream, and that is why it is so effective, as it has been shared by the rest of the audience at one time or another. Its extra connotation of insanity feeds upon a common preconception, as we have seen.

We cut to the back of Janet's head as she continues to walk down the corridor. At the sound of her name being called by another woman, she turns, and we are presented with a shot of the long corridor from her point of view. It is quite empty but for pools of light from the lamps overhead. Janet looks to the other side of the corridor, listening to the voice that says, "Janet. You've come to help me. Come, darling. You know where I am." We see Janet's bare feet walking and follow her into a cell where an older woman (whom we later learn is her mother) smiles and greets her with, "Now they've got us both. We're both mad!"

This recurring nightmare has, not surprisingly, unbalanced Janet, who is obviously still disturbed by a much earlier event in her life when her mother murdered her father on her eleventh birthday. Such a crime is far more resonant than would have been the equally terrible but perhaps less psychologically significant murder of her mother by her father. The Elektra complex involved here should not be underestimated; neither should the father's representation of the girl's animus. The mother has symbolically killed Janet's animus along with the very real object of her incestuous desire. Sangster no doubt arranged this instinctively, but it was a choice that has a resonant meaning, and its implications would not be the same if the mother had been the victim. To confirm this psychological situation, Francis later shows us Janet giving her guardian, Mr. Baxter (played by David Knight), a somewhat passionate and rather more than merely filial kiss. He may not be her real father, but she projects all her Elektra complex onto him. (Margaret Fuchs in *Blood from the Mummy's Tomb* is similarly "in love" with her father, and has even "killed" her mother, who died giving birth to her. That story requires the removal of the mother to emphasize Margaret's relationship with her father.)

Janet's trauma makes even more sense when we place it in the overall context of the film's post–Romantic aesthetic. The idea of being haunted by a past trauma was of particular interest to Romantic writers because of their concern with the unconscious and with memory, and their belief in the past and death as gateways to the imagination. Hoffmann constellated these concerns early in the history of the movement. In "Mademoiselle de Scudéry," Cardilac's mother has a traumatic experience, comparable to Janet's, when a cavalier, who wears a flashing jeweled chain around his neck, dies in her arms. The mother has been obsessed by the jeweled chain and wants to possess it, and that obsession is passed on to her son, as he explains in his account of the affair:

> There he crushed her in embraces to which she yielded willingly enough as long as she could touch the glittering chain. But then, suddenly, the cavalier reeled backwards and, dragging my mother down with him, fell to the ground. Whatever the cause—perhaps he had had a stroke, perhaps it was something else—no matter, the man was dead. All my mother's frantic efforts to release herself from the corpse's stiffened embrace were futile. His glazed eyes, their vision forever extinguished, were fixed upon her, and she lay there, on the ground, clutched in the dance of death by her staring cavalier. Finally her piercing cries for help reached the ears of some merrymakers in the distance. They ran up to her and succeeded in freeing her from the arms of her ghostly lover.
>
> The horror of the whole experience brought on a serious illness. My mother's life and mine were both despaired of. But she recovered, and her *accouchement* was easier than anyone had dared hoped. Perhaps because all the terror of that dreadful incident had left its mark upon me. My evil star had risen, and had sent down on me a light that would kindle in me. My evil star had risen, and had sent down on me a light that would kindle in me one of the strangest and most devouring of passions.[11]

This passion is Cardilac's obsession with jewels, passed on somehow congenitally from his mother. Similarly, Janet will repeat her own mother's crime by wielding a knife herself. Her obsession is with her father and a latent desire to kill "the mother" in vengeance for her father's murder. The villains of the plot exploit this matricidal obsession by terrorizing

Janet with glimpses of a particularly intimidating mother figure, played by Clytie Jessop. Janet's real mother has been judged to be insane and is now incarcerated in an asylum (an echo of the situation in *Maniac*). The implication of the film's opening nightmare sequence is that the mother wants to destroy her daughter—to have her locked away just as she has been locked away. This, at least, is what Janet fears.

Freddie Francis' atmospheric use of lighting during this sequence is repeated in his various skillful articulations of the family home, High Towers, where steps, shadows, doors and corridors are used to equal effect. In fact, the exterior and main hall of High Towers is a version of the set later used for Castle Dracula in *Dracula—Prince of Darkness*. That film is famously one of Hammer's "Back-to-Back" productions, where the sets were re-dressed for Don Sharp's *Rasputin the Mad Monk* of the same year; but *Nightmare* could also claim to be a "Back-to-Back" with *Dracula—Prince of Darkness*. The connection is highly appropriate given the Gothic atmosphere of the house in *Nightmare*, which Francis actually exploits far more atmospherically than Fisher in the Dracula film. Again, monochrome photography enhances the mood, but Francis also uses shadows far more evocatively than Fisher, and his prowling camera moves down corridors, upstairs and towards doors far more dramatically than the much-lauded tracking shots of *Dracula—Prince of Darkness*.

Before Janet returns to High Towers, we are again treated to shots of Oakley Court and its riverside location, this time photographed in six inches of snow ("a bitch to shoot," Sangster recalled[12]), but it all looks very beautiful in its Victorian Gothic way. This time, Oakley Court stands in for Janet's school, but it is in the totally studio-bound High Towers that the really frightening events occur. Janet's teacher Mary (Brenda Bruce) accompanies Janet back home where the family housekeeper, Mrs. Gibbs (a rather ambivalent Irene Richmond), tells the backstory, which is simultaneously dramatized. Francis juxtaposes the image of the murder weapon (a knife) with Janet's birthday cake. In some shots of the cake's candles, he blurs them to create a more dreamlike quality—and this technique will recur when the event is repeated by Janet on her sixteenth birthday: Mrs. Gibbs wheels in another birthday cake (with 16 counted candles on it) but on that occasion it is not the candles but Clytie Jessop, playing Baxter's wife, who is shrouded in blurred focus. Again, it is Francis' inventive visual effects, echoing those of *The Innocents*, that distinguishes his approach from Fisher's highly effective but rather less sophisticated literalism.

Long before that sixteenth birthday party, however, Janet is persecuted by various nocturnal visions of Clytie Jessop, wandering about High Towers in her nightgown—a veritable Woman in White if ever there was one, and providing yet another echo of nineteenth-century Gothic via Wilkie Collins' celebrated novel of that name. Collins describes his mysterious apparition as "a solitary Woman, dressed from head to foot in white garments, her face bent in grave inquiry on mine."[13] Jessop is a little more disconcerting than that, with a scar on one of her cheeks, but the literary heritage is clear. Janet is woken by this "dream" and follows the woman into the corridor where she "wakes up." Of course, she has not been asleep at all but, as she puts it, "Where does the dream finish

11. Dreams and Visions in Nightmare

and reality begin?" This is indeed an interesting question, not that we are meant to abstract it into the realm of metaphysical enquiry, but it was one which Hammer would later explore in somewhat surreal manner in the *Hammer House of Horror* TV episode "Rude Awakening" (dir. Peter Sasdy, 1980). This stars Denholm Elliott as a man who dreams he has killed his wife and then actually does it, even though he still thinks he is dreaming. Janet finds herself in a similar predicament, and she wonders if the Woman in White is real or imaginary.

The Woman in White later appears at the foot of her bed and beckons Janet to follow her. Intrigued and terrified, Janet follows her into another room where she discovers her sprawled on a bed, stabbed through the heart, with a birthday cake (11 candles flickering upon it) by her side. Such a replay of Janet's childhood trauma has predictable results. (The bed is, incidentally, the same piece of furniture that graces the Harcourts' hotel bedroom in *The Kiss of the Vampire*.)

Like Eleanor Ashby in *Paranoiac*, Janet is looked after by a nurse who turns out not to be a nurse at all. This nurse, played by Moira Redmond, is called Grace (a somewhat ironic name given her distinct lack of it). She is very convincing, however, and seems to be the epitome of loving care. Though we are not yet meant to know that she is co-villain with Janet's guardian Mr. Baxter, Redmond gives us various telling facial expressions to suggest her duplicity. Mr. Baxter is also a convincing liar and insists that he won't let anyone take Janet away to an asylum.

The third nocturnal visitation begins with a close-up of the door handle to Janet's room being turned. Janet again slips out of bed to investigate, walking down more dark corridors. This time, it is the Woman in White's shadow that she follows, as it looms over walls and paneling. The bedroom in which she experienced her last shock, is empty. It is the same bed on which her father was murdered, and to remind us of this we hear the soundtrack of that childhood scene repeated.

Back in her own bedroom, the old horror awaits her: The Woman in White is discovered, stabbed once more and lying next to Janet's clown doll with its pronounced Pinocchio nose. Dolls, curiously undead creatures that they are, sometimes appear sinister because although they have no life of their own, they are invested with life by the active imagination of children. They also suggest innocence which in this instance has been profoundly contaminated by events.

"How can you dream about someone you don't know?" Janet asks, questioning her own sanity. On the morning of Janet's birthday, she has her fourth encounter with the Woman in White, but this time it takes place in broad daylight. Having overcome a momentary anxiety on opening a wardrobe to remove a dressing gown, she goes downstairs and observes a shadow thrown from an alcove window.

Later, Janet smashes a mirror with her portable radio. We have already encountered mirrors as symbols of a split personality. Here the mirror is also used to suggest Janet's presumed psychosis. The radio represents her attempt to live in the normal world outside her over-stimulated imagination. It is, indeed, her only reliable connection with the world. By using it to smash the mirror, it might be said that she is using reality to smash her apparent insanity—those persecuting illusions that are as convincing as a reflection and which she wants to believe have no real substance. Unfortunately, the attempt fails. Instead she smashes reality and she uses a shard to slash her wrist, now unable to endure either reality or illusion.

The specialist brought in to look at her is an unwitting lynchpin of the villains' plan. They need him to witness Janet's murder of Baxter's wife. A cake and a knife to cut it with are wheeled in by Mrs. Gibbs. The knife glints provocatively in the harsh light, obviously signaling danger in such a significant close-up. Everyone gathers around to wish Janet a happy birthday—including, after having been introduced, Mrs. Baxter (Clytie Jessop again). As she steps forward, Janet is convinced that she is the same specter as the Woman in White. She grabs the knife and stabs her. Freud famously suggested that "all elongated objects, such as sticks, tree-trunks and umbrellas (the opening of these last being comparable to an erection), may stand for the male organ—as well as all long, sharp weapons, such as knives, daggers and pikes,"[14] and there is a case to be made for interpreting this one as such. Janet cannot strike her real mother, but she can use her father's phallus to rape this evil mother substitute. All the plotters want, however, is a reliable witness to Janet's carefully induced homicidal behavior.

As Janet is taken away, we see what should be impossible: The apparently dead Mrs. Baxter is seen staring out from an upper window of the house. The shot echoes the school photograph in *Les Diaboliques*, in which the apparently dead headmaster similarly appears. But all is soon explained as we watch Grace peel off her Mrs. Baxter mask. Asking us to believe that a latex mask is as fluid and expressive as Clytie Jessop's real face is an old-fashioned dramatic conceit, and it stands up to as much scrutiny as the disguises in *The Merchant of Venice* and *The Marriage of Figaro*. We don't need to question it too much but we do respond to its effect, which is far more uncanny than the mere grotesquerie of the mask in *Paranoiac*. This is due to the verisimilitude of the mask, and the sense of duality it implies. In effect, both villains have been wearing masks throughout, pretending to be something they most definitely not and thereby betraying the trust of others—surely one of the most unforgivable things anyone can do.

The last we see of Janet is a shot of her in her asylum cell. After Mrs. Baxter's funeral, the second part of the story begins, and this involves the unmasking of the villains by the chauffeur (George A. Cooper), Mary and Mrs. Gibbs. They all suspect what has been going on but now they need proof.

Henry and Grace embrace in a hotel bedroom. "In law, we're guilty of nothing," Henry laughs, but soon things start to go wrong. The plan of Mary and the two servants is to make Grace jealous of Henry and drive them apart. A bar man at the hotel is bribed to say that Mr. Baxter has been to the hotel before with another woman. Henry denies this, but Grace grows increasingly suspicious. Back at High Towers she and Henry have an argument. The electricity fuses blow. Grace wanders about with a candle and is startled by a disembodied laugh, which is followed by the vision of another Woman in White. Grace shouts that whoever is responsible won't frighten her, but she later stumbles over Janet's Pinocchio doll in a corridor, and gradually her nerves are frayed to shreds. There

11. Dreams and Visions in Nightmare

is also an interesting aerial shot of her entering the parents' bedroom, which echoes, in its curious sense of vulnerability and unnerving foreshortening, a similar aerial shot in *Psycho*. We have more billowing curtains, slamming doors and shock responses.

Grace phones the asylum to inquire about Janet. A voice (in fact the chauffeur's) informs her that Janet has escaped and could be dangerous. As befits a film with the title of *Nightmare*, there are several shots of people asleep, dreaming fitfully. On one occasion, Grace wakes up to see a knife glinting on her bedside table. There are more threatening laughs and ghostly visions and Grace is eventually convinced that Janet has come back to kill her at Baxter's behest. So on edge does she become that even a chiming clock startles her. Another tracking shot takes us to the door of Janet's room behind which her old radio is playing. The camera here echoes of the tracking shot in Hitchcock's *Rebecca* as it moved towards the doorknob of Rebecca's bedroom.

In the end, Grace stabs Henry and the conspiracy against her is revealed. The final shot shows us Baxter lying dead next to Janet's Pinocchio doll—innocence and corruption lying side by side. As Sangster put it, "An interesting point in the structure of the story is that it deals with two separate cases of a woman being driven to commit a mad act, first Janet then Grace."[15] Both mad acts are the result of sexual anxiety: Grace's sexual jealousy and Janet's unresolved Elektra complex. That element is subliminal in *Nightmare*. In Hammer's next thriller, *Fanatic*, it is overt.

12

The Oedipus Complex in *Fanatic*
(dir. Silvio Narizzano, 1965)

Silvio Narizzano's *Fanatic* is a mirror image of Hitchcock's *Psycho*—ironically so, as Tallulah Bankhead's puritanical, cosmetic-hating, vegetarian, sexually repressed religious fanatic, Mrs. Trefoil, has removed all the mirrors from her creepy rural retreat. This is quite the opposite of the mirror-bestrewn environments of *Psycho;* but, as we shall see, Mrs. Trefoil's relationship with her dead son is indeed an inversion of Norman Bates' relationship with his dead mother. Mrs. Trefoil's hated of mirrors also resembles that of Count Dracula, who similarly says of Jonathan Harker's shaving mirror in an early chapter of Bram Stoker's famous novel; "It is a foul bauble of man's vanity. Away with it!"—and he it out of the window.[1] These are precisely Mrs. Trefoil's sentiments. Dracula casts no reflection, but unfortunately Mrs. Trefoil still does, and she no doubt does not wish to be reminded of what age has done to her. Once, she had been beautiful and glamorous, but she has long since cast those days aside as sinful. Even so, the memory of them remains, along with the vestiges of her former personality....

Fanatic is an Oedipal drama of considerable proportions. Unlike the equally Oedipal *Psycho*, Narizzano's narrative is a black comedy right from the start, beginning with a sequence of unusually arty main titles in which a pink mouse is pursued by a green cat. The mouse is accompanied by scurrying figures for flute and xylophone in Wilfred Joseph's suitably irreverent, harpsichord-dominated score. The cat is accompanied by a rather louche trombone, suggesting Mrs. Trefoil's similarly louche past. If she is the cat, Stefanie Powers, as Patricia, is the mouse. Patricia even wears a pink coat in the opening shots to emphasize the connection. Later in the film, when her suitcase is rifled through by Mrs. Trefoil's housekeeper, more pink garments are revealed. Similarly, Mrs. Trefoil is often photographed against green light, and such color symbolism was about as close as Hammer ever got to Hitchcock's complex red and green imagery in *Vertigo*.

Narizzano is on record as hating Joseph's score, feeling that it overplayed the comedy he intended: "Wilfred liked the idea of a harpsichord," Narizzano explained. "He thought it had a quaint Victorian feel—which suited the Tallulah character because she was living in a backwater. Everybody thought it was a cute idea. I disliked the music intensely."[2] But perhaps the black comedy was forced on Narizzano by the performance style of his star. "She was at the stage in her life when she was camping everything—even serious plays," he explained. "So, in this one, she was quite atrociously camping. If I'd done it with Flora Robson, I would've maybe attempted to make a much more realistic film."[3]

As is the case with both *Psycho* and *Dracula*, the villain of *Fanatic*, Mrs. Trefoil, lives in the depths of the country. Symbolically speaking, this suggests that the setting represents a part of the subconscious that has been repressed and to which one must make a special journey if one is to confront it. But Mrs. Trefoil is not a total recluse. She has companions: lecherous Harry (played by Peter Vaughan), his unhappy wife Anna (Yootha Joyce), and a halfwit odd-job man called Joseph (Donald Sutherland). The subconscious harbors many fears and anxieties. Harry is Mrs. Trefoil's only remaining relative now that her son, Stephen, has died, and Harry hopes to inherit the estate when Mrs. Trefoil dies. Meanwhile, he bides his time and, bored by his long-suffering wife, seduces whatever younger women he can find in the local pub. The utterly dependent Anna can do nothing but put up with this situation and do as she is told.

Mrs. Trefoil presides over interminable prayer meetings, having been shown the error of her ways by her formidably benevolent husband, whose portrait dominates the staircase. In her youth, however, Mrs. Trefoil had been, like Miss Bankhead herself, a glamorous actress of somewhat unconventional morals and reputation. Indeed, makeup artist Roy Ashton recalled having great difficulty removing the encrusted layers of cosmetics from Bankhead's features when preparing her for this well-scrubbed and distinctly unadorned role. "Those are redheads," he observed. "She's so dirty she

Poster for *Fanatic* (dir. Silvio Narizzano, 1965). A nicely rendered pair of scissors slash a portrait of Stefanie Powers.

hasn't developed blackheads or whiteheads. She's developed redheads under all that smear lipstick."[4]

Mrs. Trefoil has repressed her past to such an extent that she has gone quietly crazy in the process. Her very name suggests how much she has allowed her Christian reorientation to overcome her: "Trefoil" means "three-leafed" and is an architectural symbol much associated with Christian architecture due to its symbolic representation of the Holy Trinity.

Into this frightful situation comes Stefanie Powers' Patricia, who has just arrived from America where she was engaged to be married to Mrs. Trefoil's son. However, she decided against marrying him just before he committed suicide and she has now decided to visit Mrs. Trefoil to set the record straight before marrying another man. This is her big mistake. As in *Dracula*, a game of cat and mouse ensues. (Indeed, in Gerald Savory's 1977 adaptation of Dracula for BBC television, Harker actually shouts, "Count, you are playing cat and mouse with me!") Mrs. Trefoil is determined to purge Patricia of her sinful ways. She insists that Patricia change out of her "sinful" red sweater during morning prayers and forces her to remove her equally sinful red lipstick. At first these eccentricities are amusing, then rather annoying, but later they become terrifying. As Patricia observes, Mrs. Trefoil is actually taking her revenge upon her for taking her son away from her. In fact, *Fanatic* is what might have happened in *Psycho* if Mrs. Bates had been alive and Norman Bates was dead. Mrs. Trefoil talks to the memory of her dead son, whose portrait she keeps draped in the cellar, surrounded by the regalia of her former theatrical life, just as Norman talks to and dresses up as his dead mother.

It is the Oedipal basis of both *Psycho* and *Fanatic* that explains the uncanny effect of both stories. The surface themes of murder and captivity are certainly fraught with horror and tension but they are not in themselves uncanny according to Freud's interpretation of the term. It is the Oedipal element—that aspect of the psyche that, in Schelling's phrase, ought to have remained secret and hidden but has come to light—which gives these dramas their particularly unnerving fascination and grotesque quality. As Freud explains with regard to the story of Oedipus:

> Here is one in whom these primeval wishes of our childhood have been fulfilled, and we shrink back from him with the whole force of the repression by which those wishes have since that time been held down within us. While the poet [or, in our case, the filmmaker], as he unravels the past, brings to light the guilt of Oedipus, he is at the same time compelling us to recognise our own inner minds, in which those same impulses, though suppressed, are still to be found.[5]

Norman Bates, of course, kills Marion Crane in *Psycho*, but instead of killing Patricia, Mrs. Trefoil tortures her. She locks her up in her bedroom, deprives her of food and, grotesquely reads from the Bible while waving a pistol at her. Recalling the famous scene in *Dracula* when Jonathan Harker (locked in by the count) throws a letter from his bedroom window, hoping that the Szgany gypsies below will deliver it, Patricia (locked in by Mrs. Trefoil) shouts to Joseph, asking him to deliver a postcard with an appeal for help. But, as happens in Harker's case, she is betrayed (Joseph shows Mrs. Trefoil the card), and

Mrs. Trefoil redoubles her religious zeal. Similarly, Dracula calls Harker's plea for help written out in shorthand "a vile thing, an outrage upon friendship and hospitality!"[6] before burning the missive. Mrs. Trefoil is much more violent. She slaps Patricia and insists, "You shall repent!"

Patricia also emulates Harker's desperate attempt to climb out of the bedroom window by tying bedsheets together. Her escape is foiled on this occasion by Harry, who pursues her as she swims across the river, circling her with his motorboat. It seems there is no escape from Castle Trefoil, as there seemed to be no escape from the no doubt trefoiled architecture of Castle Dracula.

Mrs. Trefoil eventually relents sufficiently to feed Patricia tasteless pap ("God's pure food") but she does this, as she conducts all her interactions, while holding her prisoner at gunpoint. She also orders Anna to cut up Patricia's finery, and this is when the film's first overtly horrific moment occurs, when a pair of scissors impales Patricia's shoulder during the ensuing struggle. Yootha Joyce's performance as Anna here is perhaps the most subtle and finely graded one in the film. Here is a woman who has allowed herself to be compromised by her own weakness, essential decency and sense of duty. Anna is also deeply worried about the police finding out about Mrs. Trefoil's skullduggery, but is too involved in it to extricate herself from the nightmare. (*Nightmare*, incidentally, was the title of the original novel by Anne Billsden on which the film is based.)

In a later scene, Mrs. Trefoil forces Patricia to write a letter to Alan telling him she is safe. (Dracula instructs Harker to do the same thing: "Write to our friend ... and say, if it will please you, that you shall stay with me until a month from now."[7]) Anna appears almost as much of a prisoner as Patricia. "Please, miss," she gasps as she wrenches Patricia's arm behind her back, "you must write it." Her tone of voice expresses genuine concern and regret at the situation, for Anna is more truly trapped than any of the characters, and it is therefore quite appropriate that she should be the one to stab Mrs. Trefoil in the back at the end of the film. More sinned against than sinning, she has no option but to do whatever Mrs. Trefoil demands while simultaneously putting up with her lecherous husband in the hope that one day he will inherit Mrs. Trefoil's estate. She certainly has no money of her own, and Patricia uses this sad fact to bribe her way to freedom. "I'll give you a thousand pounds," she offers. Anna's expression suggests how sorely she is tempted. "I'll give you two thousand," Patricia adds, but Anna is too dependent a personality to take the situation into her own hands—and besides, Mrs. Trefoil has a gun and is listening. Worse is to follow. Desperate, Patricia now hopes to entice sex-starved Harry to her room, knock him out and snatch back her car keys; but Mrs. Trefoil bursts in just as Patricia's plan backfires, and Harry is soon dispatched by three bullets from Mrs. Trefoil's pistol. Significantly, the secret chamber in the cellar where this murder occurs is lit with green light. When Mrs. Trefoil appears from behind the door, she is bathed in pink light, making us wonder if she is now the mouse that has been cornered, but as soon as she shoots Harry and licks the knife he was holding, the green light returns, followed by an entirely scarlet screen for a few moments.

Now that Mrs. Trefoil has committed murder, she wanders about like Lady Macbeth, washing the blood off her hands. If she wasn't mad before, she certainly is now. She curls up on Stephen's bed (his room is kept as a shrine) and clutches his Teddy bear. "Stephen!" she sobs, "why did you ever leave me?" And now Narizzano begins to show us the truth about Mrs. Trefoil's past and personality. She takes a slug of secreted alcohol and paints her lips, before smearing the lipstick off in a grotesque ring about her mouth. The old personality will not be repressed forever, and Mrs. Trefoil is reverting to type. Patricia realizes exactly what is going on: She shouts at her tormentor, "Nobody had to take Stephen from you. You drove him away.... I see exactly why he killed himself."

Mrs. Trefoil is shocked by the revelation of suicide, hitherto unsuspected by her. And this leads to the dénouement in which Patricia's fiancée Alan (Maurice Kaufman) comes to the rescue. He arrives only just in time. Mrs. Trefoil has determined that after being purified by prayer, Patricia must "die, die, my darling," so that she will be able to join Stephen in paradise. She takes Patricia to her secret chamber in the cellar, where the portrait of Stephen is enshrined amid all the costumes and memorabilia of her former life. Despite her dismay at the personal parallels suggested by the production design of this scene, Bankhead gives everything she had to this climax, draping herself before Stephen's portrait, weeping, distraught, and utterly insane. Saved in the nick of time by Alan, Patricia escapes, and it is left to Anna to stab Mrs. Trefoil in the back.

Mrs. Trefoil's subterranean domain is an eloquent expression of Jung's dream of the psyche as a house, its lowest level being the depths of the subconscious. This cellar, filled with Mrs. Trefoil's past, is more than a physical repository of ephemera, it is also a manifestation of her psychological repression, a vivid symbol of her own unconscious, and an appropriate place for her to die, if we are to interpret death as a symbol of transformation. Here, confronted by the past she has repressed but not forgotten, or even willingly renounced, she truly confronts herself and, in death, achieves individuation and integration of the psyche, even though it is too late for her to benefit from such knowledge in the world of the film's narrative.

One final thing remains to be said, and this takes us right back to the beginning of the film: The opening shot shows us a cruise ship, which cuts to a dockside shot, followed by a conversation in a car between Patricia and Alan. These opening shots establish conventional "normality" and also a sense of freedom, which is soon to be taken away in the claustrophobic, distinctly abnormal environment of Mrs. Trefoil's home with its Gothic traceries, multi-colored stained glass and resident simpleton Joseph. But Alan is a television producer, and Narizzano takes the trouble in these opening shots to have him drive to the premises of "Allied Television" where he deposits several cans of film. From the point of view of the plot this serves absolutely no function, as the exposition material could easily have been put over in the car, but the inclusion of "Allied Television" and Alan's cans of film suggest not only the submerged conceit of the film in which Tallulah Bankhead, a star famous for her colorful lifestyle, plays another actress who has renounced a colorful lifestyle, but also something more about the voyeuristic nature of film in general.

Mrs. Trefoil is indeed a version of Bankhead. In the cellar scenes we even see photographs of the young Bankhead, which serve as photographs of the young Mrs. Trefoil. We are also shown mementoes of her former life: brightly colored clothing, soda syphons, bottles of Bols Advocaat, draperies suggesting a bordello, etc. According to Peter Proud, the production designer, "We made a palpable effort to get a Tennessee Williams feeling of dilapidated charm" for this set (Bankhead appeared as Blanche DuBois in Williams' *A Streetcar Named Desire* in 1955), but the outraged star felt this was all an unnecessary intrusion of her privacy. She was equally unhappy about the film's American title *Die! Die! My Darling*, which exploited her well-known conversational usage of "Dahling."[8] But such personal identification had not apparently worried her when she appeared in Hitchcock's *Lifeboat* (1944), where she also interpolated "dahling" into the script at regular intervals. Indeed, Donald Spoto suggests that her role in that picture "is nothing so much as Bankhead herself,"[9] so perhaps the character of Mrs. Trefoil hinted at something repressed (or at least hidden) in Bankhead's own life, which touched a rawer nerve than her role in the Hitchcock film. It is an intriguing notion, and there is certainly something about her relationships with Greta Garbo, Joan Crawford, Marlene Dietrich and Alla Nazimova, to name but four of the women in her life, which suggests a possible bisexuality that she may not have wanted to acknowledge in public. There is certainly a strong element of sado-masochism in Trefoil's relationship with Patricia which may have meant more to her than merely performing a role for the money.

By merging the real-life persona of its star with the fictional Mrs. Trefoil, and framing the whole story with the imagery of television and cans of film, *Fanatic* plays with other levels of meaning. Hitchcock played with the convention of stardom by killing off his female star, Janet Leigh, halfway through *Psycho*, just as Narizzano plays with the screen image of Bankhead by inverting and then exploiting it in *Fanatic*. Both films also throw back the viewers' own sense of morality into question. As we watch Mrs. Trefoil abduct and torture Patricia (not to mention the activities of Norman Bates), we become just as much of a voyeur as the villains we wish to see defeated. As Spoto says of *Psycho*, "It's an indictment of the viewer's capacity for voyeurism and is own potential for depravity." *Fanatic*, like *Psycho*, is "a ruthless exposition of America Puritanism"[10] Spoto suggests that *Psycho* also satirizes the traditional role of the mother "and the embarrassed secretiveness that surrounds both lovemaking and the bathroom."[11]

Similar preoccupations concern *Fanatic*. The mothers in both films have destroyed their sons—Norman Bates has become a psychopath; Stephen Trefoil has killed himself. And *Fanatic* is even more explicit than *Psycho* about secretive guilty pleasures, all of which have been literally locked up in Mrs. Trefoil's basement. By prefacing his story with references to television and cans of film, Narizzano is being even more explicit than Hitchcock about the voyeurism of the audience, and the ambivalence of the medium. When Narizzano told producer Anthony Hinds, "I don't like all this blood,"[12] he was voicing concerns about how far cinema can go, and how dangerous it might be. Both *Psycho* and *Fanatic* seem to be paraphrasing Baudelaire's "Hypocrite lecteur—mon semblable—mon frère," but Narizzano leaves his audience to make up their own minds.

13

Architecture in *Hysteria*
(dir. Freddie Francis, 1965)

Of all Hammer's "mini-Hitchcocks" *Hysteria* is the most obviously indebted to Hitchcock. With its use of mirrors, a knife, shower scenes, the idea of duality, and birds (in the case of *Hysteria*, these are, deliberately oddly, toucans), it obviously references *Psycho* and *The Birds*. *Hysteria* makes no pretense at visual poetry, but it does achieve some very polished prose. For Jimmy Sangster, who again wrote the screenplay, it was "very much the mixture as before, something I was beginning to get rather fed up with. And I think it showed,"[1] but this is to underrate the film's considerable flair and Freddie Francis' effective use of somewhat obvious borrowings. More importantly, it reflects something of the spirit of the times in its approach to location and interiors.

The spinning concentric circles of the opening titles obviously reference the opening titles of *Vertigo*, and the plot device of a man suffering from amnesia also echoes the plot of *Spellbound* and *The Full Treatment*. It contains a scene in which the innocent hero is discovered holding a knife in front of a corpse, a similar situation to the one that sets in train the motion of events in Hitchcock's *North by Northwest*. (Mel Brooks satirized that plot device in his 1977 film *High Anxiety*.) *Hysteria* also features an apparently trustworthy psychiatrist who, like Dr. Prade in *The Full Treatment*, turns out to be the villain of the piece, and such a reversal of expectation again reminds us of de Sade, particularly his 1791 novel *Justine*, which similarly features a sadistic surgeon. The psychiatrist in *Hysteria* is played by Anthony Newlands, whose features manage to combine an echo of Christopher Lee's malevolence with Dirk Bogarde's wholly benevolent medic Simon Sparrow from the Doctor films.

But there is more to this intriguing film than echoes of Hitchcock. It is also a study in loneliness. It's set largely in the penthouse of an unfinished tower block, and the atmosphere of alienation felt by many people in Britain who were experiencing high-rise living in apartment blocks for the first time made this film particularly relevant to its initial audiences in the mid–1960s, few of whom, however, achieved the kind of luxury lifestyle portrayed in the film. However, such decor nonetheless appealed to the aspirations on offer in '60s Britain.

Hysteria is also interesting in its use of jazz in Don Banks' score, which intensifies the film's sense of modernity, speed, youth and glamour. This upbeat, modern sound starts the film off with refreshing brio: The spinning spirals it accompanies have no significance apart from their visual excitement (which fed off the pop art of the time). Whereas spirals have immense significance for the themes and imagery of *Vertigo* the spirals of *Hysteria* are simply a signification of speed, wheels and, most important of all, the genre of "psychological thriller" which Mel Brooks later exploited in the publicity imagery for *High Anxiety*. Combined with Banks' jazzy score, they do however get the film off to an exciting start, especially as they are later intercut with key scenes from the action, when the protagonist is attacked and involved in a car accident. Each clip ends in a freeze frame, contrasting with the rapid motion of the succeeding spirals. Banks was an

Poster for *Hysteria* (dir. Freddie Francis, 1965), with *Vertigo*-style concentric circles entangling representations of Robert Webber and Lelia Goldoni.

exponent of what was known at this time as "The Third Stream," a phrase coined by the American composer Gunther Schuller to describe the fashion for combining jazz with more traditional styles of art music. In this score, a jazz idiom predominates, but the cues are very much tailored to the requirements of the action. They provide both traditional "suspense" underscoring and more overt jazz interludes. The tempi of the cues match the various speeds of the action, and this happens from the very beginning.

A slow, languid saxophone accompanies the opening title card, but the pace immediately picks up with the introduction of the spinning disc. The font of each card is sharp and sans-serif, deliberately signaling modernity and sophistication. The last spiral significantly fades into the first shot of the movie proper: Robert Webber's head. In fact, the middle of the spiral precisely overlays his eye, summoning yet more memories of *Vertigo*. Webber plays Mr. Smith, an amnesiac, and as the film is largely about his state of mind, it is appropriate that we should start with a shot of him with his eyes closed, trying to remember who he is.

The psychiatrist is first presented in an ambivalent manner, his face half in shadow, half in light, an image that gives us our first indication that though he appears benevolent, he is in fact quite the opposite. Mr. Smith is unable to remember very much at all. He sums up his therapy session by saying, "I was born four months ago by the side of the road. Anything that happened before happened to somebody else. I can't remember a thing." He also adds, philosophically, "Without a past I have no future." But he does have a present with which to discover the past and move towards a future, and that opens up a variety of narrative possibilities: *Everything* is a mystery. "Take what happens *as* it happens," the psychiatrist counsels, which is pretty much the situation of any member of the film's audience. We are all amnesiacs when watching a film. We put ourselves away and enter the lives of the characters on screen, willing participants in whatever plot the screenwriter wishes to involve us with. Not knowing who you are or what will happen next is disorientating certainly but also rather exciting. "How long can a man live in a void without going nuts?" Smith wonders, and that is a leading question in this story because it is precisely what the psychiatrist wants to happen to him. His parting shot to Smith, "The mind is capable of all sorts of devilment," applies more to him than to his patient.

Amnesia is a very a useful plot device, as Hitchcock demonstrated in *Spellbound*. Hitchcock also exploited the idea of a corrupt psychiatrist in that film but, as I mentioned earlier, the idea for that kind of character really originates in the Marquis de Sade's novel *Justine*. Justine is a model of virtue, the kind of heroine to whom Mrs. Radcliffe subjected all the terrors of her Gothic plots. But de Sade was taken in neither by the happy endings of the Radcliffe novels, nor the punishment of their villains. Real life, he argued, simply isn't like that. In real life, virtue is often the last thing to be rewarded. Indeed, as the subtitle of the novel points out, virtue frequently brings positive misfortune. Justine is the most unfortunate of all virtuous heroines. She stumbles from one disaster to the next, encountering on her path a variety of pedophiles, sadists, serial killers, misers and sexual perverts. In the end she is struck by a bolt of lightning as though even the Almighty is exasperated beyond endurance by her patient suffering and relentless virtue. One of the libertines Justine encounters appears at first to be a good man. Like Prade in *The Full Treatment* and the psychiatrist of *Hysteria* he seems perfectly respectable. Indeed, Rodin, as de Sade's doctor is known, even looks like these two Hammer doctors, Anthony Newlands in particular: "Rodin was a man of 40, with dark eyes and heavy eyebrows, a quick penetrating glance, and a strong healthy form. His features and manner seemed to indicate a libertine temperament."[2]

But Rodin, rather than alleviating pain, takes pleasure in flogging and torturing young girls. "He did not know when to stop. His intoxication reached the pitch of depriving him of any further use of reason."[3] De Sade indulges in the most obscene fantasies, anticipating the crimes of Dr. Mengele at Auschwitz. In a later edition of the novel he even included a remarkable description of Rodin performing a Caesarean operation on a pregnant woman whilst simultaneously indulging in coitus with her, "so that he may attain orgasm at the moment he tears the child from her," as his translator describes it.[4]

For all the accusations from the critics that its films were for sadists only, Hammer rarely matched de Sade's imaginative inventiveness. The birth of the demon baby at the end of *To the Devil a Daughter* (dir. Peter Sykes, 1976) approaches it, but nowhere in *Hysteria* or *The Full Treatment* do we have exhibitions of medical depravity on de Sade's scale. We do, however, have doctors who quite happily commit murder, attempt to induce insanity in their patients and blame them for their own crimes; so their behavior is hardly any better than Rodin's more flamboyant psychopathic and proto–Nazi indulgences. As was the case with *The Snorkel*, 1960s culture was still coming to terms with what had happened in Germany only twenty years earlier. As we have seen, Erle C. Kenton's *Island of Lost Souls* (1932) had begun the process by throwing Nazi shadows over H.G. Wells' 1896 novel. Charles Laughton's performance of a crazed vivisectionist is indeed an astonishing premonition of the crimes Mengele would perpetrate only a few years later. As David J. Skal observes, the various mad scientists of the Universal horror films during the 1940s are a kind of cinematic therapy for the traumatized:

> By indulging sadism in the guise of dispassionate science, the pointless and atrocious medical "research" carried out by the Nazi doctors remarkably paralleled the typical activities of the mad movie doctors of the thirties and forties. In the movies, crazed scientists invented devices of mass destruction, or conducted cruel experiments, often to create races of new, altered, or superior beings.[5]

The "bad" psychiatrists of *The Full Treatment* and *Hysteria* are the more sophisticated responses to these European traumas.

Smith has one piece of evidence about who he was: the torn photograph of a glamorous woman (Lelia Goldoni) that was found on him after the accident. He has no idea who she is, but he intends to find out. He says goodbye to his nurse, Gina (Jennifer Jayne), who will later play an important role, and sets off for his new life. This is less of an immediate problem than it might have been as he has a mysterious benefactor who has paid for his treatment and now presents him with the use of a luxury penthouse apartment. As he can't remember where his own home is, he decides to accept the offer.

The first thing he does is hire a private investigator to discover the identity of the mysterious woman in the photograph. Previously seen as the stuffy family solicitor of the Ashby family in *Paranoiac*, Maurice Denham plays his role in this movie as a seedy English version of Charles Vanel's Fichet, the detective in *Les Diaboliques*. He wears a bow-tie, has a comb-over and occupies premises in Charing Cross Road. Though seeming to be a bumbler, he is quite capable of looking after himself and rooting out the truth. After arranging terms, Smith heads for his new residence, the penthouse apartment at Richmond Court. Our introduction to this new sequence is an aerial shot of the deserted car park. Francis presents this as a grid of white oblongs; in one of them, Smith stands as though trapped in a web. Indeed, Smith *is* about to be trapped in an equally rigid plot which very nearly destroys him. Francis zooms in to him as he looks up at the unfinished apartment block. Built in modernist style, it is vaguely reminiscent of the office block, Centrepoint, in London's West End, which was left untenanted for five years after its completion in 1965. It was designed by the architect Richard Seifert; John Betjeman described it as a "flashy and international style of crystalline concrete."[6] *Hysteria* is, indeed, its exact contemporary.

In the mid–1960s, modernism and local planning was ripping apart many British towns in the name of progress. Northampton and Newcastle-upon-Tyne were just two notable examples. Newcastle's Labour politician T. Dan Smith was even found guilty of bribery and corruption in 1974, having received £156,000 from the architect George Poulsen to give the go-ahead for redevelopment plans to turn the Georgian town into what he suggested should be called "The Brasilia of the North." Northampton also suffered because of the profit motive, with redevelopment demolishing many much-loved architectural landmarks. It was a mood that Betjeman captured in his poem "Executive":

> I do some mild developing. The sort of place I need
> Is a quiet country market town that's rather run to seed.
> A luncheon and a drink or two, a little *savoir faire* -
> I fix the Planning Officer, the Town Clerk and the Mayor.
>
> And if some preservationist attempts to interfere
> A "dangerous structure" notice from the Borough Engineer
> Will settle any buildings that are standing in our way -
> The modern style, sir, with respect, has really come to stay.[7]

The apartment block in *Hysteria* is unfinished, unoccupied, very modern, alienating and unwelcoming—experiences very much shared by many ordinary members of the public who reacted with dismay to such modernist experiments. But the Penthouse apartment (the only part of the building that *is* finished) is also very luxurious and obviously desirable. The tensions between American-style, up-to-date luxury and old-fashioned nostalgia for townscapes that were rapidly vanishing, is thus rather economically reflected in all of this. We have an American star in an English setting, European modernism contrasting with the antiquated Charing Cross Road environment of the private investigator. Indeed, as we watch Smith walk towards the tower-block, we see behind him a row of Victorian terraced houses in the distance across a busy road.

Inside, step ladders and pots of paint indicate the building's incomplete state, and the emptiness emphasizes Smith's isolation not only from others but also himself. He takes an elevator to the penthouse in a sequence that foreshadows Van Helsing's similar ascent in Alan Gibson's *The Satanic Rites of Dracula* (1973). It also has certain things in common with the elevator sequence that opens *The Nanny*, as we shall see. In all three cases, the elevator doors open onto a mystery, which is intensified in the case of *Hysteria* by the odd toucans, who squawk threateningly from their cage in the otherwise unnervingly quiet vestibule. They are flanked by two chilly rubber plants and a sofa, which does not invite repose. The reference to the avian symbolism of *Psycho* is blatant, and like the spirals of the main title, it has no function other than to signal the genre of the psychological thriller to which this film belongs and to inject a mildly unnerving sense of the grotesque. Dr. Ravna's caged jackdaws in *The Kiss of the Vampire* have a similar grotesque function, as does the disturbing portrait bust we will encounter in *Fear in the Night*. The elevator seems to have a life of its own because it goes down as soon as Smith puts the key in the door of the apartment. This suggests that there is someone else in the building, as indeed there is.

Don Banks' languorous, saxophone-dominated jazz now accompanies our first view of the apartment itself, the decor of which has much in common with the luxurious interiors of the James Bond films, which were in their first classic phase at this time. Francis undercuts the comfort and serenity with some shots of the very predatory cacti that punctuate it. These suggest that something rather prickly lurks amidst the soft upholstery. Francis takes his time to let Smith and the audience grow accustomed to this new environment, the camera gliding around its various features, somewhat in the manner of an estate agent. The walls are adorned with modern art, and there are goldfish in large tanks flush against the walls. There is plenty of space, elegant lighting—even automatic wardrobe doors revealing neatly folded shirts. Their embroidered monograms of "C.S." suggest that they have been prepared especially for Mr. Christopher Smith, as he is known by the hospital staff. Most of all, there is a very luxurious bathroom. Not only were bathrooms of this quality a relatively new concept in English life at that time (many people still had to endure the dreaded outside loo) but bathrooms also suggest the horrors of *Psycho*. Again like *Psycho*, the flat is adorned with mirrors, which suggests there is a great deal of illusion going on here.

Smith lies down and falls asleep. Times passes, as indicated by a fade and Banks' vibraphone glissando, and Smith is awoken by the sound of an argument next door. "You're trying to tell me I'm mad. Say it long enough and I shall start to believe it," shrieks the male voice. This is exactly the method adopted by Smith's enemies. Indeed, the two voices are those of Anthony Newlands and Lelia Goldoni, whose characters turn out to be those villains. The woman in the argument screams, prompting Smith to run to the rescue. The toucans in the vestibule are strangely unimpressed, and when Smith goes to the adjacent room he finds it empty, filled not with an arguing couple but only with shadows, step ladders and paint pots.

He then hears the elevator descend, and rushes out to catch it but misses whoever was in it. We have actually already heard the footsteps of this stranger. They were walking about when Smith woke, and belong to the woman in the photograph (Goldoni), who in collusion with the psychiatrist is setting Smith up to make him appear to be the killer of the psychiatrist's wife. It is a familiar plot, and though intriguing, it is not so much the plot as the *style* of the film along with its references to other films of the period that makes *Hysteria* interesting.

The next scene reflects the world of fashion photography that was so very much part of 1960s swinging London. Indeed, the year after *Hysteria* was released, Michelangelo Antonioni deconstructed the whole phenomenon in *Blow Up*, wherein David Hemmings plays a photographer who is unable to distinguish between illusion and reality. A similar confusion is played out in *Hysteria* but without the intellectualism. Smith finds another photograph of the mysterious woman on the floor when he returns to his apartment. The name of the photographer is printed on the back this time, and in the next scene Smith pays him a visit. The photographer is played by George Woodbridge (who played the hypnotist Zoltan in Freddie Francis' *The Evil of Frankenstein* the previous year). A model is posing in a bra and underclothes, providing some very mild titillation. Woodbridge's photographer would appear to be gay, however. "Why come here with this aggressive, masculine attitude?" he snaps as Smith. "Unless you need that sort of thing." But in the end, the photographer reveals that the woman in the photo was murdered in Smith's penthouse apartment. "She was stabbed," he explains, and as if we needed any more reminders of *Psycho*, he concludes by adding, "Her body was wrapped in the plastic curtain of a shower cubicle." The photographer's final expression as Smith leaves suggests that he is involved in the conspiracy—or merely paid to say his piece. Either way it doesn't matter much as we don't hear from him again.

Smith wanders through the gray, misty city streets and then catches sight of the same mysterious woman whom he has just been told has been murdered. Lelia Goldoni poses by her car and the character she plays gives Smith plenty of opportunities to see her. He runs after her but she disappears, as people do in this kind of film. There are more shots of Smith wandering alone, and again the sinister apartment block is presented looming vertiginously over him.

After an altercation between Smith and the private detective, who resigns from the case (or so we think), there is another "invisible" argument in the deserted apartment next to his own. Once more he runs next door, and Francis has the shadows of the sinister toucans thrown eerily over the walls of the vestibule. Smith discovers that the shower in his own apartment has been left running, *Psycho*-style. He also picks up a blood-stained knife and we are led to believe that he might literally be caught red-handed for a murder he has not committed, just like Cary Grant in *North by Northwest*. In fact, this plot element has a much longer lineage than that, and was again articulated by E.T.A. Hoffmann in "Mademoiselle de Scudéry": Cardillac's assistant Olivier watches Cardillac kill a victim, then hurries to help and is discovered by the police who, for a moment, jump to conclusions. "Why, this is Olivier Brusson, the journeyman, who works for our worthy Master René Cardillac. Yes, he would make a fine murderer, indeed! And isn't it just like a murderer to stop and lament over his victim's corpse until someone comes along to arrest him."[8]

Hysteria doesn't go down that road just yet, but as Mr. Smith washes the blood off his hand, Francis echoes Hitchcock's image of blood swirling down the plughole at the end of *Psycho*'s infamous shower scene. Then, as Smith opens the bathroom cabinet, the mirror inside reflects Goldoni standing in his apartment. "You're supposed to be dead!" he gasps, thus referencing yet another classic Hollywood film. This time it is Otto Preminger's *Laura* (1944) in which much the same thing happens to Dana Andrews' police detective. He has been investigating the murder of a beautiful woman, who then appears as if by magic in her own apartment after he has fallen asleep in it.

In *Hysteria*, the woman introduces herself as Denise James and explains that her husband was the driver of the car involved in the accident that led to Smith's amnesia. The photograph, she suggests, must have belonged to her husband. (But what about the second photo?) She insists that the photographer who said she was murdered was wrong, and she denies having been seen by Smith in the street earlier. She feels guilty about the accident, as her husband was drunk at the time. She apparently felt responsible and therefore paid for Smith's treatment and lent him this flat in which to convalesce. She is his secret benefactor. All this is a pack of rather unconvincing lies, as we will eventually find out, but it propels the plot along. Smith discusses the shower and the bloody knife with her; she puts them down to his imagination, but, of course, she is the one responsible. It is also Denise who switches on the tape recording of the arguing neighbors, recorded by both her and the psychiatrist with whom she is in love. These are all devices to make Smith think he is losing his mind.

Smith takes Denise out to dinner, where they are observed by the private investigator, who is still on the case and suspects that Denise is involved. Then a flashback sequence is inserted. "Inserted" is the appropriate word for its rather perfunctory appearance. It is necessary for the plot, but it is rather awkwardly handled. Denise tries to get Smith to remember what happened and says he must go back to the very beginning. The words "very beginning" are repeated on the soundtrack in time-honored style to suggest a trip down memory lane, but in fact Smith isn't remember anything. It is the audience who is doing that—for now the brief sequences we were shown during the main title sequence are explained to us. Smith was in France with a girl. She steals his money. Her male accomplice chases him. He escapes, and ends up hitching a lift from a rich English girl, who smuggles him back to England. Awkwardly, this girl has now fallen in love with him and wants to marry him, so Smith escapes from her while she is re-fueling her car. He hitches another lift, and it is this car that is involved in the accident.

Back in the apartment, Denise is cutting bread with the same knife Smith saw by the shower, covered with blood. Francis seems to be referencing his own *Nightmare* here, lighting the blade until its gleams white. Denise deliberately displays the knife to disturb her victim but professes that she simply bought it when furnishing the flat. "You mean I didn't see this the other night covered in blood?" Smith asks. "I don't know what you saw the other night," she replies. He starts to repeat the words of the recurring argument from next door and, knife in hand, staggers towards Denise. She screams. The toucans squawk and we assume Smith has stabbed Denise in a deranged fit of mania. He regains consciousness with blood on his hands, makes his way to the shower and now discovers a corpse beneath the running water.

At this juncture, Gina, the nurse, appears and Smith confesses that he has killed Denise. In fact, he hasn't done any such thing. The body in the shower is that of the psychiatrist's wife. Gina soon finds this out, removes the body and brings the psychiatrist back to the apartment. There, he promptly punches her in the face in a striking scene that reveals for the first time his villainous nature. Smith has now disappeared and the plan becomes much more complicated than intended. When Denise appears, she and her accomplice argue. Denise says, "You couldn't arrange for your wife just to disappear. Oh no, you had to complicate the whole thing so that a hundred things could go wrong."

"We both agreed it was a good idea."

"You agreed. I said this thing was dangerous from the beginning."

"It couldn't possibly have gone wrong. As soon as the drug wore off, he would have discovered my wife's body and run. I know him. Well, he's gone all right. So's the body."

"What? Well, is she [Gina] involved?"

"That I don't know. I didn't allow for her."

"You didn't allow for anything, my darling."

The psychiatrist still thinks they will get away with it if they can bring Smith back. He knows where Smith is and has arranged to pick him up. Meanwhile, Denise will put Gina in the shower to replace the missing wife. Having wrapped Gina in the shower curtain, she attends to her makeup in the bathroom mirror and, in a nice piece of visual symmetry, she sees Smith suddenly reflected behind her, just as she was reflected behind him in the earlier scene. "You look as though you've seen a ghost, to coin a phrase," he smiles, now knowing exactly what's been going on. In fact, he has known for some time. Denise pulls a gun but decides to knock him out with a martini bottle instead. She is prevented from hurling him off the balcony by the arrival of the detective.

The finale, in which the doctor returns to the apartment with the intention of stabbing Gina, is again straight out of *Psycho* (his shadow behind the shower curtain, the gleaming knife), though with little of Hitchcock's inventiveness. By this time, Smith has replaced the corpse of the psychiatrist's wife back in the shower and Gina is safe. The film ends with a parting shot of the glamorous apartment, but by now we are presumably aware that all that glistens is often far from being gold.

14

Domesticity and *The Nanny*
(dir. Seth Holt, 1965)

Some of our most exquisite murders have been domestic, performed with tenderness in simple, homey places like the kitchen table.[1]

Jimmy Sangster's screenplay for *The Nanny* was based on the 1965 novel of the same name by Evelyn Piper. She also wrote *Bunny Lake Is Missing*, which was filmed by Otto Preminger, and starred Laurence Olivier in the same year as Hammer's film. Sangster confessed that he "never met Ms. Piper but I'm eternally grateful to her for writing the book."[2] It is probably just as well he never met Evelyn Piper because not only did he considerably alter her book, he also improved on it.

There are many ways in which Sangster's screenplay differs from Piper's much more crudely violent novel. To begin with, Piper's novel is set in New York. Sangster moved the action to London for quite practical reasons: Hammer was based at Bray in Hertfordshire, and a modern dress story was obviously so much easier and cheaper to film in London. But, in fact, only the beginning of the film uses locations. The rest is claustrophobically set-bound, so it would have been perfectly viable to set the action in America. That Sangster deliberately chose not to go with the American setting suggests that he wanted to retain the traditional English "Gothic" resonance that had made Hammer so successful in the first place, and he reinforces this by having an exterior shot of Joey's ivy-covered school, with its battlements and Oakley Court–style *porte cochère*; but he also wanted to say something about English society. There is certainly horror a-plenty in Piper's novel, but by transposing even only some of the mayhem in the novel to an affluent English setting, with repressed English characters, the horror is in fact intensified, as it is all the more unexpected. Bette Davis furnishes Nanny with an English accent, and presents the role in a much more ambivalent, psychologically complex manner than in the Piper novel, which has her perpetrating her crimes far earlier on than in the movie. It also seems more natural to have an English nanny working in an English environment rather than an English nanny working in America.

Nanny's motivation in the novel is also rather different from her motivation in the film. In the novel, it is Joey's baby brother Ralphie, not his sister, who is accidentally killed. Piper's Nanny has nothing to do with Ralphie's death. She does not run the bath, unaware that Ralphie is lying there dead. Instead, it is Virgie who discovers the boy's body. And in the book, there is no doubt about how the accident happened. The reason Nanny wants to kill Joey in the book has nothing to do with trying to silence him and thus hide her responsibility for the child's death. Instead, she is motivated by several other concerns. The fact that Joey has always been willful and stubborn and has "set himself against Nanny" is one of them; and when she learns about psychopaths, having encountered a book on the subject in the surgery of Dr. Meducca, who lives below the Fanes' apartment, she puts two and two together to make nine. Also, she believes that if she can dispense with Joey (her plan is to drug him and then hang him, thus making it appear as though he committed suicide), she will be able to stay with Virgie and not be sent away, which is what the psychiatrist and Mr. Fane think would be for the best, given Joey's aversion to her. Sangster kept the motif of hanging for an early scene in the film when Joey (William Dix) plays a cruel trick on one of the staff at the home for disturbed children to which he has been sent, but there is no suggestion that Nanny intends to hang him in the film. Instead, Sangster reprises the motif of drowning when Nanny drags Joey off to the bathroom at the end of the film. Not only does this create formal symmetry, it also reinforces the echoes of the shower scene in *Psycho* and all the implications of vulnerability that bathrooms suggest.

Poster for *The Nanny* (dir. Seth Holt, 1965), showing Bette Davis in the title role, with Jill Bennett as Penelope Fane writhing in the throes of a heart attack. Above them both is William Dix, as Joey Fane, playing with his hangman's noose.

Sangster also tightens

up the family relationships, turning Piper's Mrs. Gore-Green into the film's Aunt Pen (played by Jill Bennett). Sangster explains that Nanny was Aunt Pen and Virgie's childhood nurse. He also cuts out the more extreme depravities of the novel, increasing the plausibility of the story. Also, by using an upper-middle class English setting, Sangster was able to inject some light satire of the English class system into the proceedings. Mr. Fane becomes a Queen's Messenger, played with exasperated patrician restraint by James Villiers. His ineffectual character is almost as weak as that of Wendy Craig's Virgie, and does indeed reflect the kind of society that John Osborne, eight years earlier in *Look Back in Anger*, had satirized as "phony." According to him, it was a society populated by people like Jimmy Porter's brother-in-law Nigel, whom Jimmy dubs "the chinless wonder from Sandhurst" and "the Platitude from Outer Space."[3] The Fanes have no idea how to control Joey, and all Mr. Fane can do over a particularly trying dinner table scene, when Joey refuses to eat Nanny's meal, is to storm out and eat at his club. This proves fortunate for him, as he consequently avoids being poisoned by one of Nanny's pies, but it is also the last we see of him in the film, which is unfortunate for the audience, as Villiers' excellent performance is so enjoyable.

In the novel, both Mr. and Mrs. Fane are poisoned by Nanny's pies. This is made quite explicit, and Piper clearly describes Nanny mixing the Ipecac into the filling, just as later she mixes sleeping pills into Joey's cinnamon on toast. In the film this poisoning is presented in a much more ambivalent manner, and we are not sure, at first, if it really is Nanny who has done the dreadful deed or if Joey is the culprit. As was the case with his adaptation of Josephine Tey's novel for *Paranoiac*, Sangster delays important information to increase suspense; and instead of having Mr. Fane poisoned, Sangster has him taken away on official business, thus clearing the stage for Aunt Pen to help Nanny look after Joey (and die in the process) while both parents are absent. In the novel, Penelope is not a family relation at all. She is called Mrs. Gore-Green and is an English lady living in America, who had been brought up by Nanny in England. Mrs. Gore-Green's daughter, Alethea, is Mr. Vane's secretary and mistress, and it is through this connection that Nanny gets her job with the Fanes. In the film, the immature and neurotic Virgie has been brought up by Nanny from birth, but in the novel, the birth of her younger son Ralphie proved such a strain that a nanny was needed to help Virgie to cope. She has since become utterly dependent on Nanny (a feature Sangster retains), and Nanny realizes that her future is safe so long as Virgie still needs her. When Nanny finds out about Mr. Fane's affair with Alethea, she uses it as ammunition in her campaign to stay with Virgie at all costs (for where else has she to go at her age?).

Piper's major subplot about the psychopathic daughter of the doctor is also missing from the film. Both characters make it into Sangster's screenplay, but they are presented in a very different manner and given different names. In the novel they are called Dr. Meducca and Robbie, who become Dr. Medman (Jack Watling) and Bobby (Pamela Franklin) in the film. Franklin's Bobby is an innocent tomboy whose only sins are the occasional secret cigarette and some boyfriend fantasies. She tries to help Joey, but Roberta Meducca is a psychopathic nymphomaniac who exposes Joey to radiation from her father's Fleuroscope, explaining that it will "warm him up." (Joey isn't harmed as he doesn't like the noise it makes.) Roberta is also a drug addict, and tricks Virgie into giving her an emerald ring to pay for more marijuana. She "helps" her escape from the hospital after the poisoning, and takes her to her fence, Leo, who threatens them both with violence when Virgie explains that her finger is too fat to remove the ring. So Roberta takes her back to her father's office below the Fanes' own apartment where she drugs her, before attempting to cut off her finger with a scalpel. She then threatens her with a pistol, shaves off all Virgie's hair, seduces the Irish doorman, and unsuccessfully attempts to force him to have sex with Virgie, before she is shot by the police.

None of this, of course, would have been appropriate for a thriller set in 1960s Britain, and so it all had to go. The resulting vacuum was filled by Sangster's re-working of Nanny's motivation for attempting to kill Joey. We learn about her abandoned daughter, who has just died from an abortion. We see Nanny returning to the Fanes' flat in a distracted, guilt-ridden state, inadvertently causing the drowning of the perhaps already dead infant. Joey's observation of this is again only implied. Her attempt to drown Joey at the end of the film, brilliantly intercut by Seth Holt with flashbacks of the earlier accident, is thus explained as the product of a deranged but not criminal mind; after all, Nanny stops short of actually killing Joey and pulls him from the water just in time. Nanny survives but is a broken woman. In the novel, she is killed (some time before the end), having tripped over the rope Joey has tied as a tripwire over the threshold of his door. Nanny was on her way to smother him with a pillow, a detail Sangster retains for the film, but which does make one wonder why she bothers to drown him as well—but, of course, Sangster's needed to echo *Psycho*. The drowning sequence is anyway much more spectacular than a mere smothering would have been.

Though Joey survives in the film, in the novel he is injected with morphine by Dr. Meducca, who wants to rid the world of another little psychopath like his daughter. Joey is held in his mother's arms as the doctor injects him, Virgie thinking her son is being given a dose of penicillin. All that would have been far too grotesque even for a Hammer film, and so vanished without trace. Even as it stood, Sangster was forced to add an optimistic epilogue, reuniting Joey with his mother in her hospital bed, all ending happy ever after. Having seen the original version, the head of Twentieth Century–Fox insisted, "You can't end a movie that way. It's too downbeat. Have everybody leaving the theater in a bad mood. Cheer 'em up, for Christ's sake. Give 'em a happy ending."[4]

The Nanny is a domestic tragedy. Most of the action takes place within the confines of a luxuriously appointed but somewhat claustrophobic apartment in London. Though the complete opposite of a Gothic castle, the apartment block of *The Nanny* is nonetheless imposing: a severe neo-classical facade by Nash in a fashionable area of London. Holt makes sure we have no doubts about this, providing us with an imposing shot of the facade's columns as Nanny enters it. Richard Rodney Bennett's music also subtly informs us that this is an unsettling place. Being a domestic tragedy, *The Nanny* belongs to a venerable tradition. *Hamlet* is perhaps the most famous domestic tragedy of all—as well as being one of the most overtly Gothic, set within the claustrophobic confines of Elsinore

Castle. *The Nanny* has certain things in common with Shakespeare's play. Joey is an infant Hamlet, devoted to but alienated from his mother. Nanny resembles King Claudius (who killed Hamlet's father). She has killed Joey's sister, admittedly by accident, but Joey suspects that she is now intent on killing him as she can no longer endure the fact that he knows what actually happened. Bobby has a role similar to that of Horatio in Shakespeare's play. Together, she and Joey try to stand up to Nanny (just as Horatio helps Hamlet confront the Ghost of Hamlet's father). Joey, also like Hamlet, sets out to trap Nanny's conscience. The role of poison is another shared theme. Hamlet accidentally poisons his own mother. Joey is (falsely) accused of poisoning Mrs. Fane. He even pretends to commit suicide at the beginning of the film, thus providing a crude paraphrase of Hamlet's "To be or not to be."

The film opens in a very ambivalent manner. Holt focuses on a group of children playing on a roundabout in a playground setting. There is no music—an absence that increases the ambivalence, as we have no aural signifiers to help us locate the kind of genre to which this film belongs. All we hear are the cries of the children. It is a bright sunny day, and the sun casts a crisp shadow of the roundabout and the children on it. Holt then focuses solely on the shadows—a significant decision, as by this means he suggests that there are darker things about to be revealed than the sunny images of innocence suggest. Over this shadow image the first title card appears: "A Seven Arts/Hammer Production." Presumably, we have read the reviews and we know about Hammer's reputation along with that of Bette Davis, but still we have no confirmatory music to say what kind of film this is. Then Davis' name appears, followed by the title of the film, but there is still no music. This only begins when we see Davis walking behind the children. (If you look closely you will also see soldiers with their horses behind a fence in the distance, though these are merely bystanders and have no symbolic role.) Bennett's score features a harpsichord in a comparable, though much more sophisticated way to Wilfred Joseph's use of it for *Fanatic*. The harpsichord in both cases suggests a certain old-fashioned quality, and Bennett combines this with a melody that resembles a child's nursery rhyme. The harpsichord's connotation of innocence will ultimately be utterly corrupted, but at the moment all seems sunshine and tranquility in the park.

There is also a vague echo of J.M. Barrie's *Peter Pan*, a play to which I will be returning in Chapter 19. *Peter Pan* has a famous connection with Kensington Gardens, where Peter "lived a long time among the fairies."[5] The lost boys of the play are "the children who fall out of their prams when the nurse is looking the other way. If they are not claimed in seven days they are sent far away to the Never Land."[6] Though the opening scenes of *The Nanny* were filmed in London's Regent's Park, they nonetheless remind one of Kensington Gardens in *Peter Pan*. The play's tension between innocence and corruption, the theme of parents coming to terms with the loss of a child, the Lost Boys' longing for their mothers, and the distinctly pedophile tendencies of the creepy Barrie himself, all inform *The Nanny* to a greater or lesser extent.

During the rest of the main title sequence we watch Nanny feeding the ducks, enjoying the sunshine and buying flowers (she is watched in the background by members of the public who point at the camera crew). Nanny seems eminently trustworthy, and we are thus furnished with the film's first theme of trust. But Bennett's score takes on a more somber mood as we cut to the Corinthian columns on the neoclassical façade of the building in which the Fane family lives. Holt's name appears over this, as he invites us inside to witness the unfolding domestic tragedy. We cut to an interior shot and, as in *Hysteria*, hear the soulless whirr of the elevator motor, after which the elevator doors open and Nanny walks into frame.

Bill Fane is arguing with Virgie, but Nanny ignores this and goes quietly about her business. She stows her purchases in the kitchen and tidies her hair in her bedroom where the camera lingers on (and Bennett's more atonal style accompanies) an array of silver frames on the chest of drawers. The frames display pictures of all the children Nanny has cared for during her career. The last photo, on which the camera lingers longest, is of Virgie and her now dead daughter, Susie.

Virgie is too frightened to fetch Joey back from his school, and persuades Nanny to go in her place. While Nanny is getting ready, Virgie looks at Nanny's photos and Holt obliges with the film's first flashback to a time when life was happy and Susie was still alive. Susie says, "When I grow up..." and the phrase is repeated on the soundtrack as its irony reverberates in Virgie's memory. We therefore have our second clear theme of grief.

Next, we cut to the exterior shot of Joey's school. Maurice Denham as Dr. Beamaster, the psychiatrist-in-chief, explains to Mr. Fane that they have all sorts of children at his institution: "We have paranoia, schizophrenia, ambivalence, withdrawal, sibling rivalry. You name it, we've got it." It sounds like a roll call of the subjects covered by Hammer's previous psychological thrillers, but *The Nanny* takes perhaps the most psychologically interesting approach of them all. Joey has been sent to this school because he wouldn't sleep or eat. Though Beamaster and his staff have cured these external problems, no one is sure that the underlying difficulties have been dealt with. As we shall eventually learn, Joey's only real problem is Nanny herself, but no one suspects that. Even so, Dr. Beamaster is closer to the truth than he thinks when he says that Joey has "an inborn antipathy to middle-aged females." The reason for such a comment is that Joey pretends to have hanged himself when his teacher, Mrs. Griggs, comes to fetch him. It is a strikingly shocking image that will recur in Sangster's later *Fear in the Night* (a film which is set entirely in a school environment).

Joey will not sit next to Nanny in the car, and as he is driven away Dr. Beamaster confesses, "I hate to admit failure, but with young Joey, I'm afraid..."

"He was a monster," says the young staff member standing next to him.

"Oh, don't be uncharitable, Sarah. Our job is to search out their little devils and exorcise them. I'm afraid we've failed Joey—failed him miserably."

This is nothing short of the truth, as no one will believe that Joey is the victim of his deranged Nanny, whom everyone else thinks is sweetness and light. When Joey is reunited with his mother, Holt makes sure that we see him as a healthy, genuinely affectionate little boy. He beams at his mother and runs to her embrace, but he won't sleep in the room Nanny has prepared for him. He moves his bed linen to a smaller room and makes up his own bed. (Holt uses a hand-held camera to follow him about to create an even more claustrophobic feeling of domestic confinement.) Neither will Joey allow Nanny even to touch his things, particularly his rope, which he hides beneath his pillow. This is one of the several sinister signals that suggest Joey might be a psychopath, especially when we see him tying a hangman's noose in it while listening to his record player.

Mr. Vane is shocked when Joey asks him to sack Nanny, but does his best to remain patient without really listening to his son's point of view. "You can continue playing your records but not so loud, there's a good chap." As an indictment of upper-class inability to communicate meaningfully, this line says it all.

Aunt Pen arrives for a drink and necessarily informs the audience of her weak heart. During this monologue, Joey plays with a clockwork robot shown to us in close-up. As in *Taste of Fear*, Holt again monumentalizes the mundane to increase suspense in a prosaic environment. Later, Joey asks his aunt if it might be possible that she could die from her condition. When he learns that she could, he wonders if Nanny could drop down dead as well. This statement not only encourages our suspicions that he truly is the psychopath his teachers believe him to be but also plays with our adult discomfort at any discussion about death in the company of children.

A dismal dinner follows when Joey again refuses to eat. Ever-tolerant Nanny defends his behavior: "Nanny understands. She's on your side," she smiles. "No, you're not," Joey replies. Sangster now dispenses with Mr. Fane by sending him away on his Queen's Messenger business, after which Joey insists on having a key to the bathroom, terrified that Nanny will try to drown him. He makes Nanny swear not to come in when he's bathing. William Dix is excellent at pouting and staring in an ambivalent manner, so we are always unsure if he is telling the truth or not. Distraught and exhausted, Virgie weeps on her pillow, and when Nanny comes in to inquire after her, Virgie asks her to brush her hair in a scene reminiscent of the similar moment in Hitchcock's *Rebecca*.

Next morning, having locked himself in his room for the night, Joey cuts himself a slice of bread and jam, later stealing the leftovers from his father's breakfast. Ever-observant Nanny asks why he is doing this, to which Joey replies: "You wouldn't poison him." Nanny's expression in response to this accusation is somewhat darker than before, but still inscrutable. Doubts, however, are now definitely raised about her, especially as, just before, Joey has told Bobby Medman that everyone blamed him for killing his sister Susie. He has always denied this.

But Sangster won't let Joey off the hook as easily as this. In the next scene, a milkman is nearly killed when Joey hurls a window box of flowers off the fire escape. "He's a homicidal nut!" the milkman shouts, and later Nanny reprimands Joey with a marked threat: "I had hoped things would improve between you and I while you were away. They haven't, have they? I will give you one more chance, Master Joey. One more chance," and she is as good as her word.

Bobby is reading the teenage magazine *Jackie* in her bedroom. *Jackie* was well-known at the time for its liberal tips about teenage sex, which have since been criticized by today's more pedophile-obsessed society. Bobby tells Joey how stupid his prank with the milkman was and how lucky he was to have Nanny to stand up for him. She refers to her as Mary Poppins, and indeed Nanny *is* a dark shadow of Mary Poppins, the Walt Disney film adaptation which had appeared only in the previous year (1964). Together, they decide to frighten Nanny by placing a doll face-down in the bath. When Nanny sees this, it triggers all the memories of Susie's death and finally tips the balance of her sanity.

Virgie threatens to tell Joey's father what he has done, but Joey responds with a threat that he will "do something" if she does. This has a similarly chilling effect to Mr. Mocata's threat that "something will come for Simon and the girl" in Hammer's adaption of *The Devil Rides Out*. In fact, it is Nanny who is about to "do something," and in the next scene we watch her making steak and kidney pies. She has poisoned one of them, and we are led to believe that she is identifying the poisoned pie with Joey's initial, cut out in pastry. In fact, it is Virgie's pie that has been poisoned. Joey is seen walking into the kitchen to imply that he is the guilty party, but when he refuses to eat and is sent to his room by his mother, Nanny feeds Virgie the poisoned pie to make sure it takes effect. By this means, she will be able to blame Joey for his mother's illness and have him sent away again.

An intriguing literary parallel to this scene brings us back, yet again, to a passage from E.T.A. Hoffmann's "Mademoiselle de Scudéry" in which a similar poisoning exploit is recounted:

> The most sacred bonds were riddled by doubt and the most appalling mistrust. The husband trembled in fear of his wife, the father of his son, the sister of her brother. Dishes which a friend put before his friends remain untouched on the table, while wine sparkled untasted in the glasses. Where formerly good humor and mirth had prevailed, savage glances now spied about for a secret assassin. Fathers of families were observed shopping for provisions in remote districts with uneasy looks and movements, and preparing the food themselves in the first dirty eating-house they came to, since they feared evil and treachery in their own homes. And yet even the greatest and most thorough precautions were often of no avail.[7]

Dr. Medman later asks Joey what he has used to poison his mother. Joey denies having done so, and during the interview, we see Nanny look furtively at the doctor, then at Joey's pillow and finally, while plumping it up, putting her hand in the pillow slip to plant the bottle of icapecuana. It falls out onto the bed as she lifts the pillow and Joey is apparently caught red-handed. Virgie is taken to a hospital but Joey insists he cannot be left alone with Nanny, so Aunt Pen is called in to stay the night.

Pen agrees to play draughts with Joey, and once more Holt is able to use a mundane object to create a powerful sense of shock. When Nanny offers to make a hot mug of cocoa for them, Holt cuts to a close-up of the draughts clattering over the board and a shot of Joey's face expressive of sheer terror. "I'll make it all in one jug," Nanny assures him. The scattered draughts also become a metaphor of the collapse of order in the house that night. The first thing that goes wrong is that Joey runs to Aunt Pen soaking wet, accusing Nanny of having tried to drown him—and this isn't, apparently, the first time. Aunt

Pen has a spasm as a result and Nanny helps to administer one of her pills. Next time, she will not be so helpful.

Joey goes back to see Bobby, and in another flashback we learn how Susie died. The *Psycho* imagery of the bathroom is played to the fore here, though the violence is purely accidental. The vulnerability and coldness of the bathroom in both cases, however, is a powerful component of the unnerving atmosphere. Susie plays with her doll and prepares to bathe it. First, the doll falls in, soon followed by Susie, who lies unconscious, hidden from view by the shower curtains that are drawn against the side of the bath. Nanny returns from her unauthorized afternoon off and runs the bath water, unaware that Susie is lying face down beneath the rising water. Joey is playing with his train which, like the robot earlier, conveys a frightening sense of inevitability. Nanny parts the bath curtains and we immediately cut back to Joey and Bobby. The masterful Holt denies us any shot of Nanny's reaction.

Bobby then takes Joey to her father's surgery but there is no larking around with the x-ray machine as in Piper's novel. On the contrary, Bobby is very concerned that Joey doesn't touch it as "it's dangerous," but together they fantasize about over-exposing Nanny with x-rays. The flashback continues: We see Nanny imagining that she is bathing the living Susie, and when Joey tries to phone for help, Nanny grabs his hand and prevents him. Now we all know the truth, Joey is revealed as heroic and plucky rather than psychotic and selfish. Later that night, he barricades himself in his room and we cut to a shot of Nanny in her rocking chair, with sinister shadows behind her, resembling a wicked step mother in a fairy tale. There is also a shot of the deserted hall of the flat in the middle of the night.

Heartbeats pound on the soundtrack as the camera wanders over the sleeping form of Aunt Pen. Suddenly, the heartbeats stop and Pen wakes up in a cold sweat. She goes to the kitchen to make a cup of tea, and Holt perfectly captures the disorientation, coldness and desolation of waking up at three in the morning. On her way to the kitchen, Pen observes Nanny clutching a pillow to her breast, listening at Joey's door, and remembers that Nanny doesn't approve of giving children cushions because they might "overlay" themselves—a word lifted directly from the novel. Pen, who now understands that Joey has been right all along, has an argument with Nanny during which she suffers a violent heart attack. Watching impassively, Nanny this time does not oblige with any pills. Harry Waxman's hand-held camera follows Pen crawling along the floor just as it followed Joey moving his bed linen earlier in the film. As Pen drags herself back to the bedroom, Nanny tidily picks up her shoes—a rather nice touch showing how old habits die hard even during a catastrophe. Similarly, when Pen is dying on the bed, Nanny carefully places a pillow under her head and covers her with the eiderdown to make her death as comfortable as possible. She even moistens a flannel to bathe her forehead. "Master Joey wants to get rid of his old Nanny," she explains. "I gave Master Joey his chance."

Nanny then introduces the last flashback, which is entirely Sangster's invention and makes Nanny the victim of circumstances and her own devotion to duty rather than the evil murderer of Piper's novel. She responds to a message from a doctor who has been nursing her daughter Janet. Janet is the victim of an unclean abortion and when she knew she was dying she asked to see her mother. Nanny, of course, has been too busy looking after other people's children to look after her own illegitimate daughter, which might be interpreted as yet another indictment of the British class system.

Holt chooses a desolate, shabby street for Nanny to walk distractedly along after her upsetting interview with the doctor. Still distressed by the sight of Janet's corpse when she returns to the Fanes' apartment, she mechanically runs the bath water, without drawing the shower curtains back. A large Teddy bear looks on impassively as she walks down the corridor, eloquently signifying the death of innocence.

When the flashback ends, Nanny adds, "I can't have Joey tell on his old Nanny.... Being a Nanny is based on trust." And this film is indeed about the betrayal of trust and the purging of grief. In one particularly brilliant shot, Holt has Nanny peer through the opening of Joey's doorway, her eye looking down at the sleeping boy like the unnamed watcher in Poe's murder story "The Tell-Tale Heart": "I turned the latch of his door and opened it—oh so gently! And then, when I had made an opening sufficient for my head, I put in a dark lantern, all closed, closed, so that no light shone out, and then I thrust in my head. Oh, you would have laughed to see how cunningly I thrust it in!"[8] Bette Davis is at her most frightening here, as she intones the famous line, "You mustn't make it difficult for Nanny, Master Joey."

Joey trips in the struggle between them and is knocked unconscious. Nanny lifts him in her arms and Bennett's harpsichord is utterly corrupted with its note clusters as she attempts to drown him. This climax is far more disturbing than the *Psycho* shower scene, for not only are we horrified by this attempted murder of a child, but we are also responding to Nanny's deranged deliberation, which, presented as it is in every detail, is much more worrying than the shadowy presence of Norman Bates and his stylized stabbings. Suddenly coming to her senses, Nanny changes her mind and pulls Joey out. He runs off and Nanny, utterly crushed, lies on the floor, weeping. All that remains is the happy ending forced on Sangster against his will.

15
Homophobia in *The Witches*
(dir., Cyril Frankel, 1966)

The Witches is ostensibly a story about the occult, but there is nothing really supernatural going on here. Its occult aspect is really about belief rather than magical phenomena, which latter are singularly absent. As its title suggests, *The Witches* is also, on a deeper level, a discussion about female sexuality and really belongs to the category of Hammer's psychological thrillers. Men play a subservient, even neutered role. Alec McCowen's failed priest, Alan Bax, is a mere accomplice to Kay Walsh's Stephanie Bax, the real villain of the piece, who aims to transplant her soul into the body of a schoolgirl. The idea of using a younger woman to ensure the survival of one's own ego is already a sexual idea—homosexual pedophilia indeed. There is a further layer of repressed lesbianism in her relationship with Joan Fontaine's Gwen Mayfield, the new headmistress of the village school.

Miss Mayfield is recovering from a nervous breakdown. On the surface, this is due to a traumatic native uprising in Africa. We are not shown exactly what happens to her there, but the schoolroom where she works is invaded by a witch doctor wearing a terrifying mask. Has Miss Mayfield been raped? Does this turn her against men and sexuality altogether—or has she always been more interested in women? Her later relationship with Stephanie is very much a servant-mistress relationship with Stephanie coming out on top (until her eventual, ignominious end); but there are other female characters in the film who elaborate the gay subtext. Gwen Ffrangcon-Davies plays Granny Rigg, an older woman, a much more "obvious" witch than Stephanie, who has a somewhat split personality. She is under the control of Stephanie but also protective of her granddaughter, whom Stephanie intends to sacrifice. Ffrangcon-Davies' genuinely disturbing performance emphasizes the film's matriarchal atmosphere, which reaches its climax in the occult ceremony itself, in which Stephanie's incantation resembles a long-repressed female orgasm. The orgasm ends in a Liebestod when Miss Headerby slashes her own wrist and splashes Stephanie with blood, thus destroying the "spell" and Stephanie herself. This could be interpreted as the *petit mort* of consummation, which rather undermines the sense of resumed normality attempted in the film's final scene. There, the film's sexual tension is merely rejected rather than resolved, and lesbianism is thus labeled as "abnormal," undesirable and alien.

Such an interpretation sends the film in the opposite direction of Basil Dearden's homosexual blackmail drama *Victim*, starring the gay though very much "in the closet" Dirk Bogarde, which was released in 1961. *Victim* was a major breakthrough in the positive presentation of homosexuals on screen. As Bogarde's biographer John Coldstream explains, the Secretary of the British Board of Film Censors, John Trevelyan, felt that "most intelligent people came to the matter 'with sympathy and compassion, but to the great majority of cinema-goers homosexuality is outside their direct experience and is something which is shocking, distasteful and disgusting.'" Coldstream adds, "In the very week that Trevelyan gave the writers his thoughts about their first full script [of *Victim*] the Wolfenden Report was debated in the House of Commons and, he said, indicated that a majority was still opposed to the compassionate treatment of homosexuals."[1] *Victim* went on to make a difference. Indeed, in 1968 the Sexual Offences Act was passed through Paliament, decriminalizing homosexual acts. Coldstream concludes,

> Lord Arran, who had introduced the legislation in the House of Lords, wrote to Dirk that he had just seen *Victim* for the first time—on television—"and I just want to say how much I admire your courage in undertaking this difficult and potentially damaging part." He said he understood that it was in large part responsible for a swing in popular opinion, as shown by the polls, from forty-eight percent to sixty-three percent in favor of reform. Lord Arran concluded: "It is comforting to think that perhaps a million men are no longer living in fear."[2]

The Witches did not serve the cause for gay women at all. It treats lesbianism very much as part of "the other." Stephanie Bax is destroyed and, climactically, "normality" is somewhat crudely imposed on all the villagers—not least Gwen Mayfield herself. It seems odd that the blood-smeared trauma of the occult ceremony does not induce in her another nervous eclipse. Instead, the final moments suggest that nothing untoward has happened at all. Alan Bax loses his dog collar and stops running tapes of organ music in his statue-littered bedroom (instead we have an upbeat orchestral cue from Richard Rodney Bennett), and the implication is that he and Miss Mayfield will get together and have a child to fill the desk left empty by Ronnie Dowsett (Martin Stevens), a boy who has been a victim of village witchery. Hammer would address lesbianism again in the 1970s with its Karnstein vampire trilogy, but its approach to the subject was really only an opportunity to indulge in male-oriented female nudity. As Ingrid Pitt so succinctly puts it in her autobiography when reminiscing about her part in *The Vampire Lovers*, "It's so easy to make men happy."[3]

Duplicity is another important theme in *The Witches*, and again this film has certain things in common with Hitchcock's approach, not least in its star Joan Fontaine, who had found herself in a similar victimized role in *Rebecca*. Stephanie Bax also breezes about her ancestral pile not unlike another Mrs. Danvers. Indeed, Miss Mayfield's relationship with Stephanie is very like that between the predatory Mrs. Danvers and the preyed-upon Mrs. de Winter. When discussing whether there are witches in the village,

Stephanie concedes the poszsibility: "It's a sex thing, deep down, of course. Mostly women go in for it—older women." But Miss Mayfield fails to see the irony here. At first Stephanie merely suggests that they collaborate on a newspaper article, but she ends up with the altogether more ambitious proposal of extending their lives together into the twenty-first century by means of witchcraft: "Gwen, you could help me. Someone intelligent, as fastidious as I am myself. And there's just time for you to learn the rites."

The Witches is perhaps Hammer's most sustained etude on the conflict between appearance and reality in the sense that it is actually about very little else. Its witchcraft element is technically no more than a MacGuffin, and the final ritual scenes are nowhere near as integral to the overall plot as the occult element of *The Devil Rides Out*, for example. The principal question that director Cyril Frankel wants his audience to ask is "What is going on?"

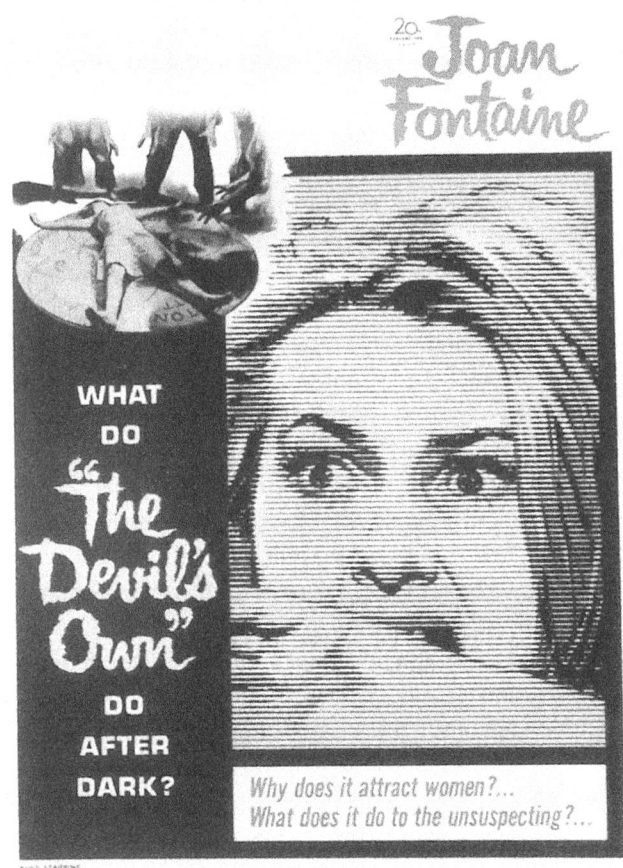

American poster for *The Witches*, retitled *The Devil's Own* (dir. Cyril Frankel, 1966), with Joan Fontaine on a bad-hair day.

Can we trust the apparently trustworthy, and what are the apparently untrustworthy characters hiding? Very few people in the village of Heddaby are as they appear. The ones who look most sinister prove to be the most benevolent (such as Alan Bax and Mrs. Curd, the butcher's wife, played by Viola Keats). Conversely, the seemingly benevolent ones are the real villains, Stephanie Bax being the prime contender. Only Duncan Lamont's grotesque Sweeney Todd butcher, Bob Curd, and crosseyed Granny Rigg exude ambivalence from the start, and Granny Rigg is anyway later redeemed as being the victim of a false doctrine.

The story is straightforward. Stephanie Bax believes that she can reincarnate her personality and intelligence in the body of young Linda Rigg (Ingrid Brett). But Linda is spending too much time with Ronnie Dowsett, a boy in her class at school. This is worrisome for Stephanie because the medieval ritual she plans to use to attain her ends specifies that the new host of her old soul must be a virgin, so Ronnie is dealt with by means of sympathetic magic: Granny Rigg sticks pins into a doll and leaves it in a tree. The next morning, Ronnie is taken to the hospital. When his father discovers who is responsible, he is dispatched more conventionally by being thrown in the lake.

Miss Mayfield, recovering from her nervous collapse, thinks that the rural tranquility of Heddaby is just the place to get back to normal, but she couldn't be more mistaken. Heddaby may look idyllic, especially in the golden summer weather in which the film was shot, but it is too good to be true, harboring, as it does, an entire coven of witches under the thrall of crazed Stephanie Bax. The village church is in ruins (always a bad sign in such films—think of *The Wicker Man* [dir. Robin Hardy, 1973]), and the place is filled with gossipy, sharp-eyed women. When Miss Mayfield begins to suspect the truth behind Mr. Dowsett's death, Stephanie intervenes. She diverts a flock of sheep to trample over footprints by the lake which suggest that the unfortunate man was indeed dragged there and murdered. Significantly, it is sheep who do the dirty work. By so doing, they invert their traditional connotation of innocence, which Frankel had nicely set up in an earlier scene showing rehearsals for a school play, where the sheep occupy the idyllic background. Having conveniently obliterated the evidence, Stephanie then elaborately goes to the trouble of importing the African fetish objects seen in the prologue and by this means causes Miss Mayfield to suffer another nervous breakdown. (This scene is surely one of the film's most implausible moments.)

Stephanie is still being presented to us in a wholly benevolent light at this stage, and we are still being led to believe that it is Alan, with his fake dog collar and mania for organ music, who is the real villain. Anyway, Miss Mayfield is packed off to a nursing home (Oakley Court again), where she discovers that she has lost her memory, just like Dr. Ballantyne in *Spellbound*. Indeed, the nursing home scenes are a home counties reworking of *Spellbound*'s Green Manors mental asylum, and just as Ballantyne recovers his identity, so too does Gwen. Her Proustian petite Madeleine is a girl visiting another of the patients, who brings with her a doll which reminds Gwen of the voodoo doll that was responsible for Ronnie's illness. Miss Mayfield eventually manages to escape, and she is driven away through Oakley Court's main gates, which we last saw in *The Man in Black*.

The suspense Frankel creates in the escape sequence echoes the various predicaments of Cary Grant's Roger Thornhill in Hitchcock's *North by Northwest*. As Spoto describes Thornhill's predicament in *North by Northwest*, "The accumulating images of entrapment (in limousine, jail, elevator, hospital room, hotel room, even a cornfield and at the national monument) express what might be called his emotional or even spiritual condition of entrapment."[4] Similarly, Miss Mayfield initiates nothing. She is merely a pawn in the hands of others. Her only intervention in anything is in her recommendation that bright Ronnie Dowsett should stay in the village and be coached by her, rather than be sent away to a crammer. Supposedly sinister Alan Bax wants the boy to go away—as it turns out, for purely benevolent reasons—and Miss Mayfield's genuine concern for the boy's welfare results in him being victimized by Granny Rigg. He would indeed have been better off going away, as Alan originally observed.

Both *The Kiss of the Vampire* and *The Witches* demonstrate how aspects of the psychological thriller can sometimes motivate or at least affect other, related genres. These films are among Hammer's best because of this cross-fertilization. The straightforward revenge plots of Hammer's Dracula series have none of the suspense and psychological excitement of *The Kiss of the Vampire*, while Hammer's other foray into the occult, *The Devil Rides Out*, lacks the ambivalence that makes *The Witches* a more intriguing and subtle affair, if less sensational and glamorous than the much-lauded Wheatley adaptation. There is very little overt horror in both *The Kiss of the Vampire* and *The Witches*, and this is wholly appropriate for films that are, in fact, studies in terror and suspense. Consequently, they are all the more compelling.

16
Doppelgängers in *Crescendo*
(dir. Alan Gibson, 1970)

Doubles and impostors appear in several of Hammer's thrillers. They also feature in *Les Diaboliques* and Hitchcock's *Strangers on a Train* (1951). Even during Hammer's early years, as we have seen, *The Man in Black* featured Sid James impersonating a gruff odd-job man and gardener. But Hammer's most spectacular foray into the world of the doppelgänger is surely Alan Gibson's *Crescendo*, the story of a composer's widow, Danielle Ryman (played by Margaretta Scott), who attempts to perpetuate her dead husband's musical genius by mating her deranged son, Jacques (James Olson), with a girl, Susan (Stefanie Powers), who resembles the former's dead wife, Catherine. Unfortunately, Jacques killed Catherine after discovering that she was having an affair with his identical brother Georges (also played by James Olson). As Jimmy Sangster observed after providing his own synopsis of his screenplay, "Reading that back, one wonders how some of these films ever got off the drawing board."[1]

Again, the ghost of E.T.A. Hoffmann hovers over this film. Hoffmann was fascinated by doubles, and they make their appearance in the appropriately entitled "The Doubles," an 1821 story about two identical men who fall in love with the same woman. One line from Hoffmann's story sums up the motivations of the paralyzed brother in *Crescendo*: "It is only too certain that I have a second self, a double, who persecutes me, who wants to swindle me out of life and rob me of Nathalie."[2] Hoffmann also knew the value of gradual plot revelation. The situation of his story, like that of *Crescendo*, is explained little by little after initial predictions and suggestions. In "The Doubles" a raven and a mysterious woman offer hints of what is to come: "Murder is close behind you! Save Nathalie!" and the raven echoes this with "'Murder! Murder!' in a hideous croak."[3] Sangster and Alfred Shaughnessy, the screenwriters of *Crescendo*, similarly create a sense that all is not what it seems to be, and Gibson's direction includes many oblique glances and significant stares from characters in the know to suggest that Powers' Susan is not in safe hands. We are also shown three dream sequences which are deliberately confusing. Olson's dual roles are not explained at first, and neither is the identity of the mysterious woman with whom both men seem to be in love. This too has its parallel in Hoffmann's "The Doubles":

16. Doppelgängers in Crescendo

A double-bill poster advertising *Taste the Blood of Dracula* (dir. Peter Sadsy, 1970) and *Crescendo* (dir. Alan Gibson, 1970). James Olson wields an axe.

> "Yet," argued the desire burning within him, "is it not possible that it is my double who is practicing the delusion by passing himself off for me, and that I am the one for whom Nathalie has always been intended, bound to her by the most mystical destiny?"[4]

The anxiety regarding identity here was of particular concern to Romantic artists. Théophile Gautier's 1835 novel *Mademoiselle du Maupin* plays rather provocatively with this problem, having its eponymous heroine dress up alternately as a man and as herself, and then simultaneously fall in love with a brother and sister who do not realize that they are in love with the same person. ("He came many times into my room with his declaration on his lips, but dared not utter it; for really it is difficult to speak of love to some one who is dressed like yourself and is putting on riding boots."[5]) The homosexual subtext of all this understandably appealed to Oscar Wilde, who was a great admirer of Gautier's novel. There is no sexual ambiguity in *Crescendo* but there is considerable ambiguity of identity as we wonder exactly who is who. At the end of the film, the deranged brother, Jacques, tries to kill Susan but he is ultimately shot by his own mother. In the similar psychological environment of "The Doubles," the hero Deodatus significantly meets his beloved Nathalie in a Gothic ruin and explains:

"The other meant you harm. He is my double and he tried to kill you; the bullet hit me instead. It wounded me but it has healed; my true self is still alive! Tell me, Nathalie, that you believe in that self, that you love the self who is not called George!"

"My poor George," Nathalie exclaimed. "What has happened to you? But no, no! You are excited, overwrought! Be calm, be yourself, like the George I have always known."

Nathalie embraced him again; and holding her pressed close to his heart he said: "Yes, Nathalie, it is I: I am the one you love! No one shall attempt, no one shall dare, to tear me away from this heaven of bliss! Nathalie, we must escape—I must put you beyond his reach. Fear nothing, it is I, his true self, who will kill him!"[6]

Crescendo also has much in common with *Taste of Fear* and, consequently, with *Les Diaboliques*. Sangster was disenchanted with the film, feeling it was one variation too many on a well-worn theme, but that is to deny its many interesting qualities, of which the theme of the double is the main but not only one. Like *Taste of Fear*, *Crescendo* is again set in France; the prologue suggests the Carmargue location of *Maniac* with its wide open skies, beach location and shots of Olson riding a horse. The prologue even briefly includes a shot of horse rustlers holding long staves as in the scene from *Maniac* when the guilty lovers first attempt to drown the embarrassing corpse they find in the back of their car. *Crescendo* also has a mysterious villa with a swimming pool (much larger than the one in *Taste of Fear*), as well as a sinister chauffeur (this time a psychopathic one as well, played with frightening intensity by Joss Ackland). There is another enigmatic femme fatale (Margaretta Scott taking over from Ann Todd), mysterious piano music drifts through the night, and last but not least, the action revolves around an imperiled young woman.

An important element is the score by Malcolm Williamson, which nudges the film into a venerable category of what one might call "piano thrillers," the grandfather of which was *Dangerous Moonlight*. Richard Addinsell's "Warsaw Concerto" from that film has gone on to have a life of its own (a fate not shared by Williamson's attempt at an equivalent in *Crescendo*), but whereas Addinsell's piece was based on the idiom of Rachmaninoff, Williamson's "concerto" is a swaggering blend of symphonic jazz and Hubert Bath's "Cornish Rhapsody" from *Love Story* (dir. Leslie Arliss, 1944). *Love Story* was, as its title clearly points out, a romance rather than a thriller, but it too rode the considerable ripple that was stirred by *Dangerous Moonlight*. So too did Bernard Herrmann's "Concerto Macabre" for *Hangover Square* (dir. John Brahm, 1945), Charles Williams' "The Dream of Olwen" from *While I Live* (dir. John Harlow, 1947) and Nino Rota's music for *The Glass Mountain* (dir. Henry Cass, 1949). *Crescendo*'s musical supervisor Philip Martell also wanted to feature the great jazz saxophonist Tubby Hayes; he shares the solo performing credits with pianist Clive Lythgoe, who had made something of a specialty of interpreting Gershwin. It is Hayes we hear first, during the pre-credits dream sequence, for which Williamson provides an aural equivalent to Gibson's slow-motion camerawork by using vibraphone and high-pitched, wandering strings over which the sax plays with the main theme. We watch Olson (as Georges) riding up to a row of drying lobster nets at the end of which stands a mysterious woman in a pink dress with a pendant resting on her bosom. Olson embraces her and another figure appears, also played by Olson, whom we later learn is his deranged twin brother Jacques. The lobster nets perhaps suggest that both of them—and the girl—are trapped in a love triangle and that they might all share the same fate as the lobsters. This certainly happens to the girl because Jacques shoots her. Georges looks down at her face, which has become a decayed, skeletal horror. Then, back in real time, he wakes up screaming from his nightmare.

Now the other characters are gently introduced. Georges is brought his breakfast by the maid, Lillianne (played by Jane Lapotaire). Their nasty, exploitative relationship is hinted at by various kinds of smiles, which only attain significance when we know what is really going on between them. The maid goes out and has a few words with Danielle, Georges' equally deranged mother. Ackland's chauffeur, Carter, has been sent off to collect Susan from the station and in the next shot we see a train hurtling towards us. This ultimate cinema cliché is reminiscent of the Lumière brothers' *Arrival of a Train at La Ciotat Station* (1895), which caused audiences to run out in panic, fearing they would be flattened. Rather different fears are being pandered to in *Crescendo*, however, the title of which zooms out of the distance along with the train as Williamson's big piano concerto theme takes center stage.

The French landscape through which Carter drives Susan looks somewhat less glamorous than that of *Taste of Fear* and the car in which Stefanie Powers is brought to the villa is a long way from the Rolls-Royce that brings Susan Strasberg to hers. Perhaps this reflects the fact that France was no longer quite the aspirational location it had been only ten years earlier, thanks to the establishment of mass tourism. Even so, the location is intended to be glamorous. Sangster mentions that notes by Michael Carreras, who produced the film, point to the fact that a Camargue setting was intended but was faked. He admitted that "the Camargue was a very dramatic area, but the story could have been located anywhere and certainly didn't gain anything from the location."[7] This suggests that Hammer was now desperate to rekindle old successes, and that, as Sangster observed, "the word 'lifeless' had begun to describe the whole Hammer scene."[8] Sangster also thought Scott MacGregor's impressive set was also a little lifeless, but one of MacGregor's production designs so impressed Philip Martell that he asked if he could buy it from him. MacGregor presented it to him specially framed and it hung on Martell's living room wall until he died.[9] It is indeed one of Hammer's most impressive and extravagant sets, an elaboration and expansion of Bernard Robinson's composite set for *Taste of Fear*. It is not necessarily an improvement, as it is not used anywhere near as atmospherically as the way in which Seth Holt exploited Robinson's more restrained creation. Also, *Crescendo* being filmed in color, Gibson was not able to evoke the same expressionist intensity as Holt, but the much larger swimming pool is a definite advantage here.

Susan is informed that her trunk has not arrived. Annoying though this is for her, it passes as a trivial detail in plot. In fact it is very significant, as Danielle wants her to wear the clothes left behind by the murdered Catherine. The trunk has indeed arrived, as Carter well knows, but it has been kept out of sight. Danielle also suggests that Susan should lower her hair to enhance the resemblance she has to Catherine. In a later scene we even see the maid hang up Catherine's clothes in Susan's wardrobe, including the iconic pink dress. The maid is also rather annoyed by Susan's presence as she wants to marry Georges herself, and Susan, who implies competition in that department, is one guest too many for her. The stage, so to speak, is now set.

Susan, like Penny Appleby before her, now hears piano music (a solo version of the film's main theme) emerging from the pool house–music room, and we are by now more than familiar with the Gothic connotations of mysterious music. Susan tries not to let this worry her at the moment, assuming that it is Georges at the piano. (It is presumably Jacques or a tape recording.) Georges watches her take a dip in the pool, in which she wears Catherine's bikini. Then Susan, like the good Gothic heroine she is, explains that she is an orphan. She doesn't even have the advantage of an aunt, like Emily in *The Mysteries of Udolpho*. Not being good enough for the concert platform, she has instead taken up teaching, hence her academic researches in the Ryman archive. Over lunch, she finds out that Georges is also not a good musician, despite ten years of piano lessons. The conversation between him and his mother over this subject subtly introduces some tension between them, and this is markedly enhanced by the arrival of Carter, dressed in black from head to toe like a cat burglar. Ackland does a very good job at looking sinister in a restrained psychopathic manner. He later watches Susan wander around the estate, which eventually leads her to the pool house. She peers through its distorting bottle-glass windows and sees a cobwebby candlestick and an ornate piano (reminiscent of the even more baroque instrument in *The Kiss of the Vampire*). Though there is no dripping wet corpse, as in *Taste of Fear*, this pool house will later serve a similar dramatic function.

Susan picks out the piano concerto melody at the keyboard but the next scene is played not only without music but also without dialogue. In it, Danielle gives Georges his daily injection of heroin—for, yes, Georges is a hopeless drug addict (not that we are meant to know this just yet, but it is fairly obvious). Olson and Scott give tremendous performances here. Their expressions say very nearly everything, and Olson does much more than sit lamely in his wheelchair, conveying instead immense emotional energy and physical frustration. The fact that his character is wheelchair-bound is yet another similarity this film has with *Taste of Fear*.

Back in Susan's bedroom, Susan is typing away at her master's thesis. After all, that is why she has come to the Ryman villa, as she wants to study the compositions of Danielle's dead husband at first hand. Engrossed in her work, she fails to notice the maid's annoyance at her presence. By these means, Sangster gradually introduces the reality of the situation, much as Hoffmann gradually revealed the elements of his plots. Lillianne has come to deliver a message from Danielle, who would like to see Susan before dinner, so Susan obliges. After giving Susan some of her husband's letters, Danielle explains that Georges used to be a tennis player before an accident put an end to that. She then chats about her musical family, revealing that Georges is the un-musical black sheep. Her father, apparently, was a close friend of Sibelius—an enjoyable, if absurd, little detail. Significant glances between mother and son also indicate a subtext of which Susan is quite unaware.

Georges and Susan are left alone to listen to a recording of Ryman's Second Symphony, another piece of smoochy symphonic jazz courtesy of Williamson and Tubby Hayes, during which Georges massages Susan's shoulder before he confesses that she reminds him of someone. But then his legs start to trouble him and Lillianne is summoned. "Get over here!" he shouts, shattering the cozy mood. The music stops, the idyll is over. After turning off the record player, Susan flips through a family photo album, intrigued by what Georges said about her reminding him of someone.

We cut to Lillianne ministering to Georges in his room. Lapotaire, as one would expect from a Shakespearean actor of her stature, gives another excellent performance here as a scheming nymphomaniac, who teases Georges as she pulls off her black stockings: "You must remember, my darling, it is *I* you need. It is me who helps you; it is me who makes you forget." This is nothing short of the truth as she provides him with heroin from a dealer in Arles. The injection sets Georges off on another hallucinogenic trip. Gibson puts things into slow motion again and we see Georges swimming in the pool. When he pulls himself out, the mysterious girl in pink is sitting on a day bed. He embraces her. Jacques appears again with the same shotgun. The girl turns as the weapon is aimed at her, and this time she has Susan's face.

Meanwhile, Carter is closing down the villa for the night. He encounters Lillianne drinking in the living room; she explains that she is practicing for her future role as mistress of the house. Carter laughs and calls her a slut. Ackland is particularly disturbing here in his stillness, but when the maid reminds him that he has spent rather a long time in asylums, he grabs her face and pushes her away.

The next morning, Susan shows Danielle the photo she has found, which she thinks might be a picture of Catherine. According to Danielle, Georges "loved her too much"—the first suggestion we have that Catherine was actually Jacques' wife. At dinner that night, Susan appears in the pink dress and Georges is so upset he doesn't even wait for the first course to be served. Danielle smiles knowingly and Georges wheels himself away. Confused, Susan asks why Danielle is trying to turn her into Catherine. We seem to be re-entering Pygmalion territory, but Susan never wears the dress again.

Later, we get a replay (with differences) of the pool house scene in *Taste of Fear*. Danielle settles herself down in a chair opposite the piano. Carter lights the candles as though preparing for a religious ritual, which in a way this is, and announces that "everything is ready, madame." In comes an unidentified figure—in fact Jacques—who sits at the piano and starts to play. "There you are, my darling," Danielle smiles, adding, somewhat in the manner of a James Bond villain, "I've been waiting for you." Susan hears the piano and goes out to investigate. We see the piano again through the bottle-glass windows but we never glimpse the player—other than his hands at the keyboard. "That's right, my darling." Danielle purrs. "That's right. Strong declamatory chords, leading to the appassionata." And "Appassionata" is what Shaughnessy originally wanted to call the movie. It would have been appropriate, but *Crescendo* is better, as the whole point of the film is gradually to increase the dramatic tension to a melodramatic *fortissimo*.

Susan peers through the windows again as Williamson introduces the anxious harmony of augmented triads into the piano music. Eventually the piece disintegrates. "No, no, that's not right!" Danielle laments, before a bone-chilling scream pierces the night. By the time Susan finds her way to the door, the room is empty, but in the chair previously occupied by Danielle, there is a dummy dressed in the pink dress, with its eye ripped out and dangling over its waxy cheeks. Susan runs out and bumps into Carter whom she takes with her to investigate the mystery. The dummy has been replaced by Danielle, who explains she has been listening to a tape recording. This shuffling of motifs from *Taste of Fear* serves no real narrative function. Why a dummy, one asks? It is dramatically effective but basically redundant material, and does demonstrate the fact that this film is a copy of a copy of a copy stretching back through *Taste of Fear* to *Les Diaboliques*.

Georges later asks Susan to leave without letting Danielle know he has asked her to leave. Fond of her, he doesn't want her to be part of his mother's insane plot. Lillianne arrives with more drugs, and in the privacy of Georges' bedroom informs him that the price of the drugs has just gone up: She wants him to marry her before she will agree to provide any more heroin. After this little argument, she goes for a swim and forces Georges to watch her, but this is a taunt too far, as Lillianne soon finds herself stabbed to death by an unidentified assassin. We are led to assume it is Georges, as his wheelchair hurtles away without its inhabitant shortly before the killing; but we cannot be sure. Again, Sangster remembers his favorite film and references *Les Diaboliques* here. Whereas the murder in that film took place in a tiny bathtub, here we have a huge swimming pool in which to shed Lillianne's blood. Williamson's ascending scales also suggest air bubbles rising from the corpse.

Gibson then gives us a breather from this set-bound claustrophobia and takes us to Arles, which Susan visits to find out about her missing trunk. Apparently it was delivered to the Ryman residence two weeks before. When she confronts Danielle about this, Danielle calmly apologizes, explaining that she has only just found out that the trunk had been hidden away by Lillianne, whom she has now dismissed. All very convenient. The pool is also being cleaned out, just like its counterpart in Clouzot's film. Carter eventually refills it and Georges and Susan settle down to listen to Tubby Hayes playing a saxophone version of the piano concerto. A love scene ensues. They kiss until George pushes her away, arranges his legs and takes off the record. Suddenly in agony, he shouts, "You'd better leave me alone," and a few moments later he falls out of the chair with another shriek. Gibson now provides one of the film's more interesting images, shooting Georges' prostrate figure through a tumbled lampshade, creating a suitable mood of disorientation. Responding to Georges' desperate plea, Susan steals some soothing heroin from the ornate jewel box in which Danielle keeps it. Danielle has been watching her and later reveals the awful truth that Georges is an addict and that Susan is now an accessory to illegal drug use. Danielle has finally trapped her, and promises to keep quiet if Susan agrees to marry Georges.

Georges' third trip follows, which is interesting in its use of the Freudian staircase symbolism we have already explored. The basic situation of the dream is reprised: Georges and the mystery woman embrace, and Jacques interrupts them; but this time the action takes place in Susan's bedroom, which is accessed by a spiral staircase. Both men successively climb this, which could be interpreted along similar lines to a dream that was included in Freud's *Interpretation*: "The excitation led to an orgasm and thus revealed the fact that the whole staircase-symbolism represented copulation."[10] Be that as it may, the dream ends in the death of both Georges and the woman.

Despite everything else, Susan now believes herself to be in love with Georges, and has lost all interest in her thesis. Georges is furious with her, pointing out his unsuitability as a husband. Again, piano music drifts out of the pool house; it is introduced by a rather effective shot of the villa and pool moving from daylight to evening, with foreground shrubs rustling gently in the evening breeze. Once more, Jacques breaks down halfway through the concerto in a scene that is reminiscent of Anton Walbrook unable to remember his own Warsaw Concerto in *Dangerous Moonlight*.

And so we move towards the long-awaited dénouement in which Susan is amazed that Georges can now walk. But it isn't Georges. It is Jacques, who crazily explains to the bewildered Susan, "Mother said you'd come back tonight." A mad son dependent on an almost equally deranged mother reminds us of *Psycho*, and *Crescendo* now piles on the action. Meeting one's doppelgänger was always said to be a harbinger of one's own death, and this certainly applies to Jacques, who has been let out to rape Susan in the hope that the ensuing child will grown into a genius worthy of his grandfather and consequently finish the concerto. This fails to come to pass as Danielle eventually shoots Jacques. But before that happens he manages to kill Carter, whose experience in asylums has hitherto qualified him to keep the lunatic under control. Jacques staggers around in distinctly expressionist style like Conrad Veidt in *The Cabinet of Dr. Caligari* (dir. Robert Wiene, 1919)—all in black with staring eyes, thus adding the final film reference in Hammer's most derivative but nonetheless entertaining thriller.

17

The Past in *Fear in the Night*
(dir. Jimmy Sangster, 1972)

Fear in the Night again reprises *Taste of Fear* with its plot concerning a couple of adulterous lovers, Robert and Molly (played by Ralph Bates and Joan Collins), who try to drive a young woman, Peggy (Judy Geeson), insane. It also resembles the plot of *Nightmare* because the lovers do their best to turn Peggy into a murderer, hoping she will kill the somewhat demented but harmless headmaster, Michael Carmichael (Peter Cushing). He owns the valuable real estate of a private school that has been closed for some years; but the lovers' plot is designed to make Peggy believe it is still a going concern. They contrive to make Carmichael appear psychopathic in the hope that Peggy will kill him in "self-defense." The inheritance will then pass to Molly, the headmaster's wife, and Peggy will be put safely out of the way in an asylum. It seems more than mere coincidence that the girl is called Peggy, which is only two letters away from Susan Strasberg's Penny in *Taste of Fear*. And with its school setting and plot twists, *Fear in the Night* is the closest thing to a remake of *Les Diaboliques* that Jimmy Sangster ever penned. He also produced and directed this film, his last attempt at this particular genre for Hammer, and the one that brought him full circle back to his original inspiration all those years before.

The most important element here is the evocation of the past. All Hammer's thrillers dwell to some extent on the past: a lost past (amnesia), a hidden past (a guilty secret) or, as in the case of *Fear in the Night*, a terrifying past that one of the characters is trying to forget. (Peggy has been violently assaulted in her home and the experience has traumatized her.) "History," says Stephen Daedalus in James Joyce's *Ulysses*, "is a nightmare from which I am trying to awake,"[1] and that is precisely how Peggy feels. Everyone keeps telling her that she imagined the attack but the resulting nightmare keeps repeating itself and she begins to doubt if she can distinguish between fantasy and reality. "What if that nightmare gave you a back kick?" Joyce's Daedalus thinks, while watching schoolboys playing football. "The ways of the Creator are not our ways," he continues. "All history moves towards one great goal, the manifestation of God."[2] If God is truth here, *Fear in the Night* is also a journey towards it.

As we have seen, Romanticism in general was fascinated by the past, not only because

Poster for *Fear in the Night* (dir. Jimmy Sangster, 1972), with Judy Geeson in the grip of the petrifying prosthetic arm.

it found the increasingly industrial present unsatisfying but also because looking backwards became a metaphor for looking into submerged psychological strata of the personality. Introspection was one of the key aspects of the movement as a whole. (I again refer the reader to Jung's analysis of his own dream about a house.) Historical subjects became fashionable in the nineteenth century because they gave Romantic artists greater freedom to explore psychological motivation than from within the confines of their industrial, bourgeois present. Even in nineteenth-century settings, a historical *approach* to dramaturgy proved invaluable. By gradually uncovering what happened in the past, the motivations and personalities of the characters on stage, so to speak, could be all the more convincingly revealed.

Ibsen used this technique to shattering effect in plays such as *Ghosts* (1881) and *John Gabriel Borkman* (1896). In *Ghosts* we learn how a father's degenerate personality has been passed on to his son, in an exploration of the genetic past we all have to deal with; and we all have to deal with the ghosts of old ideas and conventions, which threaten to overwhelm new freedoms and ideals. In *John Gabriel Borkman* we learn how a social humiliation of long ago has destroyed the title character's confidence and led to his self-imposed exile from society. We are, in other words, all potential hostages to our own errors and past actions. Ibsen's dramatic technique was to start with the present and progressively peel off the layers of the past that led to the opening situation. Wagner similarly used this approach in *Parsifal* (1882). With its many narrations describing past events, *Parsifal* anticipated the technique of the cinematic flashback, of which *Fear in the Night* makes considerable use. As we saw earlier, E.T.A. Hoffmann's "Mademoiselle de Scudéry" demonstrates how a trauma, experienced by Cardillac's mother, brings on a serious illness. Peggy similarly suffers a mental illness after her struggle with the intruder. The plot of *Fear in the Night* depends upon Peggy's vulnerability caused by this trauma and much of the film's dramatic tension is built upon her anxiety that the past is *not* over and done with.

Fear in the Night is also a series of essays in nostalgia: The action largely takes place in a school left empty during the holidays with echoes of term time played on a tape recorder. (The headmaster, deprived of his vocation, nonetheless pretends still to be running it.) The film conveys an elegiac sense of time past, not least through the hauntingly lyrical flute melody provided by composer John McCabe for the scenes in which Peggy wanders through the deserted school rooms. It is vitally important that we understand the past if we are to comprehend the present, and it is the function of Hammer's thrillers in general to peel off the layers of the past to arrive at the truth. Peggy along with the amnesiac Christopher Smith of *Hysteria* must recall the true nature of the past to discover who they and other people really are.

The film starts at the end of the story, so the whole thing is one gigantic flashback containing within it further flashbacks. We open with a shot of the school playing fields and hear a tolling bell. Rugby posts stand out in the autumn light—and for anyone who has been to a public school and not enjoyed it, there is no place quite so evocative of conflict and suffering as the rugby pitches of those particular institutions. Indeed, the film exudes, throughout, the particular gloom and menace of the British public school system, often nodding in the direction of Terence Rattigan's 1948 play *The Browning Version*. In Anthony Asquith's 1951 film version of that play, Michael Redgrave brilliantly performs the role of the emotionally repressed Latin master Andrew Crocker-Harris, known as "the Himmler of the lower fifth." At first, he appears to be a dry-as-dust martinet but at the end of the play, after we have learned about his unhappy marriage and seen his essential decency, he is moved to tears by the kindness of one of his pupils. Cushing had also performed the role in a TV production in 1955 and no doubt brought his experience of Crocker-Harris to his interpretation of Michael Carmichael in *Fear in the Night*. It would have been an appropriate model, for like Christopher Lee's Dr. Gerrard in *Taste of Fear*, Cushing's Carmichael is no more than a red herring who turns out to be on the side of the angels.

Sangster also manages to reflect something of the anxiety and threat delivered by Giles Cooper's disturbing 1958 radio play *Unman, Wittering and Zigo*. This was later done for TV in 1965 and filmed in 1971 by John Mackenzie, with a youthful Michael Kitchen as the schoolboy Bungabine, just before Kitchen appeared in Hammer's *Dracula A.D. 1972*. David Hemmings plays John Ebony, an optimistic new master who soon learns that schoolboys can be truly terrifying; but it is the role of art master Cary Farthingale, whom Ralph Bates' character, Robert, in *Fear in the Night*, initially seems to resemble.

Robert says he is work-shy, just as Cary says, "There must be a peculiar knack that only headmasters possess—always finding a chap when he's idle." Robert also tells Peggy that there aren't any good-looking boys in the school, calling them all "monstrous little brutes." Similarly, when passing a dreary Latin class which is translating a line about "beautiful women," Cary tells Ebony that "there are no beautiful women in this hell," later adding that the boys "think like men, talk like men; they even smell like men." Like Crocker-Harris, Ebony is to be in charge of the lower fifth (form 5B to be precise) but it is not he who is Himmler. Instead, his entire form is basically composed of Hitler Youth, as they have all conspired to murder their previous master. There are, inevitably, many shots in *Fear in the Night* that resemble those in the film version of *Unman, Wittering and Zigo*, particularly the rows of school desks, the refectory scenes and the gym, the only difference being that there are no actual boys at Carmichael's school; but the school tie worn by everyone in *Unman, Wittering and Zigo* is, perhaps coincidentally, identical to Carmichael's tie. The tape recordings of lessons and mealtimes with which Carmichael amuses himself are also depressingly evocative not only of the real thing but also of the sounds of boys going about their business in Mackenzie's film.

During the rest of *Fear in the Night*'s main title, Sangster has Arthur Grant's camera pan around the deserted rooms of Carmichael's school, while the invisible boys sing "Lord receive us with Thy blessing/Once again assembled here." It is tempting to detect some irony in the closing lines of this much-loathed beginning-of-term hymn: "Break temptation's fatal power, Shielding all with guardian care, Safe in every careless hour." The hymn gives the film's composer John McCabe some time off, but his work load is considerable later, and adds immensely to the overall mood of the picture. The title of the film is presented as if in double exposure, the superimposed letters echoing in an effective though less sophisticated manner the fragmented lettering in the main title sequence of Hitchcock's *Psycho*. The double exposure effect suggests that this film will also involve psychological disorder. Having no boys to mess it up, Carmichael's school is rather cleaner than the depressing grime of the school in *Les Diaboliques*, but the sterile emptiness brings with it its own desolation. The camera then wanders outside again, and as the hymn comes to an end we are shown the dangling feet of a hanged man, whose identity will not be revealed until the prologue is reprised at the end of the film.

We immediately cut to a shot of Peggy talking with her psychotherapist. She explains that she has just married a schoolteacher and so feels that the time has come to put an end to her sessions. Later, when she is talking to her housekeeper Mrs. Beamish (Gillian Lind), we learn that Peggy is "quiet as a mouse"—and indeed, her role resembles that of the unnamed wife of Maxim de Winter in *Rebecca*. Like that character, Peggy marries a man she knows little about and then finds herself transplanted to a grand house with its own intimidating rituals, but with the major difference that the Rebecca figure is still there in the form of Joan Collins' Molly Carmichael. Mrs. Beamish wishes Peggy "pleasant dreams" and in a film like this such a benediction ensures that she will have quite the opposite. The camera moves through to the bathroom where a tap has been left running and a window left open. These signs, along with McCabe's oscillating terror music, ensure that something unpleasant is soon to happen, and it is significant that it happens in the bathroom, reminding us not only of *The Nanny* and *Maniac* but also, inevitably, of *Psycho*. A black-gloved hand opens the window as a telephone rings. It is Robert, apparently still at an end-of-term party. Peggy puts down the receiver, closes the bathroom window and is attacked. This is perhaps to be expected, but what we might not expect is that a prosthetic arm falls to the floor as she faints. No one believes she has been attacked, especially when Mrs. Beamish explains to James Cossins' doctor that she has recently suffered a nervous breakdown, hence the flashbacks to the psychiatrist's consulting room.

Next, we are shown a misty motorway. This is England in the early 1970s, an evocative period, and the autumnal atmosphere enhances the film's elegiac, lonely mood. Robert and Peggy have stopped off on their journey to the school for a cup of tea at a service station. Orange curtains—that very 1970s color—hang behind them, just as an orange cushion and an orange lamp shade will later punctuate the sitting room of Robert's little cottage. Robert assures his new wife that she is "safe now," but we should be able to guess that something is out of joint when we cut to a shot of him staring moodily into space by a rack of "Marble Arch" budget LPs in the foyer of the service station. Perhaps he is having doubts about his evil plan, or merely expressing his essentially heartless nature, which is otherwise skillfully disguised. When Peggy comes back, he snaps out of his reverie and confesses that he was "miles away."

The school itself is described as "Stockbroker Tudor" and, though a relatively recent fake, is worth a quarter of a million pounds. That Robert should know the value of the estate is very significant information, as that is exactly what he is after. He later admits he is not a dedicated teacher (in fact he is not a teacher at all) and wishes he had Carmichael's money. Taking Peggy on a tour of the school, they encounter one of Molly's unnerving portrait busts; Molly, like Dr. Richter in *Stolen Face*, is also a sculptor. Later we will see her portrait of Peggy, into the eye of which she sadistically twists a knife. The sculptures contrast effectively with the three sweet little Teddy bears that sit on a chair beside Peggy's bed, suggesting her childlike vulnerability. Robert assures her she is safe—and we begin to suspect that he is protesting a little too much. Peggy gets out of bed during the night and stares at the school where she thinks she can see someone wandering around. Robert suggests this might be Carmichael, who is gradually being set up as the sinister villain of the piece.

When Peggy is left alone the next day, she wanders around the empty school, accompanied once again by McCabe's melancholy solo flute theme. Its harp and string accompaniment at times resembles Ravel's *Pavane pour une Infante Défunte*, a piece that is similarly concerned with a vulnerable young woman. She looks up at the portrait of Carmichael and notices some half-eaten food on a plate in the refectory. Upstairs in one of the dorms, she hears boys' voices and goes to investigate. It seems that Carmichael is taking a lesson. This is the equivalent to the various examples of mysterious music we have encountered in previous films and, as in those instances, as soon as Peggy enters the room the voices stop. The room is revealed to be empty—empty, that is, except for Carmichael, who makes a starling entrance from behind.

"Robert said it would be all right as long as I didn't touch anything," Peggy explains. Peter Cushing perfectly times a beat before replying, "Did he?" He seems not to like Robert.

He then takes Peggy to the gym where we see a hangman's noose hanging on the wall. Carmichael is worryingly interested in knots, "especially in the study of character formation," he explains, a formulation which, after all, many public school boys have been informed about when being instructed in the handling of rifles in the CCF. He then delivers the film's best line: "Do you like tying knots in things, Mrs. Heller?"

The noose punctuates the space between them and we are left to draw our own conclusions. Like Danielle Ryman in *Crescendo*, Carmichael now observes that Peggy has beautiful hair and suggests she shouldn't tie it up. This Rapunzel motif is a persistent motif in psychological thrillers, as we saw in the hair-brushing episodes in *The Nanny* and *Rebecca*, and it not only suggests vulnerability but also an erotic subtext that contributes greatly to the tension here. "Oh! oh! what is this?" gasps Pelléas in Maurice Maeterlinck's iconic symbolist drama *Pelléas et Mélisande* of 1893:

> Your hair, your hair is coming down to me! ... All your hair, Mélisande, all your hair has fallen down the tower! ... I hold it in my hands, I hold it in my mouth.... I hold it in my arms, I wind it about my neck.... I shall not open my hands again this night.[3]

Just as the Biblical Samson's hair signified his virility, so too does Mélisande's hair stand for her sexual allure. Thus, when Carmichael unties Peggy's hair band, we are intended to interpret the act as a form of sublimated rape—at least that is the implication at this stage in the plot. It also gives Sangster an opportunity to reveal Carmichael's prosthetic arm, which he threateningly clicks into position to hold one end of the ribbon while he unties the knot with his other hand. Carmichael does indeed seem to be the man who attacked Peggy in London, but things are never so obvious in a Jimmy Sangster script.

Peggy asks if Carmichael keeps recordings of the boys to study. He does not reply to this, merely staring back at her instead. Cushing is an excellent starer. He also keeps his voice low when he does speak, maintaining a sibilant whisper, which adds immeasurably to the balefully avuncular quality of the persona he plays. With hair slightly graying, a wisp of a mustache, and spectacles that make his eyes seem quietly deranged, Cushing, as usual, gives another remarkably restrained, ambivalent performance.

Back in the cottage, Peggy is attacked a second time, and another flashback to the psychiatrist's coach suggests she might be paranoid after all. She is so disturbed by the experience that the planned dinner with the Carmichaels is now called off; but, of course, it was never on in the first place. Could it all be her imagination? Robert takes her out in the Land-Rover for some fresh air. There is a shotgun in the back, and Peggy hates guns. They drive over a bridge that had appeared in Hammer's *Taste the Blood of Dracula* two years earlier, and shortly afterwards Peggy sees the heartless Molly shoot a cute little rabbit. Molly is a brutal, catlike character and her superficial smile collapses when Peggy and Robert leave. "Do Michael and Molly get on?" Peggy inquires, and images of Molly with her kill and Carmichael staring at her flash through her mind.

True to her catlike nature, Molly now presents Peggy with the dead rabbit. She also insults her by calling her "almost a child bride." Left alone again, Peggy takes the shotgun to bed for company while McCabe selects an oboe, with its traditional signification of feminine vulnerability, to accompany her. She uses the gun a little while later when Carmichael pays a visit himself. He falls, but is not killed because, as we later learn, he has substituted the shot with blanks. Peggy locks herself in a schoolroom but the headmaster smashes his way through the door in a scene that looks forward to the famous image of Jack Nicholson in Kubrick's *The Shining* (1980). All he really wants to do is warn Peggy about the plot against her, but is obviously going about this in quite the wrong way. When Peggy fires again, his spectacles shatter to unnerving effect (an equivalent in its way to the blank white contact lenses of the headmaster in *Les Diaboliques*).

Robert returns and discovers Peggy in a very withdrawn condition. He suspects that she has killed Carmichael, but in fact Carmichael has informed her of Robert and Molly's plan. Robert looks around the school again, searching for the body and looking much meaner than before. Then he explains the situation to a certain extent, peeling away more layers of the past. The school has been closed since 1963 when a fire broke out. Carmichael was badly burned and Robert met him in the hospital where he was a medical student at the time. He looks after Michael by playing along with the game that he is still a headmaster. It is all an elaborate piece of dramatic therapy—or so he says. Carmichael's situation is very like that of John Gabriel Borkman in the aforementioned Ibsen play. Like Carmichael, Borkman paces around in his upper floor room after his life was destroyed by a different kind of disaster (ignominious fraud in his case). There are also parallels with Ibsen's *The Wild Duck* (1884), in which a similarly crushed man pretends his way through a shattered life by what is called a "saving lie."

With Peggy refusing to acknowledge that she has killed Carmichael, Robert discusses the problem with Molly in a scene that removes all the deception in one swoop. Their plan is revealed, but Molly shouts, "Why do you have to be so devious? Why couldn't you have just taken him out into the woods and shot him?" This is very much the same complaint that Lelia Goldoni's Denise hurled at Anthony Newlands' Dr. Keller in *Hysteria*. Anyway, they decide to force a confession from Peggy and prepare a suicide note for her to leave when they have finished with her. But Peggy is literally saved by the school bell. This now starts tolling as it did at the beginning of the film—a point in time we have at last caught up with. Carmichael plays cat and mouse with Robert, taunting him through the public address system. He reveals that he knew about Robert and Molly's little plot all along. He even spilled blood from the dead rabbit on the cottage floor to make it look as though Peggy had killed him. Thinking Carmichael is hiding under one of the dust sheets, Robert fires the shotgun at him, but it turns out to be Molly whom Carmichael has gagged and bound. Frenzied by the frustration of his plan, Robert grabs the hangman's noose from the gym with the intention of stringing up Peggy on it, but Carmichael kills him before he can harm her. When the police arrive, Peggy walks away in an understandably dazed state and the film ends with the hymn it began with, but this time the camera reveals whose legs are dangling from the tree: They are Robert's.

18

Insanity, Incest and Christianity in *Demons of the Mind*

(dir. Peter Sykes, 1972)

Originally designed as a revisionist reworking of the traditional werewolf myth, *Demons of the Mind* evolved into a rather more complex study of incest and insanity. As was the case with many of its predecessors, it features a psychiatrist (played by Patrick Magee) who on this occasion is loosely modeled on the real-life persona of Franz Anton Mesmer (1734–1814—the film is set in the early nineteenth century). Unlike the psychotherapist in *Hysteria*, however, he is not the villain, though he is somewhat unnerving. Magee, with his astonishingly gravelly voice, which so precisely articulates each syllable of his dialogue, is usually rather unnerving, and his role here certainly echoes his approach to the role of the Marquis de Sade in Peter Weiss' play *Marat/Sade*. That play was premiered eight years earlier at the Aldwych Theater in London, and in his own way, de Sade was also a prototype psychologist, charting hitherto unacknowledged territory in the endlessly mutable terrain of human sexuality.

Demons of the Mind also resembles Poe's "The Fall of the House of Usher." Robert Hardy's Baron Zorn, like Roderick Usher, is afraid that insanity runs in the family. In addition, Zorn is terrified that his son and daughter are involved in an incestuous relationship; but incest, a game all the family can play, can also be seen in more positive light, as Wagner demonstrated in his opera *Die Walküre*. There, the incestuous Siegmund and Sieglinde conceive the hero, Siegfried, who will come to represent freedom and unconventionality in the later operas of the *Ring* cycle. It is this Romantic idea of incest as a metaphor for breaking the bonds of convention that the film seems to be championing. Released at the end of the optimistic era of psychedelia and free love represented by the hippie movement of the 1960s, this film nonetheless lays such idealism to rest. In the end, Baron Zorn shoots Falkenberg. He also shoots his son, but before he can bring himself to shoot his own daughter, the traditional forces of religion are paraded in the shape of Michael Hordern's priest and the usual band of angry villagers. They chop off Zorn's left hand (significantly, the sinister side) and drive a flaming crucifix through his heart. Such a dénouement suggests the death of liberalism, imaginative freedom and individualism that was to affect British society as the 1970s progressed. Although Britain may have largely invented the Gothic imagination, such an imaginative trope has always existed, perhaps necessarily, on the periphery of respectable British society. The screenwriter of *Demons of the Mind*, Chris Wicking, was very critical of this tension: "[Horror] films at that time were regarded as pretty offensive things in the great sensibility of English culture," he recalled. "I remember dinner parties and things like that and going to people who would say, 'What do you do?' And I would say, 'I write films.' 'What have you written?' And you would have to say, '*Blood from the Mummy's Tomb*.' And people would look aghast."[1]

"This is England," he observed elsewhere. "And England isn't interested in fantasy; isn't interested in imagination; isn't interested, really, in commercial pictures."[2] He was speaking of a time when Hammer was suffering a near-terminal decline, but despite the resurgence of interest and activity in Hammer's fantasy films in the internet age, horror is perhaps still best served by remaining on the periphery of the bigger picture. Horror, fantasy, science fiction and psychological thrillers with a lavish Hollywood budget are perhaps a rather emasculated commodity, absorbed as they now are, into the status quo.

Poster for *Demons of the Mind* (dir. Peter Sykes, 1972), with Shane Briant peering through the keyhole, Michael Hordern brandishing a burning crucifix and Yvonne Mitchell looking suitably anxious.

Just as we must dream in the dark, horror and fantasy films thrive best in the shadows of society.

As *Demons of the Mind* is largely about the repression of memory and its release by therapeutic means, it is appropriate that the main titles show us sepia-tinted images of not only Baron Zorn's family mansion—a metaphor, as we have seen, of the psyche itself— but also of the protagonists: Baron Zorn, his late wife, and his children Emil (Shane Briant) and Elizabeth (Gillian Hills). They are first shown when they were younger, as painted in a family portrait that hangs on the wall of Zorn's study. Those images are then contrasted with how the characters look when the action begins. The mansion itself is Wykehurst Park near Bolney in West Sussex, designed by Edward Middleton Barry, the son of Sir Charles Barry, who designed the Palace of Westminster in London. (Edward also supervised the completion of the Houses of Parliament after his father's death.) As for Wykehurst Park, Edward came up with a venerable pile in vaguely French style with Romanesque arches, but also with a general Gothic flavor provided by its turrets and steep roofs. (*Oh! What a Lovely War*, *The Eagle Has Landed* and *The Legend of Hell House* similarly featured the building.) Director Peter Sykes made full use of Wykehurst's Gothic potential, adding a stone eagle and a couple of live eagles, along with some eagle designs in the interior stained glass and an ecclesiastic eagle lectern, all of which reflect the baron's later comment, "Madness is eating us all like carrion birds." Dr. Falkenberg's very name also relates to this symbolism. He is the falcon from the lofty heights of the intellect ("Berg" = "Mountain") who will attempt to eat up the madness.

Meanwhile, madness is indeed eating up Baron Zorn, who turns out to be the real villain of the piece, despite the fact that it is his son who physically commits the film's three murders. The only clue as to the culprit at the beginning, however, is Emil's striking apricot colored shirt, which not only singles him out with what was a very fashionable color in the 1970s but also echoes the red roses that always accompany the murders. In fact, the baron's own repressed neuroses and sado-masochistic bloodlust have been psychologically transferred to his son, much as Cardillac inherited his mother's lust for jewels in Hoffmann's "Mademoiselle de Scudéry." Zorn exerts a powerful influence over his son and actually wills him to his various acts of murder in some undefined manner. We see a hand unlocking Emil's bedroom door, which, of course, belongs to Zorn, who uses his son to release his own murderous instincts while pretending to be protecting him. Thus, it is the baron who is corrupt, not his offspring. His "bad blood" is insanity. Wicking also wanted to put across a socialistic subtext, referencing a corrupt aristocracy and oppressed villagers, though in the end the villagers prove to be no more enlightened that Zorn himself.

From the very beginning of the project, Wicking was keen to take a more intellectual approach to the story. Not only did he originally want a Shakespearean quotation for the title ("Blood will have Blood") but he also wanted to include various details which cannot be seen in the finished film. One of these was to show the young medical student, Carl Richter (Paul Jones), reading Goethe's *Farbenlehre* or *Theory of Color*, to demonstrate the kind of intellectual radical he is.[3]

We are introduced to Richter when he first encounters Elizabeth, who has escaped from her Aunt Hilda's protection during a coach journey. The coach is returning them from the sanatorium where Elizabeth has been taken for a consultation with Dr. Falkenberg. Elizabeth has a brief sexual relationship with Richter before being recaptured by her family: he rows her on a lake near his woodland dwelling, and the languid shot of the oar in the water provides a symbol of the intercourse that obviously follows.

Elizabeth also has a psychic rapport with her brother Emil. Indeed, all the women in the film are psychic to some extent. When Elizabeth reaches out her hand from the carriage, we cut to a shot of Emil back at the mansion, who echoes the gesture. When she and her aunt arrive home, Baron Zorn is found by the grave of his wife reciting a slightly altered version of Psalm 38: "My loins are filled with a sore disease." It is useful to read through the whole psalm fully to understand the baron's state of mind. The most significant passages are:

> *There is* no soundness in my flesh because of thine anger; neither *is there any* rest in my bones because of my sin. For mine iniquities are gone over mine head; as an heavy burden they are too heavy for me. My wounds stink, *and* are corrupted because of my foolishness.
>
> I am troubled; I am bowed down greatly; I go mourning all the day long. For my loins are filled with a loathsome *disease*: and *there is* no soundness in my flesh. I am feeble and sore broken ... and my groaning is not hid from thee. My heart panteth, my strength faileth me: as for the light of mine eyes, it also is gone from me. My lovers and my friends stand aloof from my sore; and my kinsmen stand afar off.

The baron believes himself to be both physically and morally corrupt: Corrupt blood has caused his own insanity and the incestuous attraction of his offspring. Like David in Psalm 38, he too is alone. "He has no friends," says one of the villagers. His attempt to cure his children of their mutual attraction has resulted in their enforced separation, a state of affairs that has only increased their longing for each other. Even when they are briefly reunited on the impressive staircase of the mansion, they are soon separated. "It can only be the way I say it will be," the baron insists. That this encounter takes place on the staircase is psychologically significant, when we consider (again) Freud's interpretation of staircases as sexual dream symbols: "Steps, ladders or staircases, or, as the case may be, walking up or down them, are representations of the sexual act."[4] Emil in his '70s orange shirt can be seen as a Gothicized symbol of oppressed youth, desperate for freedom.

After the first murder, red roses are scattered over the corpse, accompanied by Harry Robinson's reverberant and highly evocative string pizzicato effect, which adds a considerable resonance to the psychotic fragmentation of the imagery. As the roses are pulled apart and scattered, so too are the musical pitches, plucked in apparently random sequences. Roses are traditionally scattered over the dead. "With dropping wings, ye Cupids come, And scatter roses on her tomb," sings the chorus at the end of Purcell's *Dido and Aeneas* of 1689, but here there is no lament or tranquility, only anguish and disorder, and the music is an essential element in conveying that sense of disorder, both of Emil's personality and the murder itself. The roses are also reminiscent of the red flowers in the graveyard scene of Hitchcock's *Vertigo*, and they serve a similar function as symbols of obsession and death; also, rather obviously, they remind us of the blood that Baron Zorn believes is tainted by insanity.

Michael Hordern's eccentric priest now makes his first appearance, muttering to himself in the driving rain. The priest is the counterpart of Zorn's misguided beliefs, against which, in proto–Richard Dawkins style, Dr. Falkenberg and Dr. Richter apply their scientific, rational approach. Whereas the priest and Zorn believe in demons of the mind, the two doctors believe in the exorcising powers of psychology. Perhaps significantly, the priest arrives in cloudy weather; Falkenberg will arrive later in the clear light of day.

Another kind of blood-letting now takes place in Elizabeth's bedroom. It is not murder this time, but nonetheless represents another form of oppression. Aunt Hilda (Yvonne Mitchell) produces a scarificator (the genuine article, according to Peter Sykes, who borrowed this particular example from the Wellcome Museum in London[5]). This she uses to purge Elizabeth's body of the bad blood that her father believes to be coursing through her veins. It of course does nothing but weaken her and draw her closer to the grave, which is no doubt Zorn's subconscious desire anyway. (Roderick Usher goes so far as to bury his sister alive, so impatient is he to cleanse his family of inherited insanity. Similarly, later in the film, Zorn stares at the family portrait and mutters, "Perhaps death is the only answer.") Emil is quite aware of what his father is doing to Elizabeth. "You're not going near her," he shouts. "You're not going to hurt her any more."

It is rather contradictory of Baron Zorn to invite the Mesmer-inspired Dr. Falkenberg to assist him in his quest: It is not blood but the brain that Falkenberg aims to cure. He does not believe in demons of the mind but rather in unlocking memories and uncovering repressed psychosexual drives. Like Mesmer, who was ostracized by his critics, Falkenberg has also been "booted out of Vienna" (the line echoes that of the much camper Dr. Pretorius in *Bride of Frakenstein* [dir. James Whale, 1935]). Mesmer's temporary cure of blind pianist Maria Theresa Paradies caused a sensation in Vienna in 1777. He realized that her condition was not physical but hysterical; her parents refused to let him continue with the treatment so the cure ultimately failed, and this, combined with accumulating resentment and gossip, finally forced Mesmer into exile. Like Falkenberg, he was distrusted by the medical establishment of his day. As his biographer Vincent Buranelli explains, "Every cure made him more notorious."[6]

The coach that brings Falkenberg to the Zorn residence crashes in the forest, in a moonlit, rain-soaked scene that would be echoed the following year in Freddie Francis' Gothic adventure *The Creeping Flesh*. In that film, the coach is carrying an ancient, fossilized skeleton—the personification of evil. The coach in *Demons* is carrying quite the opposite kind of passenger, for accompanying Falkenberg is that young man of highly enlightened, liberal ideas, Dr. Richter. While he goes off to fetch help, Emil is once more released from his room and there is another murder with more rose petals and pizzicato. Then, Falkenberg arrives at the mansion. "Well, where is my patient?" he asks and, on cue, Zorn appears. Zorn has sent for Falkenberg to treat his son, but it is indeed Zorn himself who is the real patient here, and Falkenberg has already worked this out for himself. When, some time before, Elizabeth was sent to him for treatment, he realized that there was nothing wrong with her. Her weakness and disorientation—even her incestuous feelings—were all Zorn's doing. Confusingly, Zorn's shirt is covered with blood. At first, this suggests that he is the murderer. The supposition is strengthened due to our having just seen him remembering his wife's suicide, her naked body similarly covered in blood; but the blood stains are due to his having helped to dispose of his son's latest victim, which he later submerges in the lake.

Now Falkenberg sets up his Mesmeric equipment in Zorn's study. The paraphernalia resembles Mesmer's infamous "banquet," which consisted of a tub of magnetized water from which metal bars, bent at right angles, protruded. The ends of these were then applied to whatever part of the anatomy needed to be "cured." What Mesmer was actually doing was using hypnosis as a method of alleviating hysterical pain. The "banquet" itself merely created a placebo effect. The "banquet" in *Demons of the Mind* is a portable version of Mesmer's larger apparatus, with a clockwork device that spins a candle around the 360 degrees of a circle, the purpose of which is to induce hypnosis. Falkenberg explains: "The basic principle of my work assumes the existence of a universal fluid—a force uniting all living things, which this magnetic apparatus can harness to bring your innermost secrets to the surface."

Like Mesmer, Falkenberg knows that hypnosis works but does not understand what it is or how it works. As Buranelli points out, when a subject was hypnotized, "Deep layers of his personality revealed themselves during the trance. He could recall long-forgotten events, often far back in his childhood, by somehow switching from the conscious mind to his subconscious."[7] Zorn tells Falkenberg about "the legends of insanity and incest" in the family, and confesses to feeling like an animal at times, prowling in the night, affected by the moon. "A bloodlust courses through me," he admits. He sees himself as an evil demon of the forest. In other words, he is describing the symptoms of lycanthropy, but we are not expected to assume that he physically transforms into a werewolf, Oliver Reed–style. Wicking was very much a horror revisionist, intent on exploring the psychological reality behind such fantasy myths, and Zorn's problem is entirely psychological. We see a close-up of his eyes with the hypnotizing candle revolving within it—another visual echo of the main title of *Vertigo*—as he confesses to "dreams of sexual fear." Again he expresses his fear that his children have inherited his own madness. It was to protect them from this illness that he married a healthy peasant woman; but he drove her to madness and suicide, and he is now convinced that the children have succumbed to the family malaise.

Buranelli usefully observes, "Mesmerism coalesced with the other elements of Romanticism—excessive individualism, passionate protest, uncanny fantasy, Gothic horror, and sentimental belief in nature,"[8] adding that Poe was fascinated by its "artistic usefulness. Mesmerism, will dominating will, thought transference, sleep-waking [*sic*], occult knowledge—these moved his imagination and made him feel that they could be the ingredients of popular literature."⁹ Horror films are similarly fascinated by hypnosis because of its ability to access repressed aspects of the psyche. This can lead to schizophrenic activity that may be interpreted as just that or, as in the case of Roger Corman's *The Tomb of Ligeia* (1964), as the actual invasion of another personality from beyond the grave into a living mind. (Elizabeth Shepherd's Lady Rowena in that film is regressed back to her childhood and then overwhelmed by the personality of the dead Ligeia, who plans to return from the grave via Rowena's body. A similar sort of thing happens in *Blood from the Mummy's Tomb* but without the hypnosis element.) Hammer frequently had recourse to hypnosis. In *The Devil Rides Out* both Christopher Lee's Duc de Richelieu and Charles Gray's Mocata indulge in it, either to dominate others and extract information from them or to access higher spiritual powers. In *Hands of the Ripper*, Eric Porter's psychoanalyst, Dr. Pritchard, hypnotizes Angharad Rees' Anna to uncover her childhood trauma, but ends up triggering the spirit of her father, Jack the Ripper, who lives within her. In *The Evil of Frankenstein*, Peter Cushing's baron witnesses a stage performer called Zoltan (played by Peter Woodthorpe), whom he employs to access the disturbed brain of his creation; but Zoltan uses his power to force the creature to steal things for him, which ultimately leads to murder.

Right at the beginning of horror films, hypnosis featured in *The Cabinet of Dr. Caligari*, again in order to control the will of others. In fact, this is not strictly possible, as no one can be made to do things under hypnosis against their own will. That aspect of the popular image of hypnosis was created largely by George du Maurier in his 1894 novel *Trilby*, which introduced the character of Svengali to the world. In fact, as Robin Waterfield explains, hypnotism only works if there is a willing rapport between hypnotist and the subject: "All hypnotism must be consensual to a degree: you cannot be hypnotized unless you want to. In fact, it is arguable that the hypnotist's role is not to *do* anything as such, but just to facilitate your own spontaneous entry into a trance state. All hypnosis may be self-hypnosis."¹⁰

The peasants of *Demons of the Mind* use less sophisticated methods of keeping the powers of evil at bay. A scarecrow, personifying death, is driven, scapegoat-style, from the village. "We carry death to the fires of hell," the villagers and children chant. "All is well. All is well." Boys rap out a rhythm on drums in a shot somewhat reminiscent of equally enthusiastic fellows of the Hitler Youth in Leni Riefenstahl's *Triumph of the Will*, and the comparison, even if unintended, is apt, as the irrational power of ritual is what Sykes and Wicking are presumably demonstrating here. The prostitute played by Virginia Wetherell is also persecuted by the villagers but is eventually invited to the mansion to take part in a psychological experiment, of which more in a moment. Before that happens, however, Emil attempts to make contact with Elizabeth, who is locked in an adjacent room. As he moves a large mirror it cracks, distorting his reflection in a time-honored visual metaphor for mental disorder, but brother and sister eventually manage to overcome this obstacle, embrace and kiss rather more passionately than perhaps they should. And it is because of this unnerving development that Zorn shouts at Richter, when he arrives, that it would have been better if Elizabeth had never been born. He now blames his apparently healthy peasant wife for this: "There is a heritage of disorder in her blood, which to my inexpressible grief Elizabeth has fallen heir to as my son did before her," but Zorn is wrong. It is his own madness that has affected everything around him, including the house, which Sykes has photographed at oblique angles to suggest (very successfully) its malign atmosphere.

Falkenberg insists that the attraction between Zorn's children is quite natural given the violent death of their mother, and proposes the aforementioned experiment involving the prostitute, who is dressed in a blue gown and made to impersonate Elizabeth. Such a substitution will apparently give Falkenberg an enhanced opportunity to work on Emil's incestuous feelings at one remove, but unfortunately it all goes wrong. The experiment also vaguely echoes the scene in *Rebecca* when Maxim is outraged with his new wife's appearance at the top of the stairs, dressed in a costume identical to the one Rebecca wore at a previous Manderley ball. In *Demons of the Mind* it is Emil who stands at the top of the stairs. The prostitute is with Aunt Hilda. Understandably disturbed by Emil's confusion ("Is she Elizabeth or not?" he wonders), she runs out. Emil chases her and, outraged by having been tricked, murders her as well. Falkenberg now accuses Zorn outright: "Emil is the instrument of your lust. You let him out so that he could kill." Zorn is more concise and relies on Shakespeare: "Blood will have blood." And indeed it does. After Emil kills Aunt Hilda, he snatches the real Elizabeth. Zorn shoots Falkenberg in a spectacular murder scene (perhaps one of the most shocking death scenes in any Hammer film). He also dispatches Emil but, as already mentioned, fails to finish off Elizabeth before the villagers stake him in a ritual act that demonstrates in no uncertain terms the overthrow of enlightenment and scientific inquiry in the most gruesome fashion. Christianity (or at least a particularly unenlightened form of it) is the ultimate victor in a film Richard Dawkins should wholeheartedly endorse. The ultimate message follows Nietzsche's virulent condemnation of Christianity with remarkable accuracy:

> One should not embellish or dress up Christianity: it has waged a *war to the death* against this *higher* type of man, it has excommunicated all the fundamental instincts of this type, it has distilled evil, the *Evil One*, out of these instincts—the strong human being as the type of reprehensibility, as the "outcast." Christianity has taken the side of everything weak, base, ill-constituted, it has made an ideal out of *opposition* to the preservative instincts of strong life; it has depraved the reason even of the intellectually strongest natures by teaching men to feel the supreme values of intellectuality as sinful, as misleading, as *temptations*. The most deplorable example: the depraving of Pascal, who believed his reason had been depraved by original sin while it had only been depraved by his Christianity![11]

19

Peter Pan in *Straight on Till Morning*

(dir. Peter Collinson, 1972)

Hammer's final psychological thriller (before the re-formed company's *The Resident* in 2011) was an oblique, and very bleak, response to J.M. Barrie's *Peter Pan* 1904 play and 1911 novel. The title derives from a line spoken by Peter Pan after Wendy asks where he lives: "Second to the right and then straight on till morning."[1] The film adapts this line when Brenda (Rita Tushingham) asks Peter (Shane Briant) where his bedroom is. "You go up these stairs," he explains. "You take the first star on the right and go straight on till morning." There are many other overt references to Barrie's famous and troubling play throughout John Peacock's unusual screenplay for this tale of a beautiful psychopath—a kind of Lucifer figure—who kills beautiful women, takes their money (which he keeps carelessly in the kitchen drawer), and lives in a fantasy Never Never land of his own creation in which he need never grow up. It was originally designed as part of a two-film package about "Women in Terror," and was linked with *Fear in the Night*, the "Night" and "Morning" imagery of the titles deliberately providing opposing "balance."

As I mentioned earlier, the Lost Boys in Barrie's play are "the children who fall out of their prams when the nurse is looking the other way. If they are not claimed in seven days they are sent far away to the Never Never Land."[2] The personal Never Never land of Briant's Peter is his creepy bedroom where he murders his adoring women, all of whom have been polished off before the action begins. (We only catch glimpses of them in flashbacks.) Peter's personal history is sketchy, and revealed only in terms of the fairy tale imagery Brenda enjoys and to whom he relates his story. His real name is apparently Clive. His surname, according to a postman who makes a delivery, is Price. When his father died he became "King Clive" and had to grow up. "He was now king and had great responsibilities; but he didn't want to grow up, so he ran away—never to see the queen [his mother] again." He kills the women who come into his life because they apparently don't really love him, they "just want people to know [they] could catch the prince of them all." He keeps meeting these "princesses," "but they all wanted him for his beauty" and he came "to loathe beauty for what it had done to him." So he gets rid of them all. Rather like the character played by Karlheinz Böhm in Michael Powell's *Peeping Tom* (1960), who films the death throes of his victims, Peter-Clive makes tape recordings of their last moments. He has amassed quite a library of spools, which are all carefully arranged on his living room shelves.

Straight on Till Morning is very much a story about the "awfully big adventure" of death, and at one stage Peter-Clive addresses this infamous line from *Peter Pan* to his dog, who shares the name of the fairy in the play, Tinker: "What an awfully big adventure!" he laughs as he embraces the dog, which he also murders in his Never Never Land bedroom for the same reason that he killed the women. They were all too beautiful, and when Brenda washes Tinker and presents him to his owner with a pink ribbon in his hair, Tinker also become too beautiful. Immaturity is in itself a kind of death. Adam and Eve had to eat the apple from the Tree of Knowledge in order to gain maturity. If they had not, they would forever have remained God's children in the Garden of Eden. The eating of the apple was a *felix culpa* (a "fortunate crime") for it replaced the charms of innocence with the benefits of experience. A child who never grows up is dead to experience and maturity, lost as he is in his enchanting world of illusions. The final stage direction of Barrie's play alludes to this. Wendy reaches out to Peter Pan, wanting to embrace him, but he draws back. Wendy comments "Yes, I know," and leaves him behind.

Poster for *Straight on Till Morning* (dir. Peter Collinson, 1972) with portraits of Shane Briant and Rita Tushingham.

> In a sort of way he understands what she means by "yes, I know," but in most sorts of ways he doesn't. It has something to do with the riddle of his being. If he could get the hang of the thing his cry might become "To live would be an awfully big adventure!" but he can never quite get the hang of it, and so no one is as gay as he.[3]

Barrie's use of the word "gay" is not intended in its current homosexual sense, though it might be appropriate if it was, considering the longing Peter has for his mother, his penchant for male company, his inability to have children, and his exclusion from "straight" society; but Barrie's meaning is otherwise quite clear. Peter Pan is unable to form a relationship with reality. He will never be able to marry, raise a family and consequently become an adult—and these are problems Barrie suffered from himself. Impotent, unable to love, compelled to control, he was, in fact, a pedophile who took refuge in fantasy. Significantly, in one of the earlier stage directions of *Peter Pan* he insists that Peter is never touched by any one in the play. "No one must ever touch me,"[4] he insists. In other words, he is doomed to his Never Never land. The Lost Boys, whom he leads in their adventures, are similarly dead to the world. There is also a way in which they should be regarded as actually dead: children "who fall out of their prams when the nurse is looking the other way. If they are not claimed in seven days they are sent far away to the Never Never Land. I'm Captain," says Peter.

"What fun it must be," Wendy suggests, to which Peter replies, "Yes, but we are rather lonely. You see, Wendy, we have no female companionship."[5]

This problem is shared by Peter-Clive in the film, so when the gauche, un-beautiful Brenda comes into his life, he hopes for a soulmate whom he won't have to murder, who won't love him merely for his beauty. Wendy-Brenda wants him to give her a baby, even though she is just as immature as he is. Together they fantasize about this impossibility. Peter-Clive buys an elaborate fairy tale cot and an array of cuddly toys, but their love can never be consummated. They cuddle each other in bed like babes in the wood. Conversely, the "mature" characters who balance this Never Never Land fantasy (Caroline, played by Katya Wyeth, and Jimmy Lindsay, her employer, played by Tom Bell) enjoy mutually exploitative sex but do not love each other.

Peter asks Brenda about her mother so as "to remember a bit more about mine." He looks tearful at that confession, implying that there was a considerable coolness in their relationship, which reflects the plight of *Peter Pan*'s Lost Boys, all of whom are similarly looking for their mothers. Indeed, Briant's limpid, huge eyes are the most expressive thing about his androgynous face. They can weep like a true Lost Boy, but he is also very good at staring, suggesting an emptiness that no amount of murders can fill. Viewers familiar with Barrie's play will know that the Lost Boys build Wendy a house (the origin of the popular Wendy Houses still on sale for children today) and idolize her as the mother they have all lost:

> WENDY (*stroking the pretty thing*): Lovely, darling house.
> FIRST TWIN: And we are your children.
> WENDY (*affecting surprise*): Oh?

OMNES (*kneeling, with outstretched arms*): Wendy lady, be our mother! (*Now that they know it is pretend, they acclaim her greedily.*)
WENDY (*not to make herself too cheap*): Ought I? Of course it is frightfully fascinating; but you see I am only a little girl; I have no real experience.
OMNES: That doesn't matter. What we need is just a nice motherly person.
WENDY: Oh dear, I feel that is just exactly what I am.[6]

The story about a boy who never grows up is in some ways a kind of infantilized version of Ibsen's play *A Doll's House* (1879) in which Nora wakes up from her childish fantasy of a marriage, realizing that if she is to become a real woman, she must leave her domineering and patronizing husband and "grow up." She leaves her doll's house of a home—which one might see a parallel of in Barrie's play with its childish Wendy House— and starts her life in the cold, real but ultimately more rewarding world of maturity.

In *Straight on Till Morning* the opposite happens. The psychopathic Peter-Clive sinks deeper into his infantile psychosis, murdering women, being irresponsible with money and even more unrealistic about reality. The action begins with a pre-credits prologue. The first shot shows the rooftops and chimney pots of working class housing in Liverpool (though it was in fact shot in London). Such an opening suggests the kind of kitchen-sink realism with which Rita Tushingham had become associated since her starring role in *A Taste of Honey* (dir. Tony Richardson, 1961). Against this grim reality we hear a voice-over of Brenda telling a fairy story. This is the fantasy to which she hopes to escape. She refers to a magic garden (a reference, perhaps, to the Garden of Eden, where all infantilism belongs). She longs to find a handsome prince, and lies to her worried mother (Claire Kelly) that she is pregnant and wants to find a father for her baby. The mother is left alone to wander gloomily through her daughter's empty bedroom.

The main titles, with Roland Shaw's vibes and rhythm jazz accompaniment, depict the London of the early 1970s at a time when London had just begun to stop swinging and was uneasily contemplating a much less optimistic period. We see Brenda emerge from Earls' Court tube station and bump into Peter. Collinson's erratic and rapid cross-cutting during the scene that follows is unlike anything in any previous Hammer film and not only reflects the psychotic split personality of Peter himself but also the somewhat fragmented spirit of the times, which was simultaneously looking backwards and forwards, and anxiously shuffling from one foot to the other in an attempt to believe that nothing had changed. In a sense, the 1970s were a kind of Never Never Land themselves, which was being ruthlessly wrenched towards the realization that the optimism of the 1960s was well and truly over.

Significantly, Peter is looking at a child's comic featuring the popular BBC children's TV show *The Magic Roundabout*, which was also popular with a great many young adults at the time. The scene's soundtrack dialogue and atmosphere is continually interrupted by Peter's interior monologue, in which he arranges his thoughts in terms of fairy tale phrases. Collinson also intercuts scenes in which Peter entertains his last female victim (played by Annie Ross)—a drunk, Elizabeth Taylor parody of a woman, dependent, maudlin, wealthy—and expendable. "For new games we need new magic," Peter tells her. When he turns out the light, the woman stumbles. "What are we going to do?" she asks. "Never never mind," he replies. "Where are we going?" she asks as she follows him upstairs. "Never Never Land." The door closes, she screams, and we cut back to the opening situation with a shot of Peter nearly knocking down Caroline, who crosses the road in front of his car. The whole sequence is a masterpiece of cinematic invention, and the most experimental thing Hammer ever filmed. Collinson repeats the process later, intercutting Brenda's visit to a housing benefit office with shots of Caroline and Jimmy making love. Brenda looks down at a real little lost boy, who is eating a chocolate. He has chocolate all over his mouth. Collinson is also careful to include an Indian couple, the woman wearing a sari, reflecting the changing population of London at a time when many more immigrants were settling in the city.

Brenda finds herself a dingy flat, which is very different from her fantasy of a fairy tale castle, and it doesn't take her long to find herself a job in Jimmy's boutique, where she encounters Caroline. Caroline offers her a room in her house. This is hardly a fairy tale castle either, but Brenda is convinced she will find "the prince of princes" who is "waiting for her." Back in Peter's house, he burns the portrait of his last woman. (One thinks of Robert Browning's poem "My Last Duchess" with its line "That's my last Duchess painted on the wall,/Looking as if she were alive.")

In the boutique, Brenda meets Joey (James Bolan) who isn't quite the prince of princes, but seems a possible stepping stone to that ideal. Swinging London was largely defined by its party culture. Alan Gibson's comparable psychopath drama *Goodbye Gemini*, made two years earlier, is punctuated with party scenes, and Collinson obliges with a party scene in Caroline's house. Brenda proves to be a gauche, clumsy embarrassment who tries to hit it off with Joey while Jimmy has an argument with Caroline. Jimmy is angry with Caroline because Brenda's presence in the house will seriously cramp his style. Later, Brenda goes out to buy cigarettes and the somewhat opportunistic Caroline takes Joey rather than Jimmy to bed. When Brenda returns and hears them at it in the bedroom, her fairy tale dreams suffer another blow.

Wandering through the brutalist exterior walkways of Dennis Crompton's South Bank Centre, Brenda cuts a very forlorn figure. Filmed at night, the situation looks even more bleak. We hear Annie Ross singing the film's title song "Straight on Till Morning, All Through the Night," the melody of which appears in similarly muted form in later sections of Shaw's underscore. In the midst of this architectural nightmare, more the environment of Dr. Who and the Daleks than of people, Brenda comes upon Peter's dog, Tinker. Peter watches her from a walkway overhead. He calls out the dog's name but Brenda doesn't hear him. Instead, noticing an address on Tinker's collar, she thinks of a plan. She takes the dog home, gives it a bath, ties a pretty pink ribbon in its head and thus unintentionally signs its death warrant, for she now returns the dog to the beauty-hating Peter.

Art director Scott MacGregor made sure that Peter has appropriate pictures on the wall of his hall: a collection of prints by the seventeenth-century French printmaker Jacques Callot (incidentally, a great favorite of E.T.A. Hoffmann). They are from Callot's series *Les Grandes Misères de la Guerre*, which depict the atrocities and violence unleashed on civilians during the Thirty Years War. There are tortures, battle scenes, atrocities, and, in the eleventh and most famous print of the group (which takes pride of place in Peter's arrangement of them), a group of corpses are shown hanging from a tree. These seem singularly appropriate decorations for such a disturbed personality, whose apartment is in a terrible mess, as Peter doesn't believe in housework. "Cleaning up is a woman's job," he says, which again echoes the general sexual stereotyping of Barrie's play in which women are devoted mothers and men die "like English gentlemen." Peter realizes what Brenda has done: "You went to a lot of trouble to meet me in my house," and she explains that she wants him to give her a baby. The naive unreality of the situation certainly has the quality of *Peter Pan* despite the 1970s setting with its inevitable orange lamps and white plastic swivel chairs. Together, they forge a bargain: If Brenda will clean up and look after Peter "then," as Peter obliquely puts it, "we shall see." Brenda has given herself a fairy tale name of Rosalba, but Peter calls her Wendy, hoping, like the Lost Boys, that she will be a mother for him, someone who will not merely want his own beauty but care about him as a person. Fortunately, Brenda is not beautiful. But first, Tinker is sacrificed on the altar of this new un-beautiful relationship. Tinker is now too beautiful, and so the unfortunate animal is slashed with a Stanley knife in a truly disturbing scene. Even more worryingly, Peter makes sure the dog's yelps of terror are captured on his tape recorder.

And so Brenda moves in. She compliments Peter on his spiral staircase—a fashionable feature in homes of the time, but also, as we are now very much aware, a Freudian symbol of sexuality. In this case, the sexuality is repressed, indeed stunted, but it is nonetheless there. Peter now presents Wendy with a "Wendy House" by giving her the spare room in which a cradle has been installed. They play with Peter's tape recorder, into which Brenda reads her ridiculous fairy tales. She tries to talk to him during the night but Peter sends her away—a sexual rejection that leads her wistfully to brush her hair like Virgie in *The Nanny* but with no Nanny of her own to comfort her.

Meanwhile, Caroline has been visited by Brenda's mother, who is understandably worried about her strange daughter. When Caroline finds Tinker's lead with its address tag, she pays Peter a visit. This is a big mistake, as Caroline is beautiful, and while Brenda is out on a shopping trip with Peter's money, Caroline is invited in for a coffee. She licks her lips provocatively and the clock ticks neurotically, intercut with Brenda's desperate attempts to make herself beautiful with facials, wigs and new clothes. When Caroline follows Peter up the sexual spiral staircase and Peter says "you're beautiful," her seconds are obviously numbered. The Stanley knife once more does its work as Brian Probyn's camera zooms into Caroline's dead eye, yet again echoing Janet Leigh's lifeless, accusatory stare at the end of the *Psycho* shower scene.

Brenda returns looking absurd in an enormous wig, her face made up, her clothes overdone. Peter returns from disposing of Caroline's body and washes his hands, and here the '70s orange lampshade serves a symbolic function as it, and its similarly orange lead suggest the blood we cannot actually see being washed down the sink. Upstairs,

Brenda finds Peter's knife and we think she is about to discover Caroline's corpse in the wardrobe, but instead a gigantic Teddy bear (surely an apt symbol for Peter's monstrous infantility and reminiscent of the Teddy bear in *The Nanny*) tumbles out instead.

Crestfallen, Peter asks her why she has made herself beautiful. He smears her lipstick and tries to remove her wig, reducing her to her normal mousy self—which is just as well. But when Peter returns to the outside world, he reads about the missing Caroline and Brenda in the paper. The police are on his trail and something must be done about it. He refuses to allow Brenda to go out and after an argument he decides that the time has come to dispatch her as well. Peter calls his tape recordings "magic," and he now promises Brenda some particularly special magic. He leaves her alone in his bedroom and plays her recordings of his previous murders. Brilliantly edited, this scene intercuts the tape recorder with shots of Brenda flat against the wall and radiator, in a scene which anticipates the surreal claustrophobia of David Lynch's *Eraserhead* (1977). "You mustn't be beautiful," Peter cries, assuring her that he loves her. Brenda, desperate to escape, runs past the Callot engravings to find the front and later the back door locked. Peter follows her in tears, assuring her that he could never hurt her, but the eventual outcome is uncertain. Collinson implies that Brenda has gone the way of all the other females in Peter's life, by cutting to a shot of him on the bed listening to his recordings of Brenda reading out the now deeply ironic fairy tale cliché of Princess Rosalba and the Prince of Princes "Living happily ever after." We are then shown three shots of the empty house, before the final shot takes us into the empty street, and Annie Ross sings the sad little nursery rhyme title song once more.

Coming as it did towards the end of Hammer's long, immensely imaginative contribution to British cinema history, *Straight on Till Morning* was an attempt at a new direction. Unlike the following year's *Frankenstein and the Monster from Hell* (dir. Terence Fisher), which was a gloriously melancholy death knell for the Studio That Dripped Blood, *Straight on Till Morning* could, under more conducive circumstances, have pumped fresh blood into Hammer's singularly depleted veins. Unfortunately, this failed to come to pass, and Hammer, along with the rest of the British film industry, virtually disintegrated by the end of the decade.

But even if *Straight on Till Morning* had managed to change Hammer's direction, its final image of a spinning spool of tape suggests that something more than just this particular film was at an end. Britain was becoming a grimmer, less imaginative place. Collinson's vision of London in this film represents the very end of the flower-powered 1960s with its euphoric optimism. A different mood was emerging, and *Straight on Till Morning* suggested the kind of place it was going to be: a country where fantasy would be seen as infantile and the ideals of free love, anarchism and hedonism as ultimately dangerous rather than liberating. Only seven years after the release of *Straight on Till Morning*, Margaret Thatcher and the British Conservative party would root out such "immature" indulgences from British society, despite the fact that Thatcher's economic ideals flew in the face of reality and were the epitome of fantasy themselves. The prosaic ideals of a woman for whom shop-keeping was the rule of thumb and there was "no such thing as society" were the symptom, not the cause of the sick new Britain that emerged in the 1980s. The late 1970s were also less affluent times, with industrial unrest, an oil crisis, and a declining economy. As a consequence, the desire for surrealism, experimentation, fantasy, psychological exploration and most of all *imagination* also began to wither away. Hammer fought back against the new mood with its refreshingly unrealistic TV series *Hammer House of Horror* and *Hammer House of Mystery and Suspense* in the 1980s, both of which included some gripping psychological thrillers of their own. These included, in the first series, the aforementioned "Rude Awakening," "The Silent Scream" (with Peter Cushing as an ex–Nazi animal trainer who entraps an ex-con), an iron-curtain reworking of *So Long at the Fair*, with Susan George and Patrick Mower called "Czech Mate," and, in the second series, a revenge drama starring David Langdon from the long-running TV series *Upstairs Downstairs*, called "Last Video and Testament"; but most of the episodes from both series were supernatural rather than classically *psychologial* thrillers in a direct line of descent from Clouzot and Hitchcock. ("The Two Faces of Evil," for example, is about an all too real doppelgänger.)

British television has always been a useful barometer of British society. It had once been dominated by fantasy serials like *The Avengers*, it was unafraid to screen occult thrillers, its children's drama was second to none, and there were always the BBC's weekly Plays for Today. But by the end of the 1980s, the so-called age of Aquarius had turned into the nightmare of twenty-first century British television with its prosaic conformity, its reality shows, its soap operas, and interminable obsession with current affairs. What fantasy there now is, is high on digital effects but much lower on narrative conviction; and as for British cinema, it was as if Hammer had never existed.

Straight on Till Morning bravely waved goodbye to British fantasy and social optimism. It was also the last of Hammer's astonishingly effective, if often highly derivative cycle of psychological thrillers, among which are some of Hammer's very best and most underrated films.

Chapter Notes

Introduction

1. Christopher Lee, *Tall, Dark and Gruesome,* London: Victor Gollancz, 1997, p. 187.
2. Jimmy Sangster, *Inside Hammer,* Richmond: Reynolds and Hearn, 2001, p. 73.
3. Donald Spoto, *The Art of Alfred Hitchcock—Fifty Years of His Films,* London: Fourth Estate, 1992, p. 314.
4. Robert Murphy, *Sixties British Cinema,* London: British Film Institute, 1992, pp. 194–195.
5. Bram Stoker, *Dracula,* London: Constable, 1904, p. 19.
6. Thomas de Quincey, "On Murder Considered as One of the Fine Arts," http://www.gutenberg.org/files/10708/10708-8.txt
7. *Loc. cit.*
8. *Loc. cit.*
9. *Loc. cit.*
10. Søren Kierkegaard (trans. Alastair Hannay), *The Seducer's Diary,* London: Penguin, 2007, p. 61.
11. *Op. cit.,* p. 10.
12. Friedrich Nietzsche (trans. R. J. Hollingdale), *Twilight of the Idols/The Anti-Christ,* Harmondsworth: Penguin, 1981, p. 115 ("The Anti-Christ).
13. Evelyn Piper, *The Nanny,* London: Collins/Fontana, 1965, p. 59.
14. Sigmund Freud (trans. James Strachey), *The Interpretation of Dreams,* Harmondsworth: Penguin, 1983, p. 356.
15. *Op. cit.,* p. 357.
16. Ernest Jones, *Essays in Applied Psycho-Analysis,* London/Vienna: International Psycho-Analytical Press, 1923, pp. 78–86.
17. John Dover Wilson, *What Happens in Hamlet,* Cambridge: Cambridge University Press, 1970, p. 218.

Chapter 1

1. Jimmy Sangster, *Inside Hammer,* Richmond: Reynolds and Hearn, 2001, p. 25.
2. *Op. cit.,* p. 82.
3. John Fleming, "Fanatic" in *The House of Hammer* magazine (ed. Dez Skinn), Vol. 2, No. 3, London: Top Sellers, Dec. 1977, p. 22.
4. Derek Prouse, "Les Diaboloqies" in *Sight and Sound,* Winter, 1955/56, http://old.bfi.org.uk/sightandsound/reviews/releases/les-diaboliques.php
5. Lotte H. Eisner (trans. Roger Greaves), *The Haunted Screen,* London: Secker & Warburg, 1973, p. 337.
6. E. F. Benson *Night Terrors: The Ghost Stories of E. F. Benson* ("At Abdul Ali's Grave"), Ware: Wordsworth, 2012, p. 55.
7. Sigmund Freud (trans. James Strachey), *Art and Literature* ("The Uncanny"), Harmondsworth: Penguin, 1985, p. 345.
8. *Op. cit.,* p. 363.
9. *Op. cit.,* p. 364.
10. *Op. cit.,* pp. 364–365.
11. *Op. cit.,* p. 366.
12. *Op. cit.,* p. 367.
13. *Op. cit.,* pp. 372–373.

Chapter 2

1. Donald Spoto, *The Art of Alfred Hitchcock—Fifty Years of His Films,* London: Fourth Estate, 1992, p. 85.
2. Dennis Gifford, *A Pictorial History of Horror Movies,* London: Hamlyn, 1973, p. 190.
3. Spoto, *The Art of Alfred Hitchcock,* p. 299.
4. Pierre Boileau and Thomas Narcejac, *Vertigo (D'Entre les Morts)* London, Bloomsbury, 1997, p. 26.

5. *Op. cit.*, p. 79.
6. *Op. cit.*, p. 54.
7. Spoto, *The Art of Alfred Hitchcock*, p. 283.
8. Boileau and Narcejac, *Vertigo*, p. 154.
9. Jill Purce, *The Mystic Spiral—Journey of the Soul*, London: Thames and Hudson, 1974, pp. 7–9.
10. Spoto, *The Art of Alfred Hitchcock*, p. 280.
11. Hanns Eisler and Theodor Adorno, *Composing for the Films*, Oxford: Oxford University Press, 1948, p. 78.
12. Spoto, *The Art of Alfred Hitchcock*, p. 325.
13. E. T. A. Hoffmann (ed. Christopher Lazare), *Tales of Hoffmann* ("The Doubles"), New York: A. Wyn, 1946, p. 224.
14. Claude Chabrol interviewed for the television documentary *Music for the Movies: Bernard Herrmann* (dir. Joshua Waletzky, 1992).
15. Spoto, *The Art of Alfred Hitchcock*, p. 317.
16. Robert Bloch, *Psycho*, London: Bloomsbury, 1997, p. 12.
17. *Op. cit.*, p. 7.
18. Edgar Allan Poe, *The Complete Illustrated Stories and Poems of Edgar Allan Poe*, London: Chancellor Press, 1988, p. 166 ("Ligeia").
19. *Op. cit.* ("Ligeia"), p. 173.
20. Robert Donnington, *Wagner's 'Ring' and Its Symbols*, London: Faber and Faber, 1974, p. 193.
21. *Op. cit.*, p. 213.

Chapter 3

1. Edgar Allan Poe, *The Complete Illustrated Stories and Poems of Edgar Allan Poe* ("The Fall of the House of Usher"), London: Chancellor Press, 1988, p. 52.
2. C. G. Jung (trans. Richard & Clara Winston), *Memories, Dreams, Reflections*, London: Flamingo/Fontana, 1989, pp. 182–184.
3. Sigmund Freud (trans. James Strachey), *The Interpretation of Dreams*, Harmondsworth: Penguin, 1983, p. 157.
4. *Op. cit.*, p. 156.
5. Mike Murphy (ed.), ("An Interview with Francis Searle"), *Dark Terrors* magazine, no. 9, St Ives: Mike Murphy, Nov. 1994, p. 37.

Chapter 4

1. Peter Haining (ed.) *The Frankenstein Omnibus* (Villiers de l'Isle Adam [trans. Florence Crewe-Jones], "The Future Eve"), London: Orion, 1994, pp. 113–114.

2. Jimmy Sangster, *Inside Hammer*, Richmond: Reynolds and Hearn, 2001, p. 14.
3. Sigmund Freud (trans. James Strachey), *Art and Literature* ("The Uncanny"), Harmondsworth: Penguin, 1985, p. 356.
4. *Op. cit.*, pp. 357–358.
5. John Lash, *Twins and the Double*, London: Thames and Hudson, 1993, p. 17.
6. E. T. A. Hoffmann (ed. Christopher Lazare), *Tales of Hoffmann* ("The Doubles"), New York: A. Wyn, 1946, p. 234.
7. Edgar Allan Poe, *The Complete Illustrated Stories and Poems of Edgar Allan Poe* ("William Wilson"), London: Chancellor Press, 1988, p. 48.
8. Freud, *Art and Literature*, p. 358n.

Chapter 5

1. Frederic Spotts, *Hitler and the Power of Aesthetics*, London: Hutchinson 2002, p. 85.
2. Søren Kierkegaard (trans. Alastair Hannay), *The Seducer's Diary*, London: Penguin, 2007, p. 3.
3. *Op. cit.*, p. 6.
4. Spotts, *Hitler and the Power of Aesthetics*, p. 93.
5. E. T. A. Hoffmann (ed. Christopher Lazare), *Tales of Hoffmann* ("Mademoiselle de Scudéry"), New York: A. Wyn, 1946, p. 86.
6. Dirk Bogarde, *Cleared for Take-Off*, London: Viking/Penguin, 1995, pp. 18–20.
7. Hoffmann, *Tales of Hoffmann* ("Mademoiselle de Scudéry"), pp. 55–56.
8. *Op. cit.* ("Mademoiselle de Scudéry"), p. 44.
9. *Op. cit.* ("Mademoiselle de Scudéry"), p. 43.
10. *Op. cit.* ("Mademoiselle de Scudéry"), p. 54.
11. *Op. cit.* ("Mademoiselle de Scudéry"), pp. 86–87.
12. *Op. cit.* ("Mademoiselle de Scudéry"), p. 70.
13. *Op. cit.* ("Mademoiselle de Scudéry"), pp. 86.
14. Jimmy Sangster, *Inside Hammer*, Richmond: Reynolds and Hearn, 2001, p. 41.
15. Donald Spoto, *The Art of Alfred Hitchcock—Fifty Years of His Films*, London: Fourth Estate, 1992, p. 284.
16. Dirk Bogarde, *A Particular Friendship*, London: Viking/Penguin, 1989, pp. 55–56.

Chapter 6

1. Monty Norman in conversation with the author.

2. Richard Noll, *The Aryan Christ—The Secret Life of Carl Gustav Jung*, London: Macmillan, 1997, p. 60 (Richard Webster quoted).
3. Sigmund Freud (trans. James Strachey), *The Interpretation of Dreams*, Harmondsworth: Penguin, 1983, p. 174.
4. Edgar Allan Poe, *The Complete Illustrated Stories and Poems of Edgar Allan Poe* ("The System of Doctor Tarr and Professor Fether"), London: Chancellor Press, 1988, p. 547.
5. *Op. cit.*, pp. 553–554.
6. *Op. cit.*, p. 556.
7. *Op. cit.*, p. 561.

Chapter 7

1. Jimmy Sangster, *Inside Hammer*, Richmond: Reynolds and Hearn, 2001, p. 75.
2. *Op. cit.*, p. 76.
3. Robert Murphy, *Sixties British Cinema*, London: British Film Institute, 1992, p. 199.
4. Sangster, *Inside Hammer*, p. 76.
5. Sigmund Freud (trans. James Strachey), *The Interpretation of Dreams*, Harmondsworth: Penguin, 1983, pp. 559–560.
6. C. G. Jung (ed.), *Man and His Symbols*, London: Aldus Books, 1964, pp. 189–191.
7. Jane Austen, *Northanger Abbey*, Ware: Wordsworth, 1995, p. 24.
8. Ann Radcliffe, *The Mysteries of Udolpho*, London: Oxford University Press, 1966, pp. 248–249.
9. *Op. cit.*, p. 662.
10. *Op. cit.*, p. 330.
11. Austen, *Northanger Abbey*, pp. 118–119.
12. Sangster, *Inside Hammer*, p. 73.

Chapter 8

1. Jimmy Sangster, *Inside Hammer*, Richmond: Reynolds and Hearn, 2001, pp. 82–83.
2. *Op. cit.*, p. 81.
3. Edmund Burke, *A Philosophical Enquiry into the Origin of Our Ideas of the Sublime and Beautiful*, Oxford: Oxford University Press, 1990, p. 36.
4. *Op. cit.*, p. 40.
5. *Op. cit.*, p, 67.
6. *Op. cit.*, p. 60.
7. *Op. cit.*, p. 69.
8. Susan Sontag, *On Photography*, London: Penguin, 2002, p. 85.
9. *Op. cit.*, p. 188.
10. Allen Eyles, Robert Adkinson & Nicholas Fry (eds.), *The House of Horror—The Complete Story of Hammer Films*, London: Lorrimer, 1984, p. 10.
11. Sangster, *Inside Hammer*, p. 85.
12. *Op. cit.*, p. 82.
13. *Op. cit.*, p. 85.
14. *Op. cit.*, p. 82.
15. *Op. cit.*, pp. 82–83.

Chapter 9

1. Josephine Tey, *Brat Farrar*, London: Arrow, 2009, pp. 144–145.
2. *Op. cit.*, p. 135.
3. Ken Russell, *A British Picture—An Autobiography*, London: Southbank Publishing, 2008, p. 58.
4. Christopher Frayling (ed.), *Vampyres—Lord Byron to Count Dracula* (Johann Ludwig Tieck, "Wake Not the Dead"), London: Faber and Faber, 1991, pp. 165–166.
5. Gottfried Bürger, "Lenore," http://www.artofeurope.com/burger/burg1.htm
6. E. T. A. Hoffmann (ed. Christopher Lazare), *Tales of Hoffmann* ("The Vow"), New York: A. Wyn, 1946, pp. 278–279.
7. *Op. cit.*, p. 283.
8. Jimmy Sangster, *Inside Hammer*, Richmond: Reynolds and Hearn, 2001, p. 87.
9. *Op. cit.*, p. 89.
10. Dirk Bogarde, *Snakes and Ladders*, London: Chatto & Windus,, 1978, p. 237.
11. Charles Dickens, *A Tale of Two Cities & A Christmas Carol*, London: Hazell, Watson & Viney (no date), p. 405.
12. E. F. Benson, *Mapp and Lucia*, London: Black Swan, 1989, p. 270.
13. Sangster, *Inside Hammer*, pp. 89–90.
14. Hoffmann, *Tales of Hoffmann*, pp. 271–273.

Chapter 10

1. An earlier literary manifestation of a piano playing vampire occurs in Eric, Count Stenbock's 1894 story, "A True Story of a Vampire," in which Count Vardalek plays, like Carl Ravna, a Chopin nocturne "very beautifully." (See *Dracula's Guest—A Connoisseur's Collection of Victorian Vampire Stories*, ed. Michael Sims, London: Bloomsbury, 2010, p. 321.)
2. Stephen Wildman, *Edward Burne-Jones: Victorian Artist-Dreamer*, New York: Metropolitan Museum of Art, 1998, p. 15.

3. Donald Spoto, *The Art of Alfred Hitchcock—Fifty Years of His Films*, London: Fourth Estate, 1992, p. 172.
4. Paul Branch, *Chrestomathy* ("Discomforting Merrymaking: The Parties of Hitchcock"), Vol. 8 2009, http://chrestomathy.cofc.edu/documents/vol8/branch.pdf p. 20.
5. Arthur Schnitzler (trans. J. M. Q. Davies), *Dream Story*, Harmondsworth: Penguin, 1999, p. 94.
6. *Op. cit.*, p. 26.
7. *Op. cit.*, p. 45.
8. *Op. cit.*, pp. 66–67.

Chapter 11

1. August Strindberg (trans. Michael Meyer), *Strindberg Plays: Two—The Dance of Death, A Dream Play, The Stronger* ("A Dream Play"), London: Methuen, 1982, p. 175.
2. Sigmund Freud (trans. James Strachey), *The Interpretation of Dreams*, Harmondsworth: Penguin, 1983, p. 162.
3. *Loc. cit.*
4. *Op. cit.*, p. 165.
5. *Op. cit.*, pp. 214–215.
6. *Op. cit.*, pp. 156–157.
7. *Op. cit.*, p. 320.
8. *Op. cit.*, pp. 462–463.
9. *Op. cit.*, p. 472.
10. *Op. cit.*, p. 521.
11. E. T. A. Hoffmann (ed. Christopher Lazare), *Tales of Hoffmann*, New York: A. Wyn, 1946, pp. 84–85.
12. Jimmy Sangster, *Inside Hammer*, Richmond: Reynolds and Hearn, 2001, p. 91.
13. Wilkie Collins, *The Woman in White*, London: Heron Books (no date), p. 34.
14. Freud, *The Interpretation of Dreams*, p. 470.
15. Sangster, *Inside Hammer*, p. 91.

Chapter 12

1. Bram Stoker, *Dracula*, London: Constable, 1904, p. 27.
2. John Fleming, "Fanatic" in *The House of Hammer* (ed. Dez Skinn), No. 15, London: Top Sellers, Dec. 1977, p. 23.
3. *Loc. cit.*
4. *Op. cit.*, p. 22.
5. Sigmund Freud (trans. James Strachey), *The Interpretation of Dreams*, Harmondsworth: Penguin, 1983, pp. 384–365.
6. Bram Stoker, *Dracula*, p. 43.
7. *Op. cit.*, p. 32.
8. Fleming, "Fanatic," p. 21.
9. Donald Spoto, *The Art of Alfred Hitchcock—Fifty Years of His Films*, London: Fourth Estate, 1992, p. 131.
10. *Op. cit.*, p. 314.
11. *Op. cit.*, p. 327.
12. Fleming, "Fanatic," p. 21.

Chapter 13

1. Jimmy Sangster, *Inside Hammer*, Richmond: Reynolds and Hearn, 2001, p. 93.
2. The Marquis de Sade (trans. Alan Hull Walton), *Justine, or The Misfortunes of Virtue*, London: Neville Spearman, 1964, p. 153.
3. *Op. cit.*, p. 158.
4. *Op. cit.*, p. 169n.
5. David J. Skal, *The Monster Show—A Cultural History of Horror*, London: Plexus, 1993, p. 226.
6. John Betjeman, *A Pictorial History of English Architecture*, London: John Murray, 1972, p. 102.
7. John Betjeman, *Collected Poems* ("Executive"), London: John Murray, 1993, pp. 312–313.
8. E. T. A. Hoffmann (ed. Christopher Lazare), *Tales of Hoffmann* ("Mademoiselle de Scudéry"), New York: A. Wyn, 1946, p 80.

Chapter 14

1. Donald Spoto, *The Art of Alfred Hitchcock—Fifty Years of His Films*, London: Fourth Estate, 1992, p. 54 (Alfred Hitchcock in an address to the Film Society at the Lincoln Center, 1974).
2. Jimmy Sangster, *Inside Hammer*, Richmond: Reynolds and Hearn, 2001, p. 103.
3. John Osborne, *Look Back in Anger*, London: Faber and Faber, 1978, p. 20.
4. Sangster, *Inside Hammer*, p. 108.
5. J. M. Barrie, *The Plays* ("Peter Pan"), London: Hodder and Stoughton, 1928, p. 31.
6. *Op. cit.*, p. 32.
7. E. T. A. Hoffmann (ed. Christopher Lazare), *Tales of Hoffmann*, New York: A. Wyn, 1946, p. 45.
8. Edgar Allan Poe, *The Complete Illustrated Stories and Poems of Edgar Allan Poe* ("The Tell-Tale Heart"), London: Chancellor Press, 1988, p. 244.

Chapter 15

1. John Coldstream, *Dirk Bogarde—The Authorised Biography*, London: Weidenfeld & Nicolson, 2004, p. 267.
2. *Op. cit.*, p. 282.
3. Ingrid Pitt, *Life's a Scream—The Autobiography of Ingrid Pitt*, London: William Heinemann, 1999, p. 209.
4. Donald Spoto, *The Art of Alfred Hitchcock—Fifty Years of His Films*, London: Fourth Estate, 1992, p. 310.

Chapter 16

1. Jimmy Sangster, *Inside Hammer*, Richmond: Reynolds and Hearn, 2001, p. 124.
2. E. T. A. Hoffmann (ed. Christopher Lazare), *Tales of Hoffmann* ("The Doubles"), New York: A. Wyn, 1946, p. 234.
3. *Op. cit.*, p. 224.
4. *Op. cit.*, p. 253.
5. Théophile Gautier (adapted by G. F. Monkshood and Ernest Tristan), *Madamoiselle de Maupin*, London: Greening & Co., 1911, p. 301.
6. Hoffmann, *Tales of Hoffmann*, pp. 253–254.
7. Sangster, *Inside Hammer*, p. 124.
8. *Op. cit.*, p. 125.
9. Philip Martell in conversation with the author.
10. Sigmund Freud (trans. James Strachey), *The Interpretation of Dreams*, Harmondsworth: Penguin, 1983, p. 490.

Chapter 17

1. James Joyce, *Ulysses*, London: Penguin, 2000, p. 42.
2. *Loc. cit.*
3. Maurice Maeterlinck (trans. Laurence Alma Tadema), *Pelléas and Mélisande*, London: Walter Scott Publishing Co., 1910, p. 78.

Chapter 18

1. Chris Wicking commentary to the DVD of *Demons of the Mind*, Studio Canal/Optimum Releasing, 2006.
2. "To the Devil ... The Death of Hammer," documentary (dir. Marcus Hearn) for the DVD of *To the Devil a Daughter*, Studio Canal/Optimum Releasing 2006 (Chris Wicking interviewed).
3. Wicking, commentary to the DVD of *Demons of the Mind*.
4. Sigmund Freud (trans. James Strachey), *The Interpretation of Dreams*, Harmondsworth: Penguin, 1983, p. 472.
5. Peter Sykes commentary to the DVD of *Demons of the Mind*, Studio Canal/Optimum Releasing, 2006.
6. Vincent Buranelli, *The Wizard from Vienna*, London: The Scientific Book Club/Peter Owen, 1977, p. 86.
7. *Op. cit.*, p. 13.
8. *Op. cit.*, p. 219.
9. *Op. cit.*, p. 221.
10. Robin Waterfield, *Hidden Depths—The Story of Hypnosis*, London: Macmillan, 2002, p. 18.
11. Friedrich Nietzsche (trans. R.J. Hollingdale), *Twilight of the Idols/The Anti-Christ* ("The Anti-Christ"), Harmondsworth: Penguin, 1981, p. 117.

Chapter 19

1. J. M. Barrie, *The Plays* ("Peter Pan"), London: Hodder and Stoughton, 1928, p. 29.
2. *Op. cit.*, p. 32.
3. *Op. cit.*, p. 90.
4. *Op. cit.*, p. 30.
5. *Op. cit.*, p. 32.
6. *Op. cit.*, p. 49.

Bibliography

Austen, Jane, *Northanger Abbey,* Ware: Wordsworth, 1995.
Barrie, J. M., *The Plays,* London: Hodder and Stoughton, 1928.
Benson, E. F., *Mapp and Lucia,* London: Black Swan, 1989.
_____, *Night Terrors: The Ghost Stories of E. F. Benson,* Ware: Wordsworth, 2012.
Betjeman, John, *Collected Poems,* London: John Murray, 1993.
_____, *A Pictorial History of English Architecture,* London: John Murray, 1972.
Bloch, Robert, *Psycho,* London: Bloomsbury, 1997.
Bogarde, Dirk, *Cleared for Take-Off,* London: Viking/Penguin, 1995.
_____, *A Particular Friendship,* London: Viking/Penguin, 1989.
_____, *Snakes and Ladders,* London: Chatto & Windus, 1978.
Boileau, Pierre, and Narcejac, Thomas, *Vertigo (D'Entre les morts),* London: Bloomsbury, 1997.
Branch, Paul, *Chrestomathy,* Vol. 8, 2009, http://chrestomathy.cofc.edu/documents/vol8/branch.pdf
Buranelli, Vincent, *The Wizard from Vienna,* London: The Scientific Book Club/Peter Owen, 1977.
Bürger, Gottfried, "Lenore," http://www.artofeurope.com/burger/burg1.htm
Burke, Edmund, *A Philosophical Enquiry into the Origin of our Ideas of the Sublime and Beautiful,* Oxford: Oxford University Press, 1990.
Coldstream, John, *Dirk Bogarde—The Authorised Biography,* London: Weidenfeld & Nicolson, 2004.
Collins, Wilkie, *The Woman in White,* London: Heron Books (no date).
Dickens, Charles, *A Tale of Two Cities & A Christmas Carol,* London: Hazell, Watson & Viney (no date).
Eisler, Hanns, and Adorno, Theodor, *Composing for the Films,* Oxford: Oxford University Press, 1948.
Eisner, Lotte H. (trans. Roger Greaves), *The Haunted Screen,* London: Secker & Warburg, 1973.
Eyles, Allen, Adkinson, Robert, and Fry, Nicholas (eds.), *The House of Horror—The Complete Story of Hammer Films,* London: Lorrimer, 1984.
Fleming, John, "Fanatic" in *The House of Hammer* magazine (ed. Dez Skinn), Vol. 2, No. 3, London: Top Sellers, Dec. 1977.
Frayling, Chrisopher, *Vampyres—Lord Byron to Count Dracula,* London: Faber and Faber, 1991.
Freud, Sigmund (trans. James Trachey), *Art and Literature,* Harmondsworth: Penguin, 1985.
_____ (trans. James Strachey), *The Interpretation of Dreams,* Harmondsworth: Penguin, 1983, p. 356.
Gautier, Théophile (adapted by G. F. Monkshood and Ernest Tristan), *Madamoiselle de Maupin,* London: Greening & Co., 1911.
Gifford, Dennis, *A Pictorial History of Horror Movies,* London: Hamlyn, 1973.
Haining, Peter (ed.), *The Frankenstein Omnibus,* London: Orion, 1994.
Hearn, Marcus, and Barnes, Alan, *The Hammer Story,* London: Titan, 2007.
Hoffmann, E. T. A. (ed. Christopher Lazare), *Tales of Hoffmann,* New York: A. Wyn, 1946.
Jones, Ernest, *Essays in Applied Psycho-Analysis,* London/Vienna: International Psycho-Analytical Press, 1923.
Joyce, James, *Ulysses,* London: Penguin, 2000.
Jung, C. G. (ed.), *Man and His Symbols,* London: Aldus Books, 1964.

_____ (trans. Richard and Clara Winston), *Memories, Dreams, Reflections,* London: Flamingo/Fontana, 1989.
Kierkegaard, Søren (trans. Alastair Hannay), *The Seducer's Diary,* Harmondsworth: Penguin, 2007.
Lash, John, *Twins and the Double* London: Thames and Hudson, 1993.
Lee, Christopher, *Tall, Dark and Gruesome,* London: Victor Gollancz, 1997.
Maeterlinck, Maurice (trans. Laurence Alma Tadema), *Pelléas and Mélisande,* London: Walter Scott Publishing Co., 1910.
Murphy, Mike (ed.), *Dark Terrors* magazine, no. 9, St Ives: Mike Murphy, Nov. 1994.
Murphy, Robert, *Sixties British Cinema,* London: British Film Institute, 1992.
Nietzsche, Friedrich (trans. R. J. Hollingdale), *Twilight of the Idols/The Anti-Christ,* Harmondsworth: Penguin, 1981, p. 115 ("The Anti-Christ").
Noll, Richard, *The Aryan Christ—The Secret Life of Carl Gustav Jung,* London: Macmillan, 1997.
Osborne, John, *Look Back in Anger,* London: Faber and Faber, 1978.
Piper, Evelyn, *The Nanny,* London: Collins/Fontana, 1965.
Pitt, Ingrid, *Life's a Scream—The Autobiography of Ingrid Pitt,* London: William Heinemann, 1999.
Poe, Edgar Allan, *The Complete Illustrated Stories and Poems of Edgar Allan Poe,* London: Chancellor Press, 1988.
Prouse, Derek, "Les Diaboliques" in *Sight and Sound,* Winter, 1955/56, http://old.bfi.org.uk/sightandsound/reviews/releases/les-diaboliques.php
Purce, Jill, *The Mystic Spiral—Journey of the Soul,* London: Thames and Hudson, 1974.
Quincey, Thomas de, "On Murder Considered as One of the Fine Arts," http://www.gutenberg.org/files/10708/10708-8.txt.
Radcliffe, Ann, *The Mysteries of Udolpho,* London: Oxford University Press, 1966.
Russell, Ken, *A British Picture—An Autobiography,* London: Southbank Publishing, 2008.
Sade, Donatien Alphonse François, Marquis de (trans. Alan Hull Walton), *Justine, or The Misfortunes of Virtue,* London: Neville Spearman, 1964.
Sangster, Jimmy, *Inside Hammer,* Richmond: Reynolds and Hearn, 2001.
Schnitzler, Arthur (trans. J. M. Q. Davies), *Dream Story,* Harmondsworth: Penguin, 1999.
Skal, David J., *The Monster Show—A Cultural History of Horror,* London: Plexus, 1993.
Sontag, Susan, *On Photography,* London: Penguin, 2002.
Spoto, Donald, *The Art of Alfred Hitchcock—Fifty Years of His Films,* London: Fourth Estate, 1992.
Spotts, Frederic, *Hitler and the Power of Aesthetics,* London: Hutchinson, 2002.
Stoker, Bram, *Dracula,* London: Constable, 1904.
Strindberg, August (trans. Michael Meyer), *Strindberg Plays: Two—The Dance of Death, A Dream Play, The Stronger,* London: Methuen, 1982.
Tey, Josephine, *Brat Farrar,* London: Arrow, 2009.
Waterfield, Robin, *Hidden Depths—The Story of Hypnosis,* London: Macmillan, 2002.
Wildman, Stephen, *Edward Burne-Jones: Victorian Artist-Dreamer,* New York: Metropolitan Museum of Art, 1998.
Wilson, John Dover, *What Happens in Hamlet,* Cambridge: Cambridge University Press, 1970.

Documentary Films Cited

Music for the Movies: Bernard Herrmann (dir. Joshua Waletzky, 1992).
"To the Devil…The Death of Hammer" documentary on the Studio Canal/Optimum Releasing release of *To the Devil a Daughter* (dir. Peter Sykes, 1976).

Hammer's American Titles

BRITISH	AMERICAN
The Full Treatment	Stop Me Before I Kill
Taste of Fear	Scream of Fear
Fanatic	Die! Die! My Darling!
The Witches	The Devil's Own

Index

Numbers in ***bold italics*** indicate pages with photographs.

Ackland, Joss 154, 155, 156, 157
Adams, Ansel 89, 92
Addinsell, Richard 154
Adorno, Theodor 35
Alfred Hitchcock Presents (TV series) 55
And Soon the Darkness 87
Anderson, Gerry 28
Anderson, Judith 23
Andrews, Dana 134
Angel Street see *Gaslight*
The Anniversary 40
Antonioni, Michelangelo 133
Arliss, Leslie 51, 154
Arnold, Sir Malcolm 50–51
Arrival of a Train at La Ciotat Station 155
Ashton, Roy 123
Asquith, Anthony 162
Asylum 72
Austin, Jane 73, 79, 85; *Northanger Abbey* 73, 80, 85
The Avengers 182

Bacon, Sir Francis 85
Baker, Roy Ward 32, 40, 72
Bankhead, Tallulah 7, 39, 55, 122, 126–127
Banks, Don 28, 35, 129, 133
Banks, Leslie 4
Barrie, J.M. 141, 175, 176, 177, 180; *Peter Pan* 141, 175, 176–178, 180
Barry, Sir Charles 169
Barry, Edward Middleton 169
Barry, John 90
Baskcombe, Lawrence 46
Bass, Saul ***29***, 90
Bates, Florence 23

Bates, Ralph 160, 162
Bath, Hubert 154
Baudelaire, Charles 34, 108, 127
Beethoven, Ludwig van 51
Bell, Tom 177
Bennett, Compton 51
Bennett, Jill ***138***, 139
Bennett, Richard Rodney 25, 28, 35, 140, 141, 142, 146, 148
Benson, E.F. 18, 102
Bergman, Ingrid 26, ***27***
Berlioz, Hector 13, 30, 51
Bernard, James 75, 77, 109, 110
Betjeman, Sir John 132
Billsden, Anne 125
Billy Liar 116
Binder, Maurice 31
Bird, Norman 90, 91
The Birds 35, 36–37, 109, 128
Bishop, Julie 106
Black, Isobel 108, ***111***
Black, Stanley 28, 67, 90
"The Black Cat" 56
The Black Cat (dir. Edgar G. Ulmer) 106
Blackboard Jungle 11
Blackmail 22
Bloch, Robert 37–38
Blood from the Mummy's Tomb 94, 117, 168, 173
Blow Up 133–134
Bogarde, Dirk 45, 58–59, 65, 102, 106, 110, 128, 148
Böhm, Karlheinz 176
Boileau, Pierre 28–29, 31
Bolan, James 179
Bonney, John 103
Brabin, Charles 76

Brahm, John 113, 154
Branch, Paul 109–110
Brat Farrar 8, 96, 139
Brett, Ingrid 149
Briant, Shane 7, ***168***, 169, 175, ***176***, 177
Bride of Frankenstein 171
The Brides of Dracula 45, 77
Brooks, Mel 31, 128, 129
Brooks, Richard 11
Brousse, Liliane 89, 90, 98, ***107***
Browning, Robert 179
The Browning Version 162
Bruce, Brenda 118
Bunny Lake Is Missing 137
Buñuel, Luis 30
Buranelli, Vincent 170
Burckhardt, Carl 58
Bürger, Gottfried 98–99; "Lenore" 98–99
Burke, Edmund 88, 89
Burne-Jones, Sir Edward 109
Burrell, Sheila 44, 96
Bushell, Anthony 100

The Cabinet of Dr. Caligari 159, 173
Callot, Jacques 179, 181
Captain Clegg 100
Caravaggio 79
Carreras, Sir James 1, 65
Carreras, Michael 1, 24, 87–90, ***88***, 93, 94, 100, 155
Carroll, Leo G. 26
Carstairs, John Paddy 100
Casablanca 49
Cash on Demand 100
Cass, Henry 154
Cat People 2

Chabrol, Claude 36
Chagrin, Francis 64
Chekhov, Michael 26
Chirico, Georgio de 84, 93
Chopin, Frédéric 82, 85, 102, 109
Christie, Julie 116
Cilento, Diane 68, **68**
Clayton, Jack 100
Clouzot, Henri-Georges 1, 7, 11–21, **12**, 55, 59, 83, 85, 158, 182
Clouzot, Véra 12, 14
Coldstream, John 148
Collins, Joan 160, 163
Collins, Wilkie 45, 118; *The Moonstone* 45
Collinson, Peter 7, 175, **176**, 179, 181
Conan Doyle, Sir Arthur 59
Cook, Vera 110
Cooper, George A. 120
Cooper, Giles 162
Cooper, Wilkie 90, 92
Coppélia 19
Le Corbeau 11, 14
Corman, Roger 26, 113, 173
Cossins, James 164
Count Dracula—A Gothic Romance 124
Craig, Wendy 25, 139
Crawford, Joan 127
The Creeping Flesh 171
Crescendo 7, 13, 28, 30, 39, 51, 52, 60, 76, 152–159, **153**, 165
Crompton, Dennis 179
Cruise, Tom 110
The Curse of Frankenstein 11, 49–50, 58, 64
The Curse of the Werewolf 97, 103
Curtiz, Michael 49
Cushing, Peter 45, 49, 100, 160, 162, 165, 182
"Czech Mate" 182

Dalí, Salvador 26, 28, 70
Damien: Omen II 36
The Damned 100
Dangerous Moonlight 113, 154, 159
Daniel, Jennifer 106, 109, **111**
Darnborough, Anthony 106
Dauphin, Claude 7, **68**, 69, 79
Daves, Delmer 28
David, Jacques-Louis 33
Davies, Bette Ann 39, 44
Davion, Alexander 97

Davis, Bette 7, 8, 25, 39, 40, 53, 55, 137, 141, 146
Dawkins, Richard 170, 174
Day, Robert 90
Dearden, Basil 148
Death in Venice 92
Deception 49, 53
Delibes, Léo 19
Demons of the Mind 7, 167–174, **168**
Denham, Maurice 101, 131, 142
De Quincey, Thomas 2, 4–5
The Devil Rides Out 77, 144, 149, 150, 173
"The Devil's Elixir" 52
The Devil's Own see *The Witches*
Les Diaboliques (dir. Henri-Georges Clouzot) 1, 5, 11–21, **12**, 22, 33, 47, 74, 77, 78, 83, 85, 86, 94, 102, 120, 131, 152, 154, 158, 160, 163, 166
Diamond, Arnold 90
Dickens, Charles 102
Dickinson, Thorold 62, 83
Dido and Aeneas 170
Die! Die! My Darling see *Fanatic*
Dietrich, Marlene 127
Diffring, Anton 51
Dior, Christian 11
Disney, Walt 144
Dix, William 138, **138**, 143
A Doll's House 178
Donnington, Robert 38
"The Doubles" 28, 36, 52, 152–154
Dracula (dir. Terence Fisher, 1958) 4, 11, 46, 64, 81, 122–125
Dracula A.D. 1972 53, 162
Dracula Has Risen from the Grave 100
Dracula—Prince of Darkness 18, 20, 118
Drake, Tom Y. 72
A Dream Play 114
Dream Story (Traumnovelle) 110–112
du Maurier, Daphne 22; *Rebecca* 22, 24
du Maurier, George 173; *Trilby* 173
Dyall, Valentine 42

The Eagle Has Landed 169
Edison, Thomas Alva 49
Eisler, Hanns 35

Eisner, Lotte H. 16
Elliott, Denholm 119
Eraserhead 181
Evans, Clifford 106, 109
L'Ève Future 49
The Evil of Frankenstein 134, 173
Ewers, Hanns Heinz 54
Eyck, Peter van 55, 56, **56**, 59, 61, 62, 65
Eyes Wide Shut 110

Falk, Peter 18
"The Fall of the House of Usher" 26, 42–43, 167, 170
Fanatic 7, 39, 121, 122–127, **123**, 141
Farbenlehre 169
Faust 38
Fear in the Night 8, 13, 14, 133, 142, 160–166, **161**, 175
The Fearless Vampire Killers 108, 109
Ffrangcon-Davies, Gwen 147
Fisher, Terence 2, 18, 35, 39, 45, 49, **50**, 51, 58, 66, 67, 68, 77, 89, 92, 97, 100, 106, 108, 118, 181
Fontaine, Joan 22, 23, **23**, 24, 25, 55, 147, 148, **149**
Forbidden Planet 3
Forwood, Anthony 44
Francis, Freddie 1, 5, 18, 39, 96, **97**, 100, 101, 104, 105, **107**, 113, **115**, 117, 118, 128, **129**, 131–135, 170
Franju, Georges 48, 105
Frankel, Cyril 7, 26, 147, 149, **149**, 150
Frankenstein and the Monster from Hell 11
Frankenstein Created Woman 49
Franklin, Pamela 8, 139
Franklin, William 65
French, Daniel Chester 78
Freud, Sigmund 2, 9, 19–20, 34, 38, 44, 52, 54, 70, 78–79, 84, 114–116, 120, 124, 159, 169; *The Interpretation of Dreams* 70, 114–116, 159; "The Uncanny" 19–20
Fuest, Robert 87
The Full Treatment 7, 8, 9, 27, 28, 31, 39, 67–72, **68**, 76, 79, 81, 98, 128, 130, 131

Galeen, Henrik 54
Garbo, Greta 127

Gaslight 62
Gautier, Théophile 153; *Mademoiselle du Maupin* 153
Gavin, John **32**
Geeson, Judy 160, **161**
George, Susan 182
Gershwin, George 154
Ghosts 161
Gibson, Alan 7, 53, 132, 152, **153**, 154, 155, 157, 158, 179
Gilling, John 41, 97, 100
The Glass Mountain 154
Goethe, Johann Wolfgang von 38, 169; *Farbenlehre* 169; *Faust* 38
Goldoni, Lelia 8, **129**, 131, 133, 134, 166
Goodbye Gemini 179
Götterdämmerung 35–36
Granger, Farley 109
Grant, Arthur 101, 163
Grant, Cary 55, 134, 150
Gray, Charles 173
Gray, Nadia 39, 88
Green, Guy 55, 56, **56**, 74
Guest, Val 7, 9, 11, 67–72, **68**, 79

Hagen, Friedrich Wilhelm 113
Haggard, H. Rider 23
Haley, Bill 11
Hall-Say, Sir Richard 41
Hamilton, Guy 4
Hamilton, Patrick 62
Hamlet 7–8, 9, 140–141
Hammer House of Horror (TV series) 119, 182; "Rude Awakening" 119, 182; "The Silent Scream" 182; "The Two Faces of Evil" 182
Hammer House of Mystery and Suspense (TV series) 182; "Czech Mate" 182; "Last Video and Testament" 182
Hands of the Ripper 47, 173
Hangover Square 113, 154
Hardy, Robert 167
Hardy, Robin 150
Harlow, John 154
"The Haunted Palace" 42–43
Hayes, Tubby 154, 157, 158
Helmore, Tom 30
Hemmings, David 133, 162
Henreid, Paul 48–49, **50**, 51, 53
Herrmann, Bernard 30, 31, 32, 33, 34, 35, 36, 54, 154
High Anxiety 31, 128, 129
Hills, Gillian 168

Hinds, Anthony 13, 108, 110, 127
Hird, Thora 100
Hitchcock, Alfred 1, **3**, 7, 9, 11, 16, 22–40, **23**, **27**, **29**, **39**, 41, 48, 50, 55, 59, 62, 65, 69–70, 72, 79, 87, 90, 92, 106, 109, 110, 121, 122, 127, 128, 130, 136, 143, 148, 152, 163, 171, 182
Hitler, Adolf 57, 58, 63, 87
Hobart, Rose 67
Hoffmann, E.T.A. 19, 20, 28, 52, 58, 59–62, 82, 99, 105, 117, 134, 144, 152, 156, 162, 169, 179; "The Devil's Elixir" 52; "The Doubles" 28, 36, 52, 152–154; "Mademoiselle de Scudéry" 56, 58, 59–62, 117, 134, 144, 162, 169; "The Sandman" 19; "The Vow" 99, 105
Holt, Seth 1, 7, 73–86, **74**, 94, 137, **138**, 140–146, 155
Hopkins, Miriam 67
Hopper, Edward 84
Hordern, Michael 167, **168**, 170
House of Usher 26, 113
Houston, Donald **88**
Hurst, Brian Desmond 113
Huysmans, Joris Karl 108
Hysteria 5, 8, 13, 27, 28, 30, 31, 34, 35, 36, 60, 62, 71, 81, 128–136, **129**, 142, 162, 166, 167

I Walked with a Zombie 2
Ibsen, Henrik 161, 166, 178; *A Doll's House* 178; *Ghosts* 161; *John Gabriel Borkman* 161, 166; *The Wild Duck* 166
Inferno 113
The Innocents 100, 118
The Interpretation of Dreams 70, 114–116, 159
Island of Lost Souls 58, 131
Isle of the Dead 84
The Italian 73

James, Sid 44, 46, 47, 152
James Bond films 31, 133, 157
Jayne, Jennifer 131
Jessop, Clytie 30, 47, **115**, 118, 120
The Jewel of Seven Stars 94
John Gabriel Borkman 161, 166
Johnson, Fred 77, 78, 82
Johnson, Katie 17
Jones, Ernest 9

Jones, Paul 169
Joseph, Wilfred 122, 141
Journey to the Far Side of the Sun 28
Joyce, James 160
Joyce, Yootha 123, 125
Jung, Carl Gustav 23, 31, 37, 43, 46, 70, 79, 125, 161
Justine 128, 130–131

Kant, Immanuel 114
Karloff, Boris 106
Karsh, Yousuf 70, 79
Kaufman, Maurice 125
Keats, Viola 149
The Keeper 72
Kelly, Claire 178
Kenton, Erle C. 58, 131
Kidman, Nicole 110
Kierkegaard, Søren 5–6, 57
The Kiss of the Vampire 35, 69, 87, 89, 102, 106–112, **107**, **109**, **111**, 119, 132, 150, 156
Kitchen, Michael 162
Knight, David **115**, 117
Krauss, August 114
Kubrick, Stanley 110, 166

The Ladykillers 17
Lamont, Duncan 149
Lang, Fritz 12, 13, 15, 16
Langdon, David 182
Lapotaire, Jane 155, 157
Larquey, Pierre 14
Lash, John 52
"Last Video and Testament" 182
Last Year at Marienbad 93, 102
Laughton, Charles 58, 131
Laura 134
Lawrence, Quentin 100
Lee, Christopher 4, 46, 66, 72, 75, 76, 81, 83, 100, 107–108, 128, 162, 173
The Legend of Hill House 169
Legend of the Seven Golden Vampires (L.P.) 116
Leigh, Janet 17, 32, **32**, 33, 34, 35, 93, 127, 180
"Lenore" 98–99
Leroux, Gaston 59; *The Mystery of the Yellow Room* 59
Lewin, Albert 85
Lewis, Matthew 73
Lewis, Ronald 68, 75
Liberace 51
Lifeboat 127
"Ligeia" 38

Index

Lincoln, Abraham 78
Lind, Gillian 163
Linden, Jennie 8, 24, 113, **115**, 116
Lloyd, Marie 34
Lom, Herbert 58, 76
Look Back in Anger 139
Lord, Justine 90
Lorre, Peter 15
Losey, Joseph 100
The Lost Weekend 28
Love Story 51
Loy, Myrna 76
Lugosi, Bela 106
Lumière brothers 154
Lutyens, Elisabeth 99, 101
Lynch, David 181
Lythgoe, Clive 154

M (dir. Fritz Lang) 15
MacGowran, Jack 109
MacGregor, Scott 155, 179
Mackendrick, Alexander 17
Mackenzie, John 162, 163
MacMillan, Harold 65, 75
Madden, Peter 108
"Mademoiselle de Scudéry" 56, 58, 59–62, 117, 134, 144, 162, 169
Mademoiselle du Maupin 153
The Magic Roundabout (TV series) 178
Maeterlinck, Maurice 165; *Pélleas et Mélisande* 165
Magee, Patrick 167
Magritte, René 43–44
Mamoullian, Rouben 67
The Man in Black 1, 8, 14, 39, 41–48, **42**, 62, 115, 150, 152
The Man Who Could Cheat Death 51
The Man with the Golden Gun 4
Maniac 1, 24, 26, 28, 34, 39, 87–94, **88**, 99, 118, 154, 164
Manners, David 106
Marat, Jean-Paul 33
Marat/Sade 167
March, Fredric 67
The Marriage of Figaro 120
Martell, Philip 154, 155
Mary Poppins 144
The Mask of Fu Manchu 76
Mason, James 76
Matthews, Kerwin 55, 88, 90, 93
Mayne, Ferdy 108
McCabe, John 162, 163, 164, 166

McCowen, Alec 147
Mendelssohn, Felix 104
Mengele, Josef 131
The Merchant of Venice 120
Mesmer, Franz Anton 167, 171, 172
Miller, Mandy **56**, 59, 63
Milton, John 79
Mitchell, Bill 77
Mitchell, Yvonne **168**, 171
The Moonstone 45
Moore, Roger 4
Morell, André 51
The Most Dangerous Game 4
Mower, Patrick 182
Mozart, Wolfgang Amadeus 6; *The Marriage of Figaro* 120
The Mummy 92
Munch, Edvard 60, 113
Murder by Proxy 39
"The Murders in the Rue Morgue" 59
Murnau, F.W. 12, 13
Murphy, Mike 445
Murphy, Robert 2, 75
The Mysteries of Udolpho 79–81, 83, 156
The Mystery of the Yellow Room 59

The Nanny 7, 8, 13, 25, 28, 34, 35, 39, 102, 132, 137–146, **138**, 164, 165, 180, 181
Narcejac, Thomas 28–29, 31
Narizzano, Silvio 7, 13, 122–123, **123**, 125, 127
Nash, John 140
Nazimova, Alla 127
Neame, Christopher 53
Never Take Sweets from a Stranger 26
Newlands, Anthony 128, 133, 166
Nicholson, Jack 166
Nicolson, Harold 58
Nielsen, Leslie 3
Nietzsche, Friedrich 7–8, 174
Night of the Demon 53
Nightmare 2, 8, 13, 14, 15, 18, 24, 30, 39, 47, 60, 62, 102, 113–121, **115**, 135, 160
Noll, Richard 70
Norman, Monty 67
North by Northwest 87, 128, 134, 150
Northanger Abbey 73, 80, 85
Novak, Kim 28
Now Voyager 49, 51

Oakley Court 41, 44–46, 113, 118, 137, 150
Oh! What a Lovely War 169
Olivier, Laurence 23, **23**, 137
Olsen, James 6, 152, **153**, 154
Olympiade 16
O'Regan, Terence 53
Osborne, John 139

Paradies, Maria Theresa 170
Paranoiac 1, 7, 8, 9, 13, 15, 31, 39, 47, 96–105, **97**, **107**, 120, 131, 139
Parish, Robert 28
Parker, Clifton 76, 77, 84
Parsifal 162
Parys, Georges van 13, 14
Pascal, Blaise 174
Pastell, George 92, 94
Peacock, John 175
Peck, Gregory 26, **27**, 35
Peeping Tom 176
Pélleas et Mélisande 165
Penwarden, Hazel 45
Perkins, Anthony 7, **32**, 47
Peter Pan 141, 175, 176–178, 180
The Phantom of the Opera 100, 113
Pichel, Irving 4
The Picture of Dorian Gray 85
Pidgeon, Walter 3
Piper, Evelyn 8, 137, 139, 145; *The Nanny* 8, 137–140, 145
The Pirates of Blood River 93, 97, 100
Pitt, Ingrid 148
The Plague of the Zombies 41
Poe, Edgar Allan 28, 36, 38, 42–43, 53, 55, 56, 59, 71–72, 146, 167, 172; "The Black Cat" 56; "The Fall of the House of Usher" 26, 42–43, 167, 170; "The Haunted Palace" 42–43; "Ligeia" 38; "The Murders in the Rue Morgue" 59; "The Raven" 36; "The System of Doctor Tarr and Professor Fether" 71–72; "The Tell-Tale Heart" 146; "William Wilson" 28, 53
Polanski, Roman 108, 109
Portrait from Life 58
Poulenc, Francis 109
Poulsen, George 132
Powell, Michael 176
Powers, Stefanie 55, **123**, 124, 152, 155
Preminger, Otto 134, 137

Probyn, Brian 180
Proud, Peter 127
Psycho 1, 2, 6, 9, 11, 16, 17, 22, 31–40, *32*, *39*, 47, 50, 73, 75, 78, 86, 90, 92, 93, 121, 122, 123, 124, 127, 128, 133, 134, 136, 138, 140, 145, 146, 159, 163, 164, 180
Purcell, Henry 170
Purse, Jill 31
Pygmalion 48, 51

The Quatermass Experiment 11, 100
The Queen of Spades 83

Rachmaninoff, Sergei 154
Radcliffe, Ann 18, 24, 73, 74, 79–81, 83, 130; *The Italian* 73; *The Mysteries of Udolpho* 79–81, 83, 156
Radestock, Paul 114
Rains, Claude 53
Rapper, Irving 49
Rasputin the Mad Monk 118
Rattigan, Terence 162
Ravel, Maurice 164
"The Raven" 36
Rebecca 22–26, *23*, 102, 121, 143, 148, 163, 165, 174
The Red House 28
Redgrave, Sir Michael 162
Redmond, Moira *115*, 119
Reed, Oliver 7, 8, 55, 96, 97–98, *97*, 100, 101, 103, 104, *107*, 172
The Resident 175
Resnais, Alain 93, 102
Richardson, Tony 178
Richmond, Irene 118
Riefenstahl, Leni 15–16, 59, 64, 173
Riley, Bridget 31
Rilla, Wolf 100
Robinson, Arthur 54
Robinson, Bernard 75, 102, 106, *111*, 155
Robinson, Harry 170
Robson, Mark 84
Rohmer, Sax 76
Rolfe, Guy 58
Rope 1, 2, 3–4, *3*, 6, 22, 62, 109
Ross, Annie 178, 179, 181
Rota, Nino 154
Rózsa, Miklós 28
"Rude Awakening" 119, 182
Russell, Ken 97
Rye, Stellan 54

Sachs, Leonard 86
Sade, Donatien Alphonse François, Marquis de 55, 98, 128, 130–131, 167; *Justine* 128, 130–131
Sadsy, Peter 47, 83, 119, *153*
St. John, Betta 61
Le Salaire de la Peur 11, 55
"The Sandman" 19
Sangster, Jimmy 1, 2, 8, 9, 11, 13, 14, 18, 24, 50, 55, 65, 75, 76, 87, 89, 91, 93, 95, 96, 98, 100, 101, 103, 104, 117, 118, 121, 128, 137–143, 145, 146, 152, 154, 155, 156, 158, 160, *161*, 162, 163, 165
Sartre, Jean-Paul 14
The Satanic Rites of Dracula 132
Savory, Gerald 124
The Scarlet Blade 100
Schelling, Friedrich 19, 124
Schindler's List 58
Schlesinger, John 116
Schnitzler, Arthur 110–111; *Dream Story (Traumnovelle)* 110–112
Schoenberg, Arnold 36
Schopenhauer, Arthur 114
Schuller, Gunther 129
Schumann, Robert 113
Scob, Edith 48, 105
Scott, Janette 98
Scott, Lizabeth 50, *50*, 52
Scott, Margaretta *39*, 152
Scott, Peter Graham 100
Scream of Fear see *Taste of Fear*
Scriabin, Alexander 113
Searle, Francis 1, *39*, 41–42, *42*, 44–46
Seifert, Richard 132
The Seventh Veil 51, 76, 113
Shakespeare, William 3, 6, 141, 169, 174; *Hamlet* 7–8, 9, 140–141; *The Merchant of Venice* 120
Sharp, Don 106, *107*, 108, *109*, *111*, 118
Shaughnessy, Alfred 152, 157
Shaw, George Bernard 48, 51; *Pygmalion* 48, 51
Shaw, Roland 178, 179
She 90, 100
Shepherd, Elizabeth 173
The Shining 166
Sibelius, Jean 156
Siegfried 38

Signoret, Simone 14
"The Silent Scream" 182
Simmons, Jean 106
Simmons, Stan *111*
Skal, David J. 131
Slocombe, Douglas 75, 79, 82, 83
Smith, T. Dan 132
Smithson, Harriet 30, 51
The Snorkel 7, 55–66, *56*, 74, 82, 86, 131
So Long at the Fair 35, 106, 110, 182
Someone at the Door 44
Sontag, Susan 89
Souza, Edward de 106, *111*
Spellbound 9, 22, 26–28, *27*, 35, 69, 110, 128, 130, 150
Spielberg, Steven 58
Spoto, Donald 2, 24, 28, 30, 31, 35, 37, 65, 90, 109, 127, 150
Spotts, Frederic 57
Stevens, Martin 148
Stevenson, Robert Louis 67
Stewart, James *3*, 3–4, 7, 29, 48
Stoker, Bram 4, 94, 122; *Dracula* 4, 122, 124–125; *The Jewel of Seven Stars* 94
Stolen Face 48–54, *50*, 164
Stop Me Before I Kill see *The Full Treatment*
Straight on Till Morning 7, 13, 28, 175–182, *176*
Strangers on a Train 152
The Stranglers of Bombay 45, 92
Strasberg, Susan 8, 35, *74*, 75, 155, 160
A Streetcar Named Desire 127
Strindberg, August 113, 114, 115; *A Dream Play* 114; *Inferno* 113; *To Damascus* 114
Stuck, Franz von 67, 78
Der Student von Prag 54
Sullivan, Thomas Russell 67
Sutherland, Donald 123
Sykes, Peter 7, 167, *168*, 169, 171, 173, 174
"The System of Doctor Tarr and Professor Fether" 71–72

A Tale of Two Cities 66
Taste of Fear 1, 2, 8, 13, 22, 31, 35, 39, 68, 73–86, *74*, 91, 102, 103, 143, 154, 155, 156, 157, 158, 160, 162
A Taste of Honey 178

Taste the Blood of Dracula 83, **153**, 165
Taylor, Don 36
Taylor, Elizabeth 178
Taylor, Gilbert 79
"The Tell-Tale Heart" 146
The Terror of the Tongs 100
Das Testament des Dr. Mabuse 16
Tey, Josephine 8, 96–97, 98, 101, 103, 104, 105, 139; *Brat Farrar* 8, 96, 139
That Obscure Object of Desire 30
Thatcher, Margaret 181
Thomas, Ralph 66
Thorn, Ronald Scott 67
Thorne, Anthony 106
Tieck, Johann Ludwig 98; "Wake Not the Dead" 98, 102
To Damascus 114
To the Devil a Daughter 131
Todd, Ann 39, 75, 76, 154
Todorov, Tzvetan 2, 73, 76, 77, 79, 96, 102
The Tomb of Ligeia 173
Tomlinson, David 106
Torn Curtain 22
Tourneur, Jacques 2, 53
Trevelyan, John 148
Trilby 173
Tristan und Isolde 30, 100
Triumph des Willens 15, 64, 173
Tushingham, Rita 55, 175, **176**, 178
The Two Faces of Dr. Jekyll 67
"The Two Faces of Evil" 182

Ulmer, Edgar G. 106
Ulysses 160
"The Uncanny" 19–20
Unman, Wittering and Zigo 162–163
Upstairs Downstairs 182
Urquhart, Robert 49

The Vampire Lovers 32, 148
van Gogh, Vincent 92, 113
Vanel, Charles 18, 131
Vaughan, Peter 123
Veidt, Conrad 159
Vertigo 1, 5, 7, 11, 22, 28–31, **29**, 48, 51, 72, **74**, 75, 87, 90, 110, 122, 128, 129, **129**, 130, 171, 172
Victim 148
Villiers, James 139
Villiers de l'Isle Adam, Jean-Marie-Mathias-Philippe-Auguste 49; *L'Ève Future* 49
Visa to Canton 100
Visconti, Luchino 92
"The Vow" 99, 105

Wagner, Richard 30, 35, 100, 162, 167; *Götterdämmerung* 35–36; *Parsifal* 162; *Siegfried* 38; *Tristan und Isolde* 30, 100; *Die Walküre* 167
"Wake Not the Dead" 98, 102
Walbrook, Anton 62 159
Die Walküre 167
Wallis, Jacquie 110, **111**
Walsh, Kay 7, 39, 147
Warren, Barry 109, **109**, **111**
Watch It Sailor! 100
Waterfield, Robin 173
Watling, Jack 139
Wattis, Richard 53
Waxman, Franz 23, 24, 25–26
Waxman, Harry 90, 145
Webber, Robert 8, 55, **129**, 130

Webster, Richard 70
A Weekend with Lulu 100
Wegener, Paul 54
Weiss, Peter 167; *Marat/Sade* 167
Wells, H.G 131
Wells, Jerold 90
Wetherell, Virginia 173
Whale, James 171
While I Live 154
The Wicker Man 150
Wicking, Christopher 168, 169, 173
Widmark, Richard 55
Wiene, Robert 159
Wilcox, Fred M. 3
The Wild Duck 166
Wilde, Oscar 153
Wilder, Billy 28
"William Wilson" 28, 53
Williams, Charles 154
Williams, Tennessee 127
Williamson, Sir Malcolm 154, 155, 157
Willman, Noel 106, 107
Wilson, John Dover 9
The Witches 7, 13, 23, 39, 147–150, **149**
Wong, Anna May 76
Woodbridge, George 134
Wundt, Wilhelm 113
Wyeth, Katya 177
Wykehurst Park 169
Wynyard, Diana 62

X—The Unknown 75

Les Yeux sans Visage 48, 105

Zetterling, Mai 58

www.ingramcontent.com/pod-product-compliance
Ingram Content Group UK Ltd.
Pitfield, Milton Keynes, MK11 3LW, UK
UKHW050701160426
5217IPUK00038B/1799